SELF-CARE FOR LIFE

FIND JOY, PEACE, SERENITY, VITALITY, SENSUALITY, ABUNDANCE, & ENLIGHTENMENT—EACH AND EVERY DAY

SKYE ALEXANDER, MEERA LESTER, & CAROLYN DEAN, MD, ND

Avon, Massachusetts

Published by
Adams Media, a division of F+W Media, Inc.
57 Littlefield Street, Avon, MA 02322. U.S.A.
www.adamsmedia.com

ISBN 10: 1-4405-2860-8
ISBN 13: 978-1-4405-2860-6
eISBN 10: 1-4405-2922-1
eISBN 13: 978-1-4405-2922-1

Printed in the United States of America.

10 9 8 7 6 5 4 3 2 1

Library of Congress Cataloging-in-Publication Data
is available from the publisher.

The information in this book should not be used for diagnosing or treating any health problem. Not all diet and exercise plans suit everyone. You should always consult a trained medical professional before starting a diet, taking any form of medication, or embarking on any fitness or weight-training program. The authors and publisher disclaim any liability arising directly or indirectly from the use of this book.

Many of the designations used by manufacturers and sellers to distinguish their product are claimed as trademarks. Where those designations appear in this book and Adams Media was aware of a trademark claim, the designations have been printed with initial capital letters.

Interior illustration © istockphoto.com/HiDesignGraphics

This book is available at quantity discounts for bulk purchases.
For information, please call 1-800-289-0963.

CARING FOR YOURSELF

"EVERY PATIENT CARRIES HER OR HIS OWN DOCTOR INSIDE."
—Albert Schweitzer

Self-care for life. That's a tall order, but a crucial one. We often spend our lives look-ing out for other people—so much so that we forget to take care of ourselves! That stress takes a toll not only on our bodies, but also on our minds and spirits. Stud-ies show that about half of Americans feel that the amount of stress they experience has increased in the last five years, and one-third of Americans feel they are under extreme stress.

The results? Burnout, unhappiness, and mental and physical diseases. We may experience everything from headache to divorce simply because we're not taking care of ourselves in a way that will reduce stress and improve our health.

Self-care isn't something you do once a year at a spa. And it isn't something you do a few times and then drop. It's a commitment you make to yourself each and every day. Not enough time, you say? It doesn't have to take a lot of time (many of the tips in this book take only a few minutes). More than time, you simply need intention—and follow-through. Promise yourself you'll do it, and then do it.

Our emotional, mental, and physical selves are intertwined and interlinked. We have ample evidence to prove that psychological health affects physical health, and vice versa. Thinking holistically means viewing yourself as a whole being, not a col-lection of parts. In the 1970s, when Buddhist ideas seeped into Western culture, one essential message was: "I am not my liver, my spleen, my blood, nor my brain. I am all of me." It sounded revolutionary at the time, but science soon joined the chorus. You are not your individual parts; you are the sum of all your parts operating in tandem. Mind, body, and spirit are inseparable, and illness in one often produces illness in the others. Think holistically and your overall health will improve.

HOW TO USE THIS BOOK

Think holistically. That's what this book encourages you to do. Each of the 365 entries includes an inspirational quotation that you can meditate on—or just think about for a moment before reading further. Each entry is based on a special thought or theme, and follows up with specific ways you can improve your health—mentally, physically, and spiritually—with ideas based on that theme. That means for each and every day of the year, nearly 1,100 tips in all, you'll have specific actions you can take to improve your health and well-being.

The book draws upon traditions from ancient as well as modern wisdom, from Eastern systems as well as Western ones. It also provides information about recent scientific research into a variety of illnesses and treatments. This allows you to expand your thinking about what constitutes self-care and how you might achieve it.

Not every suggestion will be right for you. Try the ones that appeal. These suggestions are not intended to take the place of professional medical care. They are offered as guidelines to help you take responsibility for staying healthier, every day, in every way.

SELF~ CARE FOR LIFE

"WE ARE WHAT WE THINK. ALL THAT WE ARE ARISES WITH OUR THOUGHTS. WITH OUR THOUGHTS, WE MAKE THE WORLD." —The Buddha

Use Your Thoughts as Creative Tools

Your thoughts have the power to generate results in the material world. Quantum physics has shown that when you focus attention on molecules, your attention (mind) affects the molecules' movement. The Law of Attraction concept, popularized by Esther and Jerry Hicks, says that you can bring into your life anything you desire by focusing your mind on it.

MIND: *Focus on things you wish to bring into your life*
Put your mind to work for you. Think clearly about what you want to attract into your life. Be aware that infinite opportunities are available to you—the universe is working with you, putting wind in the sail of your dream ship to take you anywhere you want to go.

BODY: *Get a Reiki treatment*
The holistic healing modality known as Reiki channels positive, high-resonance energy into your body to help your system heal itself. Holistic healers believe mind and body are integrally connected, and that positive thoughts and emotions can actually change your body's neurochemistry to help generate healing benefits.

SPIRIT: *Create a vision board*
A vision board depicts images of things you wish to attract into your life. Cut out magazine pictures of things you want. Paste these images on a piece of poster board and display it where you'll see it often. Every time you look at your vision board you'll be inspired to acquire the things you desire.

"MOST FOLKS ARE ABOUT AS HAPPY AS THEY MAKE UP THEIR MINDS TO BE." —Abraham Lincoln

Happiness Is a State of Mind

When you think happy thoughts, you feel better. When you dwell on problems and what's wrong in the world, your emotions spiral downward. Research shows that positive thinking can help you manage stress and even improve your overall health.

MIND: *Create a happiness blog*
To improve your own happiness and that of others, consider starting a blog that focuses on happiness—or devote part of a blog you already have to the subject. By looking for positive events in your own life, your community, and the world, and writing about them, you will improve your attitude and your outlook on life. You could even spread positive energy around the globe.

BODY: *Go for a walk in nature*
Exercise increases the production of endorphins, the "feel good" proteins in the brain, so when you exercise you actually feel more positive. You'll also get fresh air and vitamin D, which helps to lift depression. As you walk, pay attention to the wonders of nature all around you—flowers blossoming, birds singing, the sun shining— and you'll soon notice your mood has improved.

SPIRIT: *Lift your spirits with rose quartz*
Healers who work with crystals say rose quartz emits gentle, uplifting vibrations that can boost your spirits. Carry a small piece of smooth, tumbled rose quartz in your pocket and rub it often to encourage a sense of joy and inner peace.

"WE DON'T SEE THINGS AS THEY ARE,

WE SEE THINGS AS WE ARE." —Anaïs Nin

See Everyone as a Mirror

We can learn a great deal about ourselves from the people around us. From a place of detachment, today observe your interactions with others—without judgment. Notice things that rub you the wrong way as well as things that inspire or enliven you. What do other people show you about yourself?

MIND: *Everyone you meet is a reflection of your inner being*
Psychoanalyst Carl Jung popularized the idea of projection, meaning that you mentally and emotionally transfer what's inside you onto everyone you come into contact with in life. Notice something you strongly like or dislike about someone you know. Realize this characteristic is also a part of you, perhaps a part you have repressed or denied.

BODY: *Listen to your body talk*
Your body reacts to your thoughts and emotions. Is someone giving you a "pain in the neck"? Is something "eating at you"? These physical reactions can be clues to what's going on with you mentally, emotionally, and spiritually. If you ignore them, they may eventually lead to health problems.

SPIRIT: *Bless everyone you meet as a teacher and guide*
Each person who comes into your life can show you something about yourself, if you remain open. Even someone who makes you angry can teach you about yourself, perhaps revealing something you hadn't noticed before. See this as a gift rather than an annoyance.

"WHEN WE FEEL THE URGENCY TO SPEED UP, THAT IS
TYPICALLY THE INSTANT WE NEED TO SLOW DOWN."

—Mark Nepo, *The Book of Awakening*

Slow Down

Our fast-paced society encourages us to keep doing more things
faster, yet the result is often increased stress and diminished quality
of life. Instead of speeding up, try slowing down. You may discover
you enjoy time with loved ones more, perform better-quality work,
and feel more relaxed. When you lower your stress level, your health
may improve, too.

MIND: *Cease multitasking*
When you do many things at once, you can't commit to doing any of
them well. According to a study published in the *American Psychological Society's Journal of Experimental Psychology*, multitasking
actually reduces productivity instead of increasing it. Make a point
of doing only one thing at a time and giving it your full attention. If
you're talking to a friend on the phone, turn off the TV. If you're eating breakfast, don't read the newspaper.

BODY: *Stop rushing around*
Life is about the journey, not the destination. Practice staying in the
moment and appreciate it for what it is right now, not what it may
become at some time in the future. Intentionally walk, drive, or speak
more slowly and see if you notice or experience things differently.

SPIRIT: *Be aware of your environment*
For five minutes stop, be still, and notice all the sounds, smells, and
images in the world around you. Notice, too, how you experience
and relate to these elements in your environment.

"THE HEART IS A THOUSAND-STRINGED INSTRUMENT
THAT CAN ONLY BE TUNED WITH LOVE."

—Hafiz, *The Gift*

All You Need Is Love

According to Dr. Daniel Amen, psychiatrist and brain-imaging researcher, people in happy, loving, affectionate relationships live longer. A study at State University of New York found that the brains of people in love were rich in dopamine, a "feel good" chemical. Love, it appears, not only makes the world go 'round, it makes us healthier as well.

MIND: *Read a love poem*
Enjoy reading a poem that inspires loving feelings in you. If possible, share the poem with someone you care about. It may be a romantic poem or one that speaks to a more all-compassionate love, such as the spiritual works of the Sufi poets Hafiz and Rumi. Allow tender, loving feelings to arise in you.

BODY: *Use a yoga exercise to open your heart*
Stand and pull your shoulders back as far as you can comfortably. Try to clasp your hands behind your back. Raise your arms slowly, keeping them straight. Feel the stretch across your chest, opening your heart center.

SPIRIT: *Send love to someone at a distance*
Close your eyes and bring to mind someone you love who is far away. Imagine a column of pink light connecting your heart to the other person's heart. Envision sending love at the speed of light along this column, and see it reaching your loved one. Sense this person receiving your love and returning it. Feel the joy that links you.

"IF YOU FEEL POOR, YOU CANNOT ATTRACT PROSPERITY."

—Esther and Jerry Hicks, *The Law of Attraction*

Prepare Yourself for Prosperity

Prosperity is both a state of mind and a state of being. If you're not as prosperous as you'd like to be, it's time to examine your attitude. Today, consider something expensive that you'd like to have. Instead of saying "I can't afford that," say "How can I get that?" Here are some other ways to increase your abundance.

MIND: *Imagine yourself rich*
The first step to becoming rich is believing you can be rich. Spend time envisioning yourself having and doing the things you would if you had an endless supply of money. See yourself driving a new car, taking a luxury vacation, living in the home of your dreams. Go ahead, indulge yourself.

BODY: *Counteract financial stress*
According to a 2008 survey by the American Psychological Association, 80 percent of Americans say the economy and financial matters are a significant cause of stress. One of the best ways to cope with stress is to meditate daily, as hundreds of studies done at more than 250 universities and research centers have demonstrated. Just fifteen minutes a day will help you feel calmer and more relaxed.

SPIRIT: *Use affirmations to increase your prosperity*
An affirmation is a short, positive statement you use to change your thinking or behavior, and to produce something you desire. Create a prosperity affirmation, such as "I now open myself to receive prosperity of all kinds" and repeat it often throughout the day.

"MANY OF OUR FEARS ARE TISSUE-PAPER-THIN, AND
A SINGLE COURAGEOUS STEP WOULD CARRY US CLEAR
THROUGH THEM." —Brendan Francis

Slay Your Inner Dragons

Are your fears keeping you from enjoying life fully? Many of the
things we fear aren't really dangerous. We constructed defenses at
an earlier time in our lives to protect us, but those defenses may no
longer be necessary or beneficial. Here are some suggestions that can
help you deal with your fears mentally, physically, and spiritually.

MIND: *What's the worst that can happen?*

In a safe place, bring to mind one fear you have that is not truly dangerous (such as speaking in public). Ask yourself, what's the worst
thing that could happen if you attempted the thing you fear and
failed? Can you live with that? If so, give it a try.

BODY: *Take flower essences to enhance courage*

Flower essences are gentle remedies made from the vital energy that
naturally exists in plants. They work on every level of your being to
induce healing. Aspen, borage, garlic, golden yarrow, and rockrose
are some essences that help you confront fears and challenges in
your life. You can purchase flower essences at health food stores and
online at *www.flowersociety.org*.

SPIRIT: *Ask a friend to help you confront a fear*

Often it's easier to do something you fear if a friend is there to provide support. Ask a trusted friend or family member to accompany you as you tackle a challenge that frightens you. That person's
energy and confidence will bolster yours.

"BE CONTENT WITH WHAT YOU HAVE;

REJOICE IN THE WAY THINGS ARE.

WHEN YOU REALIZE THERE IS NOTHING LACKING,

THE WHOLE WORLD BELONGS TO YOU." —Lao Tzu

Be Content with Life

Today, set an intention to be content with your life, just as it is right now. Instead of worrying about little annoyances or thinking about what you lack, focus on the good things in your life. Research done by Carol Ryff, a psychology professor at the University of Wisconsin–Madison, shows that a sense of well-being can reduce your risk of heart problems.

MIND: *Count your blessings*

Make a list of twenty blessings in your life. These might include such things as good health, a loving family, friends, a roof over your head and food to eat, and so on. Read the list when you've finished and feel a sense of contentment as you reflect on the many good things you enjoy.

BODY: *Move your body*

Wriggle your fingers or toes. Stretch your arms up over your head. Bend down and pick up something from the floor. Observe the amazing interaction between your muscles, nerves, joints, and tendons, and how they allow you to perform these movements. Marvel at the amazing composition your body is.

SPIRIT: *Make an offering*

One way to show gratitude—and continue the cycle of abundance—is to make an offering to a deity of your choice. Write a short prayer, like a spiritual thank-you note, to your favorite god, goddess, angel, or spirit.

"Forgiveness is a 'selective remembering'—a conscious decision to focus on love and let the rest go." —Marianne Williamson, *A Return to Love*

Focus on Forgiveness

A study published in the *Psychological Journal* in 2001 found that dwelling on past hurts increased blood pressure and heart rate. These stress reactions diminished when subjects thought about forgiveness. Practicing forgiveness in these ways can make you happier and healthier.

MIND: *Tell someone you forgive him or her*

Write a letter to someone you've chosen to forgive—even if you decide not to send it. Tell that person you forgive him or her for a particular thing that hurt you, and that it's all in the past. You may feel a sense of release as you put down the burden of anger, pain, or resentment you've been carrying.

BODY: *Activate the "Letting Go" acupressure points*

To release an emotional attachment to anger or sadness, gently but firmly press the points known in Chinese medicine as LU 1, or "Letting Go." These points are located on either side of the upper, outer parts of your chest in the indentions below your collarbones and shoulders. Press your fingers to these points and hold for about a minute; repeat several times a day to facilitate forgiveness.

SPIRIT: *Burn the letter*

If you have chosen not to send the letter to the person you are forgiving, burn it to symbolize the dissolution of the problem that stood between the two of you. As the smoke rises, it carries your intentions into the cosmos, where divine forces can act upon them.

"YOU MAY HAVE A FRESH START ANY MOMENT

YOU CHOOSE." —Mary Pickford

Start Over

Starting something new can be refreshing to mind, body, and spirit—no wonder we use the term "a fresh start." If something in your life isn't working for you—a job, a relationship, a habit—staying in that rut probably won't make things better. Instead, try a different tactic: start over. Here are some suggestions you can try today.

MIND: *Monitor your self-talk*
Pay attention to how you limit or undermine yourself with your thoughts and words. Catch yourself saying things like, "I couldn't possibly do that" or "I'm so fat/ugly/stupid" or "S/he would never be interested in me" and other self-deprecating statements. Replace negative statements with positive ones.

BODY: *Take action to implement your new beginning*
After you've decided to start something new, get busy. Thinking and talking about it are fine, but you have to put your plan into action if you want to see results. Cook a healthy meal. Go to the gym. Send out résumés. Throw away your cigarettes. Make an appointment with a therapist. Take the first step now.

SPIRIT: *Get answers with a pendulum*
If you're uncertain about your direction, you can use a pendulum to get answers. Either purchase a pendulum or make one by hanging a light weight of some kind on a chain. Hold the chain loosely, letting the bob dangle, and ask a yes or no question. Let the pendulum swing without trying to move it. Usually a side-to-side motion means "no" and a back-and-forth motion means "yes."

"WHEN RUNNING UP A HILL, IT IS ALL RIGHT TO GIVE UP AS MANY TIMES AS YOU WISH—AS LONG AS YOUR FEET KEEP MOVING." —Shoma Morita

Keep on Truckin'

Self-care means not pushing yourself so hard that you get stressed out or even sick. In 2010, the BBC reported that working overtime regularly increases your risk of heart attack. Type A people also get sick more and may be more likely to suffer from anxiety and depression. Be persistent, but don't push yourself to the breaking point. Try these strategies.

MIND: *Break tasks into segments*

Large tasks can seem daunting, but if you break a job into smaller segments and tackle only a portion at a time, it becomes manageable. For instance, don't think of writing a whole book; just concentrate on finishing a few pages a day. Or, pick one corner of the garage to clean and then finish it. The satisfaction you gain from your accomplishment will inspire you to keep going.

BODY: *Supplement your stamina*

DHEA, a hormone naturally supplied by the adrenal glands, can be diminished by disease, stress, aging, and other factors. When DHEA levels are low, you may become depressed, discouraged, tired, or ill. Some studies show that supplementing with DHEA can aid adrenal fatigue, which may give you more energy to do what you need to do.

SPIRIT: *Let Ganesh be your guide*

According to Hindu tradition, the elephant god Ganesh lends his great strength to those who need it. Acquire a figurine of Ganesh and carry it in your pocket to bolster your determination.

"IF YOU REFUSE TO ACCEPT ANYTHING BUT THE BEST,
YOU VERY OFTEN GET IT." —W. Somerset Maugham

Accept Only the Best

Are you selling yourself short? Self-care involves valuing your-self and treating yourself with respect. Self-deprecation can lead to depression, anxiety, and physical illness. Today, stop beating your-self up and do something nice for yourself instead.

MIND: *Accentuate the positive*

It's easy to get into a pattern of criticizing yourself or concentrating on your shortcomings rather than your strengths. Make a list of three things you like about yourself. Maybe you're good with animals, or you can whip up a great apple pie on the spur of the moment, or you've got nice legs. Once you've primed your mental pump, you can probably think of many more positive attributes—add them to your list. Post the list where you'll see it often: on your computer, fridge, or bathroom mirror.

BODY: *Indulge your taste buds*

Eat something truly extravagant and delicious, something you might ordinarily forego because you think it's too expensive, such as cav-iar, kobe beef steak, handmade dark chocolates, or champagne. Consume it slowly and savor every bit. As you enjoy your treat, tell yourself you're worth it.

SPIRIT: *Notice other people's vibes*

You've probably picked up on "bad vibes" emanating from some-one or simply felt uncomfortable in that person's presence, for no obvious reason. Pay attention to your impressions. You're intuitively reading that person's energy field. If you don't feel good around somebody, it's a signal—honor it. Choose to spend time only with people whose energy nourishes you.

"WHEN THE SACREDNESS OF SEXUAL UNION IS FELT, IT IS
POSSIBLE TO EXPERIENCE YOUR CONNECTION TO THE LIFE
FORCE ITSELF, THE SOURCE OF CREATION."

—Margot Anand, *The Art of Sexual Ecstasy*

That Loving Feeling

Engaging in sex regularly is one of the best things you can do for
yourself, mentally, physically, and spiritually. Studies reported on
WebMD show that sex relieves stress, boosts immunity, burns calories, improves cardiovascular health, and increases self-esteem.
Today, try the following suggestions to enhance your sex life.

MIND: *Read erotica*

It's been said that the mind is the most sensitive erogenous zone.
Read erotic literature to stimulate your mind, and perhaps give you
ideas about different ways to please yourself and your partner. If you
prefer, write your own tantalizing tales.

BODY: *Share a sensual massage*

Physical touch provides numerous health benefits. Hugging someone
you care about for just twenty seconds raises your level of oxytocin,
while lowering blood pressure and cortisol (the stress hormone). Share
a full-body massage with a partner, varying your touch from gently
stroking the skin to kneading stiffness from tight muscles. Engage in
the art of sensual touch, either as a prelude to sex or for its own merits.

SPIRIT: *Arouse your senses with scents*

Scent triggers your libido, and consequently has been used for millennia to entice and delight. Although fragrance is a personal thing,
jasmine, ylang-ylang, patchouli, and musk have long been associated
with eroticism and sexuality. Blend essential oils with a "carrier" oil
such as grape seed, olive, or jojoba, and dab some on your pulse points.

"YOU CAN'T HAVE EVERYTHING—WHERE WOULD YOU

PUT IT?" —Steven Wright

Clear Clutter

Do you waste time looking for something you know you have, but can't find because of all the clutter? Clutter adds frustration and stress to an already busy life. According to a 2008 article in the *Denver Post,* clutter can also be a sign of low self-esteem or obsessive-compulsive disorder. Today, start clearing clutter to make your life function more smoothly.

MIND: *Don't be afraid to let go*
People hoard material goods for a variety of reasons, but mostly because they are afraid to let go. We derive a false sense of security from holding on to memorabilia from the past and things we think we might need one day. When you acknowledge that your security doesn't come from material possessions, it's easier to release possessions you don't really need or enjoy.

BODY: *Open your hands*
When you grasp something tightly, your hands aren't free to accept anything else. Nor can you reach for anything so long as you are desperately clutching something else. Open your hands, spreading your fingers and palms. Imagine releasing whatever you've been gripping and allow the universe to place what you need in them.

SPIRIT: *Clear clutter, clear your life*
If you relate clutter to blockages, the cluttered areas in your home show where your life has gotten stuck, and where energy is no longer flowing freely. Clear clutter and you'll soon notice a sense of movement and freedom that allows new vitality and freshness to enter your life.

"THERE IS NO SUCH THING AS CHANCE; AND WHAT SEEMS TO US MEREST ACCIDENT SPRINGS FROM THE DEEPEST SOURCE OF DESTINY." —Friedrich von Schiller

Surrender to Serendipity

Many important discoveries and experiences in our lives come to us seemingly by chance. Scientific "accidents" have brought us numerous things of great value, including penicillin and X-rays. Today, allow yourself to be guided by serendipitous occurrences—you may find something wonderful happens.

MIND: *Notice synchronicities*
Sometimes it feels like things just line up for us, without us doing anything obvious to make it happen. Call it fate, coincidence, or what analyst Carl Jung dubbed it: synchronicity. Pay attention to positive occurrences—these show you are in sync with the universe and operating at your best. Also notice when everything seems to be going against you—blockages may appear because you're going in the wrong direction.

BODY: *Take a holistic approach to health*
Holistic healers believe body, mind, and emotions are integrally connected. Physical ailments don't just happen; they are rooted in long-standing emotional and mental conditions. Pain and illness alert us to situations that need attention on many levels. Consider consulting a homeopath, naturopath, acupuncturist, or other holistic healer to help you heal a problem.

SPIRIT: *Observe signs from the universe*
Start noticing signs. Finding a penny on the street could mean you'll soon receive money. A strong urge to call someone you haven't seen in a while could mean that person is thinking about you, too. Hunches and coincidences may indicate that the universe is communicating with you.

"THE FAMILY THAT PLAYS TOGETHER, STAYS TOGETHER."

—Anonymous

Family Fun

Care for yourself and your loved ones today by engaging in a shared activity. Family togetherness creates positive bonds that can translate into good health. For example, the National Center on Addiction and Substance Abuse at Columbia University found that teens who regularly eat dinner with family members have a lower risk of substance abuse.

MIND: *Play word games together*
Texting and other communication shortcuts may cause kids to fall down on spelling, grammar, and language skills. Playing word games together as a family is both fun and educational. Share a crossword puzzle—each person will know things another doesn't. Try Scrabble, Boggle, Word Search, and other vocabulary-improving games, too.

BODY: *Plan family activities regularly*
No matter how busy you are, make time for family fun. Once a week, schedule an exercise outing together. Go bowling, hit the batting cages, ride bikes together, play soccer, hike in the woods, go swimming. If you don't all like the same sport, rotate and let a different member choose what you'll do each week.

SPIRIT: *Engage in spiritual sharing*
If your family follows a certain faith, attend your place of worship together. If you don't subscribe to a particular religion, you can still engage in spiritual sharing. Say a nondenominational prayer before dinner. Visit a sacred historic site together. Meditate as a family. Watch a documentary about a religion in a foreign country and discuss it.

"IMAGINATION IS MORE IMPORTANT THAN KNOWLEDGE."

—Albert Einstein

Use Your Imagination

Images have a real impact on your body, according to David S. Sobel, MD, and Robert Ornstein, PhD. You can use imagination to calm stress, reduce pain, and eliminate bad habits. The more you practice, the better you'll get. Try the following techniques to develop your imagination.

MIND: *Write a short story or poem*
You may not think you are creative, but you might surprise yourself. Write a short story, essay, or poem about something you've seen today. Don't censor yourself, just let the words and images flow. The objective is to engage your imagination, not to win the Pulitzer Prize.

BODY: *Use visualization to balance your chakras*
When the body's seven main energy centers, known as the chakras, are blocked or out of balance, illness can occur. Each chakra corresponds to a particular color. Close your eyes and imagine red light glowing at the root chakra (at the base of the spine), orange at the sacral chakra (in your lower belly), yellow at the solar plexus chakra, green at the heart chakra, blue at the throat chakra, indigo at the third-eye chakra (between your eyebrows), and violet at the crown chakra (at the top of your head). Do this exercise daily to keep your energy centers functioning optimally.

SPIRIT: *Try automatic writing*
This technique lets you tap into your subconscious to discover insights your rational mind may have missed. Hold a pencil on a piece of plain paper. Close your eyes and let your hand move, without attempting to control what you're writing. Open your eyes and gaze at what you've done. What does it say to you?

"THE FUTURE IS NOT A BETTER PLACE BUT ONLY A

DIFFERENT ONE." —William Least Heat Moon, *Blue Highways*

Be Here Now

We are human *beings*, not human *doings*. Yet most of us spend more time doing than being. In his bestseller *The Power of Now*, Eckhart Tolle wrote about the creative and healing power of the present moment. Today, notice when you are in the moment and when you're thinking about the future or past.

MIND: *Keep your mind focused on the present*

It's easy to miss out on the joys of the moment when you are looking toward the future. Splitting your attention—thinking about "there" when you're "here"—drains your energy and causes stress. Practice keeping your attention on the present moment. Whenever it starts to wander, bring it gently back. Notice how you feel calmer and more centered when your focus is on *now*.

BODY: *Practice Zen*

Engage in a simple, repetitive chore such as weeding the garden or shoveling snow. Empty your mind of all thoughts and put your attention on the task. Feel your body's movements. Notice sensations: the texture of the weeds or the cool air on your face. Don't rush or let your mind wander; just take each moment as it comes. Focus on the process, not the end result.

SPIRIT: *Observe a flower*

You've heard the expression "take time to smell the flowers," right? That's good advice. Spend a minute or so enjoying a flower: observe its color, petals, delicate composition. Smell its fragrance. Notice how appreciating natural beauty calms your mind and emotions.

"BREATHE. LET GO. AND REMIND YOURSELF THAT THIS VERY MOMENT IS THE ONLY ONE YOU KNOW YOU HAVE FOR SURE." —Oprah Winfrey

Breathe Deep

Today, pay attention to your breathing and make a conscious effort to breathe deep. Although we inhale and exhale about 17,000 times each day, we usually don't give much thought to our breath. Most of us breathe shallowly, and we tend to hold our breath when we're scared. Slow, deep breathing, however, nourishes mind and body. Healthy breathing can ease pain, increase vitality, and calm anxiety.

MIND: *Proper breathing nourishes your mind*
When you breathe properly, your brain receives more oxygen and can function more effectively. Quick, shallow breathing doesn't allow enough oxygen to reach your brain, which can make you feel anxious, tired, or mentally fuzzy. When you're doing a mentally challenging task or need to think clearly, take several slow, deep breaths.

BODY: *Become aware of your breathing*
Become aware of your everyday breathing and intentionally slow its pace. Fill your lungs with each inhalation, but not to the point where it becomes uncomfortable, then exhale completely. You'll find that you go through the day with less tension and have more energy.

SPIRIT: *Embrace Spirit with your breath*
Many traditions connect Spirit with the breath. The word "spirit" is derived from the Latin *spiritus*, meaning breath. Sit quietly and turn your attention to your breathing, as you envision yourself taking not just air, but Spirit into your body each time you inhale.

"SERENITY IS NOT FREEDOM FROM THE STORM, BUT PEACE
AMID THE STORM." —Anonymous

Lower Your Stress Level

You may not be able to live a stress-free existence, but you can minimize the effects of stress by changing the way you react to outside stressors. One of the best ways to improve your mental and physical health is to reduce stress. Numerous studies have demonstrated that chronic stress weakens your immune system, which leaves you more vulnerable to illness.

MIND: *Establish personal boundaries*

If you are a person who often gets dumped on, perhaps you need to learn to set boundaries for yourself. Otherwise, people may take advantage of your generosity, and their demands could add to your stress. Establish rules at home and at work, and enforce them. Learn to say no without feeling guilty.

BODY: *Stretch at your desk to reduce stress*

How many times during the workday do you feel irritable, tense, or stressed out? To ease tension, stretch your arms up over your head and open your fingers wide. Twist slowly from side to side. Lift your legs and lower them several times. Do these simple stretches several times a day to loosen up and de-stress.

SPIRIT: *Turn a problem over to a higher power*

When a problem seems beyond your control, give it to a higher power to handle. Whatever higher power you choose—god, goddess, spirit, a guardian angel—close your eyes and imagine placing the problem in that being's hands. Feel a sense of relief come over you, knowing you are being helped.

"NOT KNOWING IS PART OF THE ADVENTURE, AND IT'S

ALSO WHAT MAKES US AFRAID."

—Pema Chödrön, *The Places That Scare You*

The Joy of Discovery

Make a point of trying something new today. Set aside the ego's arguments: "Yes, but" and "What if" and just take a chance. If you insist on knowing for certain how a matter will turn out before you attempt it, you will destroy the joy of discovery.

MIND: *Do something whose outcome is uncertain*

Remember when you were a child and every day offered a new adventure? You didn't know what the day would bring, but you embraced its infinite possibilities with enthusiasm. You still can. Strike up a conversation with a stranger. Go to a movie or restaurant you know nothing about. Try your hand at knitting, pottery, or another craft you've never attempted before.

BODY: *Go someplace you've never been before*

The joy of traveling is experiencing things you could never have experienced at home: unfamiliar people, food, scenery, language, culture. You may not be able to fly off to a foreign country, but you can go someplace in your own community where you've never been before. Become an explorer in your own town or city.

SPIRIT: *Anything could happen*

When you wake up each morning, tell yourself, "Anything could happen today, anything at all." As you go through the day, invite new possibilities into your life and remain open to whatever the universe sends your way.

> "A CHEERFUL FRAME OF MIND, REINFORCED BY
> RELAXATION . . . IS THE MEDICINE THAT PUTS ALL
> GHOSTS OF FEAR ON THE RUN." —George Matthew Adams

Create Calmness

The stress and demands of everyday life produce wear and tear on
your body. Your mind and spirit will also suffer unless you make
relaxation an essential part of your daily experience. Relaxation
requires letting go on every level. Try these suggestions to become
more at ease today.

MIND: *Become more tolerant*
Challenge yourself to keep your mind open to the opinions of someone who doesn't see things the same way you do. You may be surprised to find you have more in common than you thought. As you
become more tolerant, you'll also find you are more calm, because
you don't get angered so easily.

BODY: *Develop a bedtime routine*
Sleep deprivation is a major problem in our go-go-go society. Establishing a bedtime routine can help you sleep better. Take a warm
bath, sip a glass of milk, listen to soothing music, or do some deep
breathing to unwind. Your mind and body will soon learn this routine means it is time to go to sleep, and take the cue.

SPIRIT: *Say Aum*
This soothing mantra, which comes from Hindu Vedic traditions,
is known as the "unstuck sound." Utter it aloud to produce peace
and balance. Start by intoning Aah. Draw out the sound, letting it
vibrate within you. Next intone Ooo, without breaking between
sounds. Then intone Mmm. Hold the sound until you run out of
breath. Repeat three times.

"THE VOYAGE OF DISCOVERY IS NOT IN SEEKING NEW

LANDSCAPES BUT IN HAVING NEW EYES."

—Marcel Proust, *Remembrance of Things Past*

Step Outside the Box

Are you in a rut? Do you find yourself doing the same things over and over, or approaching people and situations in the same way? Expand your horizons today, by experimenting with the following suggestions—notice the energy boost you get.

MIND: *Brainstorm new uses for common objects*
Most of us tend to fall into a mental rut from time to time. Get those mental juices flowing and start looking at things in a new way. Choose an everyday household object, such as a spoon or facial tissue, and imagine different things you could do with it other than its familiar use. When you open your mind to new possibilities, you invite the universe to step in and bring opportunities your way.

BODY: *Eat a food you don't think you'll like*
Often we refuse to try a particular food because it sounds or looks strange. We simply assume we won't like it, but that may not be the case. Today, select a food you've never eaten before, but think you won't like—octopus, sushi, or beef tongue, for example. You might be pleasantly surprised.

SPIRIT: *Talk to someone whose views contradict your own*
Often we pigeonhole people according to their race, religion, political party, and so on. But if you keep an open mind while talking with someone who seems "different," you may discover your preconceptions were way off. You might even realize you have some common ground.

"ALL OF THE ANIMALS EXCEPT MAN KNOW THAT THE
PRINCIPAL BUSINESS OF LIFE IS TO ENJOY IT."
—Samuel Butler

Don't Worry, Be Happy

Maintaining a positive attitude could help you live longer, as a study by the Women's Health Initiative showed. The study considered more than 97,000 healthy women between the ages of fifty and seventy-four, and found after an eight-year period that the women with positive attitudes had a 14 percent lower risk of death than their negative-thinking counterparts.

MIND: *Focus on what's positive in your life*
Realize you always have a choice of whether to see the glass as half-empty or half-full. Notice how your thoughts about something affect your feelings of happiness or unhappiness. Whenever you catch yourself dwelling on something negative, gently turn your thoughts to something positive.

BODY: *Take B vitamins to make you feel more optimistic*
B vitamins can affect your mood, according to the Mayo Clinic's Daniel K. Hall-Flavin, MD. Depression may be related to deficiencies of vitamins B-12, B-6, and folate. Vitamin B1 helps the brain by acting as a building block for serotonin, a chemical that regulates mood and digestion.

SPIRIT: *Listen to music to shift your mood*
Listening to Latin or African music and other tunes with lively rhythms can make you feel more energetic and upbeat. Studies have shown that baroque and classical music tend to produce a soothing effect, calming heartbeat and pulse rate, whereas hard rock and rap do the opposite.

"A JOURNEY OF A THOUSAND MILES BEGINS
WITH THE FIRST STEP." —Lao Tzu

Get Going

Today, stop procrastinating and begin something you've been putting off. Benjamin Franklin recommended dividing a twenty-four-hour day into thirds, devoting eight hours each to work, recreation, and rest. Dr. Neil Fiore, author of *The Now Habit*, advises that making time for play in your life reduces stress levels and lets you be more productive.

MIND: *Decide on a goal*

Set a goal for yourself, either a short-term or a long-term one. It might be to lose ten pounds, finish your college degree, or take a trip to Europe. Write it down. Then break the goal down into small, manageable steps. Dedicate yourself to accomplishing the first step in your plan within a designated time frame.

BODY: *Eat eggs to build strength*

The high-quality protein in eggs may help healthy adults build muscle strength and prevent age-related muscle loss, suggests research published in a 2004 issue of the *Journal of the American College of Nutrition*. Many Americans avoid eggs for fear of dietary cholesterol; however, the benefits of eating them can outweigh the downsides.

SPIRIT: *Visualize yourself accomplishing your goal*

Sit quietly, take a few deep breaths, and close your eyes. See yourself at the end of your journey, having completed the goal you've set for yourself. Don't worry about the effort or time it may take to get there; just focus on the end result. Feel the sense of accomplishment and joy at having achieved your task.

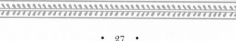

"WHEN WRITTEN IN CHINESE THE WORD *CRISIS* IS COMPOSED OF TWO CHARACTERS—ONE REPRESENTS DANGER AND THE OTHER REPRESENTS OPPORTUNITY." —John F. Kennedy

Embrace Challenges with Confidence

Many people don't achieve the success they could because they shy away from challenges. Perhaps fear of failure is keeping you from attempting something. Or high expectations set you up for disappointment. Today, take on a small challenge. Here are some tips that can help you.

MIND: *Mentally practice the challenging situation to prepare yourself*

Successful athletes often mentally envision themselves playing and winning a game as part of their training routine. This helps to improve their rate of success. Before you face a challenge, visualize yourself going through the steps. Make sure to see yourself succeeding!

BODY: *Assume "The Warrior" posture*

This yoga pose requires physical strength and balance. Stand with your legs as far apart as is comfortable, with your right leg in front and your left leg behind. Bend your right leg at the knee and keep your left leg straight. Hold your arms straight, parallel to the ground, with your right arm stretched out in front, above your right knee, and your left arm behind you. Maintain the posture for a minute or two, then change legs.

SPIRIT: *Use the runes to support your intention*

Runes are letters taken from the early Norse alphabet. Each letter has a symbolic meaning. *Uruz* means "the wild ox" and symbolizes strength. It looks a bit like a squarish, upside-down U. Gaze at this rune to strengthen your resolve.

"SUCCESS IS MEASURED NOT SO MUCH BY THE POSITION THAT ONE HAS REACHED IN LIFE, BUT BY THE OBSTACLES ONE HAS OVERCOME WHILE TRYING TO SUCCEED."

—Booker T. Washington

See Obstacles as Opportunities

Today, try to see obstacles as learning opportunities. When you look behind an "overnight success," you'll usually discover someone who has worked long and hard to get ahead. Edison may have been right when he said success is 90 percent perspiration—in other words, effort and persistence.

MIND: *Create a mission statement*
Companies usually state their core values in "mission statements." A mission statement tells customers, community, workers, and others what your purpose is and what your business is all about. You can do the same thing. Create a personal mission statement that describes your vision and goals—it will help keep you on track when challenges crop up.

BODY: *Detoxify your body*
Kale—and other *Brassica* vegetables—contains a potent nutrient that boosts your body's detoxification enzymes, clearing potentially carcinogenic substances from your body. A Netherlands Cohort Study on Diet and Cancer showed that people who ate the most cruciferous vegetables lowered their risk of colorectal cancer by 49 percent.

SPIRIT: *Clear obstacles in your home*
Can you walk easily through your home, without bumping into furniture, doors, or obstacles in your path? If not, you may be inhibiting your success. Physical blockages in your home symbolize blockages in other areas of your life. Clear obstructions that interfere with the ease of movement through your living space.

"APPROACH LOVE AND COOKING WITH RECKLESS ABANDON."

—H. Jackson Brown Jr., *Life's Little Instruction Book*

Awaken Your Appetites

The survival of all species depends on food and sex. But too often we settle for fast food and superficial sex. Anthropologist Gil Herdt, director of the Program in Human Sexuality Studies at San Francisco State University, says sexuality involves the entire person; it's not just about the act itself. Today, explore your sensuality on all levels.

MIND: *Think of sex as a gourmet meal*
According to a *Women's Health Magazine* survey, only 11 percent of couples who have been together for ten or more years experiment with new sexual positions. To keep sex from becoming boring, think of it as a gourmet meal that requires planning, careful preparation, attention to detail, and taking time to savor it. Just as you would peruse a cookbook for ideas, read books about sex to expand your sexual repertoire.

BODY: *Try a sexy herb from Peru*
Maca, an herb that hails from the Andes Mountains, may be an effective aphrodisiac. Though no large-scale tests have yet been performed, smaller studies show that it can increase libido and sperm production in men. Take maca extract in moderation to enhance your sex life; consider supplementing with 1,500 mg to 3,000 mg daily.

SPIRIT: *Discover Tantric sex*
Tantrics consider sex a sacred act, not just a physical one. It symbolizes the union of the god and goddess. Read about Tantra in books or online to transform your lovemaking into a divine experience.

"LIFE IS LIKE PHOTOGRAPHY. YOU USE THE

NEGATIVE TO DEVELOP." —Anonymous

Appreciate the Gift of Adversity

A butterfly must beat its wings against the walls of its cocoon in order to develop the strength to fly. So, too, must we encounter adversity in our lives in order to grow strong. Today, see the challenges facing you as tools for personal growth—like experiential free weights that build your life muscles.

MIND: *See the value in previous challenges*

Remember a difficult situation you faced that ultimately helped you become a better person in some way. At the time, it may have even seemed like the end of the world. However, over time you may have grown stronger or opened up to new opportunities as a result. What lessons did you learn from that effort? How can you apply that knowledge in your life now?

BODY: *Do some extra exercise*

Exercise a little longer or harder than usual. Swim a few extra laps in the pool or bike an extra mile or two. When you start to feel tired, focus on the benefits you'll gain from the extra effort. The accomplishment will give you a sense of satisfaction and confidence.

SPIRIT: *Explore the space between breaths*

When you feel overwhelmed or burdened by problems, allow your awareness to dive deeply into the space between your in-breaths and out-breaths. This is a potent place of stillness and calm, a place without boundaries. If you allow your mind to formulate a clear question now, you may receive an inspired, intuitive answer.

"ALL THINGS CARRY THE YIN AND EMBRACE THE YANG.

NEUTRALIZING ENERGY BRINGS THEM INTO HARMONY."

—Lao Tzu

A Union of Opposites

Nearly 2,500 years ago, Hippocrates, considered the father of medicine, emphasized a need for body-mind balance and encouraged his patients to employ exercise, diet, and other practices to keep their bodies in balance. The ancient system of Chinese medicine also stresses the importance of balance in health. The following tips suggest ways to harmonize opposing energies to promote well-being in your life.

MIND: *Recognize the "male" and "female" within you*
Psychoanalyst Carl Jung proposed that every man has an inner female side, which he called the *anima*, and every woman has an inner male side, which he called the *animus*. Read Jung's *Aspects of the Feminine* to learn how these inner parts of yourself play out in your life.

BODY: *Engage both yin and yang energies*
To sense *yin* energy, sit quietly and breathe slowly, deeply. Notice that you feel calm and relaxed. To sense *yang* energy, move about quickly until you start to feel your breathing speed up. Notice that you feel more active and assertive.

SPIRIT: *Gaze at the yin/yang symbol to restore inner harmony*
According to Taoist philosophy, the black half of this symbol represents *yin* energy, which is feminine, quiet, and receptive. The white half signifies *yang* energy, which is masculine, active, and assertive. Both are necessary for balance. The circle connecting the two symbolizes the Tao—the Law of the Universe.

"A PENNY SAVED IS A PENNY EARNED." —Benjamin Franklin

Money Matters

Saving money and spending money are, to use a pun, two sides of the same coin. When you see abundance as a cycle that involves circulating wealth, you realize that hoarding money signifies a fear of lack, whereas spending can indicate trust in the universe's ability to provide. The following suggestions urge you to take a new look at money matters.

MIND: *Explore your attitudes toward money*
Do you have a prosperity consciousness or a poverty consciousness? Many of us were taught that money is the root of evil, or that it's better to give than to receive. These attitudes can inhibit your ability to attract wealth. Examine your ideas about money and where those ideas came from. Once you become aware of your attitudes, you can take steps to change them.

BODY: *Send energy to your root chakra*
Many of us link security with money. According to Eastern medicine, the root chakra, at the base of your spine, is the locus of security. Sit or lie in a comfortable place and close your eyes. Send loving energy to your root chakra. Feel it gradually become warmer, stronger, and more balanced. Do this for ten minutes daily to increase your sense of security.

SPIRIT: *Plant "seed" money*
Put a coin in the bottom of a flowerpot and fill it with soil. Plant parsley seeds in the flowerpot to symbolize your finances. Water and tend the seeds regularly. As they sprout and the plant starts to grow, envision your finances growing, too.

"THE WORLD WON'T CHANGE UNTIL I CHANGE."

—James Cowan

Become a Catalyst for Change

You don't have to march carrying placards or bombard politicians with letters in order to change the world. Simply changing your own ideas and behavior will produce changes in every area of your life. Those changes will flow out into the larger world. Today, try the following suggestions and see what happens.

MIND: *Be the change you want to see in the world*

If you could change the world, what would you change? Mahatma Gandhi recommended, "Be the change you want to see in the world." If you wish people were more respectful, work at being more respectful toward others. If you wish other people were more honest, patient, responsible, generous, or kind, practice these things yourself.

BODY: *Change your daily routine*

Often we find security in sameness. To see how attached you are to your predictable routines, try changing them. When you shower, wash yourself in a different order than usual—if you generally start on your left side, begin on your right. If you normally sleep on the right side of the bed, sleep on the left. How do these simple changes make you feel? When you're ready, attempt some bigger changes. How flexible are you?

SPIRIT: *Rearrange your furniture*

According to feng shui, the ancient Chinese art of placement, moving your furniture around stimulates change in your life. If you want to instigate changes in your love life, rearrange your bedroom. If you want to change something about your job, rearrange the furnishings in your office.

"HARM ENTERS ONLY WHERE FEAR MAKES AN OPENING."

—Carol K. Anthony, *A Guide to the I Ching*

Put Fear in Its Place

Today, consider what role fear plays in your life. Some fears are natural and serve a self-protective purpose. Taking risks, however, increases your self-confidence, resilience, creativity, and competence. The trick is to determine which fears contribute to your well-being and which limit it.

MIND: *Don't let fears stifle happiness*
Assess the real danger in something you fear. Many of the things you fear may have no validity, or may never actually happen. For instance, the likelihood of being in a plane crash is minuscule, so don't reject a dream trip to Paris on the off chance of a disaster.

BODY: *Strengthen your heart*
The heart has long been linked with courage. We tell someone whose faith and fervor are waning to "take heart" and describe people who give it their all as "having heart." Your physical heart is the locus of vitality, and one way to nourish it is by drinking hawthorn tea. The herb has been scientifically proven to lower high blood pressure, ease angina, regulate arrhythmia, and improve circulation.

SPIRIT: *Look for Leo in your birth chart*
You may not have been born while the sun was in the zodiac sign Leo, but Leo's energy is present somewhere in your birth chart. Have your horoscope calculated by a professional astrologer or online service. Then see where Leo appears in your chart—this shows where you are likely to exhibit courage.

"YOU ARE THAT WHICH YOU ARE SEEKING." —Saint Francis

You're A-Okay

You can be as happy and fulfilled as you allow yourself to be. The key is accepting yourself unconditionally—just as you are, right now. Today, begin to let go of guilt and shame—which may be rooted in other people's judgments of you—so you can appreciate your own value. You'll discover that everything you seek is already within you.

MIND: *Accept yourself*
"Your level of self-acceptance determines your level of happiness," explains Robert Holden in *Happiness Now!* Self-acceptance requires a certain degree of detachment—you can't look to other people to validate you. Many of our insecurities come from an inability to fulfill our parents' expectations. Consider one expectation and examine your reasons for choosing another option. How have you benefited from walking your own path?

BODY: *Drink chamomile tea*
At the end of the day, brew a cup of soothing chamomile tea and sip it slowly. This relaxing herbal drink calms your nerves, helps you sleep, and aids digestion. As you unwind and let the stress of the day slip away, you may find you become less critical and more accepting of yourself. You can begin to value your assets and appreciate your innate goodness.

SPIRIT: *Seek insight from many sources*
Through the ages, people have turned to spiritual traditions to search for wisdom about life's meaning and purpose. Today's seekers mine ancient wisdom traditions, science, meditation, and many other avenues. Instead of sticking with only one belief system, explore a variety of sources for guidance.

"THE TRUE FEELING OF SEX IS THAT OF A DEEP INTIMACY,

BUT ABOVE ALL A DEEP COMPLICITY." —James Dickey

Enhance Intimacy

Sexual self-care isn't just about engaging in safe sex, it's about sharing intimacy on every level. Opening up to your partner about your feelings is one of the best ways to become closer to one another. Intimacy requires a willingness to be vulnerable and to trust that your partner won't hurt you or let you down. Today, try these practices to enhance your intimacy.

MIND: *Speak from your heart*
Use statements that begin with "I" rather than "you." For example, "I feel bad," not "You make me feel bad." In this way, you aren't accusing or blaming your partner, you are expressing a personal reaction with the intent of remedying the situation for the good of both parties. Be honest, but not hurtful or judgmental.

BODY: *Share sensual touch*
Take turns lovingly stroking each other's bodies, enjoying and admiring every part. Avoid the genitals in the beginning, instead caressing feet, hands, the top of the head, and so on. Go slow. Give attention to parts you rarely bother with as well as the parts you like most. Allow yourself to give and receive pleasure, without reservation or self-consciousness.

SPIRIT: *Heal old patterns*
In meditation, contemplate an old hurt that still triggers anger, sadness, or other unwanted emotions. Try to recover the memory of how that wound originated. Envision the person who first hurt you. Visualize a beam of pink light running between your heart and that person's heart, softening the old pain.

"MINDS ARE LIKE PARACHUTES—THEY ONLY FUNCTION WHEN OPEN." —Anonymous

Engage Your Mind

Today, consider how you use your mind and assess whether you've gotten into a thinking rut. Like any muscle, the brain improves when you exercise it. Engaging your curiosity and practicing methods for stimulating your gray matter can help keep you sharp well into your later years. Try the following tips for boosting your brain power.

MIND: *Use more of your mind*

Most of us use only a small portion of our minds. In a 2006 study, researcher Dr. Sara Lazar found that meditation actually increases the size of the brain's cerebral cortex, the part associated with attention and memory. Meditation also slowed age-related thinning of the cerebral cortex.

BODY: *Eat "brain" food*

According to Dr. James Joseph, a neurologist at Tufts University, blueberries can reverse short-term memory loss and slow the effects of aging by reducing cell damage created by toxins. Blueberries also strengthen the signals fired between neurons, which keeps cognitive functioning high.

SPIRIT: *Listen to wind chimes*

Listening to the pleasing sound of wind chimes can soothe and relax your mind, allowing you to access more of the intuitive part of your brain. The lack of a symmetrical tune or rhythm prevents your logical brain from trying to make sense of the sounds. In feng shui, the ancient Chinese art of placement, wind chimes are used to clear energetic blockages and to gently stimulate activity in all areas of life.

"FACTS AND TRUTH REALLY DON'T HAVE MUCH TO DO
WITH EACH OTHER." —William Faulkner

Honesty Is the Best Policy

Today, promise yourself you will be totally honest. If someone asks you something you don't want to answer, don't resort to a little white lie to save face. Say: "Why do you want to know?" or "I'd rather not respond to that now."

MIND: *Tell the truth*

Honesty develops trust between people and leads to meaningful, responsible relationships. Although telling the truth can be difficult at times, doing so removes the burden of guilt and the potential need to concoct more lies to cover up previous ones. Speaking your own truth also lets you value yourself, rather than compromising yourself to suit someone else's expectations.

BODY: *Use kinesiology to discover what's true for you*

Kinesiology lets you see which foods, medications, and supplements benefit or harm you. Hold a substance in one hand and raise your other arm. Try to hold your arm up while another person tries to push it down. If the substance you're holding is bad for you, your strength/vitality will be impaired and the other person will easily be able to push your arm down. If the substance is good for you, you'll be able to resist pressure.

SPIRIT: *Walk your own path*

One person's truth may not be another's, as the myriad religions of the world attest. Trust your own instincts and insights. Follow your own path, guided by your own beliefs, remembering that truth isn't merely the letter of the law, but the essence at its core.

"IF THE DOORS OF PERCEPTION WERE CLEANSED

EVERYTHING WOULD APPEAR TO MAN AS IT IS, INFINITE."

—William Blake

Remove Your Blinders

Set an intention to open your eyes, mind, and heart today in order
to see the world around you more clearly. This may also mean seeing yourself more clearly. Often we deny or overlook things that we
don't want to acknowledge or deal with. Don't let conditioning or
fear keep you blinded now.

MIND: *Relax perceptual training*

We see what we are trained to see, and if we aren't prepared to see
something we probably won't. When the Spanish conquerors sailed
to what's now South America, the indigenous people couldn't see
their ships because they had no conception of such things. Likewise, most of us don't see angels, ghosts, and other spirits because
we aren't open to seeing them. What would happen if you let go of
preconceptions such as these? Try it and see.

BODY: *Eat foods that contain vitamin A*

Vitamin A works to improve your vision and prevent eye disorders.
Add foods that contain lots of vitamin A and beta-carotene to your
diet to nourish your eyes: asparagus, carrots, sweet potatoes, broccoli, spinach, mangoes, cantaloupe, and apricots.

SPIRIT: *Open your "third eye"*

Close your physical eyes and turn your inner attention to the brow
or third eye chakra. This energy center is located between your eyebrows, where your nose joins your forehead. Imagine indigo-colored
light glowing there. This practice helps to increase your intuition
and insight.

"Wine is bottled poetry." —Robert Louis Stevenson

Drink to Your Health

For thousands of years, wine has been one of the most beloved of beverages, synonymous with celebrations. Many health practitioners now recommend drinking a glass of red wine per day—the grape skins contain antioxidants—which may be why wine sales in the United States are growing. Today, consider switching from beer or mixed drinks to red wine.

MIND: *See wine as a transformation symbol*
Wine is a symbol of transformation. Its creation even comes from the transformative fermentation of grapes. In mythology, the gemstone amethyst was formed when the goddess Diana turned a young devotee into a crystal to protect her from being killed by a tiger, then the god Bacchus poured wine on her and turned her purple. In the Bible, Jesus turned water to wine at a wedding ceremony. Let this symbol inspire you to transform something in your life.

BODY: *Drink to your health*
According to some studies, drinking a glass or two of red wine a day can reduce the risk of certain cancers, heart disease, and the onset of Alzheimer's and Parkinson's disease. These health benefits are tied to a type of the antioxidant known as flavonoids and the non-flavonoid resveratrol, which also help to lower LDL cholesterol and prevent blood clots.

SPIRIT: *Share a ritual glass of wine*
Many spiritual and cultural ceremonies involve drinking wine, from taking communion to toasting the bride and groom at a wedding reception. Offer a blessing as a toast, such as, "May you never thirst."

"SOMETIMES I'VE BELIEVED AS MANY AS SIX IMPOSSIBLE
THINGS BEFORE BREAKFAST."

—Lewis Carroll, *Alice's Adventures in Wonderland*

Believe Anything Is Possible

Each step in humankind's progress required believing in something the majority of people dismissed. Two hundred years ago, for instance, few people would have believed men would walk on the moon. Today, examine your beliefs about what's possible and what isn't—and how those beliefs influence you.

MIND: *Realize your ability to co-create your reality*
Many belief systems, including the Law of Attraction, tell us that we co-create our destinies in conjunction with divine consciousness. According to this philosophy, you can tap into the creative power of your own mind and the infinite potential of the universe to manifest whatever you desire. With your thoughts, you draw into your life all circumstances, relationships, and experiences.

BODY: *Tap your psychic healing power*
The next time you injure yourself slightly—a small cut, burn, or bruise—tap your psychic power to heal yourself. Use your attention to direct soothing green light to the injured site. Then instead of focusing on the injury, envision yourself completely healed. Repeat several times a day, for a minute or so at a time. Most likely, you'll find you heal more quickly than you normally would.

SPIRIT: *Believe in divine assistance*
You've undoubtedly heard stories of people accomplishing amazing feats when desperate circumstances required them to act. Some people who have done the "impossible" say they received help from a higher source. Believe that you, too, can access divine assistance should you need it.

"IT'S GOOD TO HAVE MONEY AND THE THINGS THAT
MONEY CAN BUY, BUT IT'S GOOD, TOO, TO CHECK UP ONCE
IN A WHILE AND MAKE SURE THAT YOU HAVEN'T LOST
THE THINGS THAT MONEY CAN'T BUY."

—George Horace Lorimer

Prime the Prosperity Pump

It may seem contradictory to give away money when you are trying
to increase your income. But actually, when you give what you want,
you prime the pump and tap into the universal cycle of ebb and flow.
Remember the saying, "What goes around comes around"? Try it
and see.

MIND: *Donate to charity*
If you go to the supermarket and a bell ringer is standing outside,
collecting for charity, drop some money in the bucket. As you do,
mentally affirm that the money will return to you many times over
and help you build financial prosperity.

BODY: *Strengthen your root chakra*
Eastern medicine links the root chakra (located at the base of your
spine) with security, and money is often a factor in how secure we
feel. To strengthen your sense of financial security and keep money
from flowing out too quickly, lie on your stomach and place a piece
of smoky quartz on your tailbone for about fifteen minutes a day.

SPIRIT: *Be grateful for your abundance*
The universe is rich beyond anything we can imagine, and there is
plenty for everyone. Remember that money must circulate, and that
hoarding stops the flow of abundance. Making money your god will
thwart your efforts to attract it. Express gratitude for the abundance
you have, and share with others.

"IF WE LIVE FOR TOMORROW WE WILL CERTAINLY BE

DEAD ON ARRIVAL."   —Benjamin Sells, *The Soul of the Law*

Get Grounded

Instead of running about helter-skelter today, ground your energy.
When you scatter yourself in a dozen directions, you waste your
resources, increase your level of stress, and risk burnout. You are
also less likely to accomplish your goals. The following tips can help
you stay calm and centered.

MIND: *Rein in your thoughts*
Discipline your mind so your thoughts don't keep running amok
like a hamster in a treadmill. Choose a single word, such as *peace*,
contentment, *love*, or *security*. Close your physical eyes and see
the word in your mind's eye. Contemplate the meaning of the word
you've chosen. Explore it deeply and fully. If other thoughts pop into
your head, gently nudge them aside and refocus on the word.

BODY: *Sit on the ground*
Connect with Mother Earth and her nourishing powers by sitting or
lying on the ground for ten minutes or so. Close your eyes and feel
your connection with the earth beneath you. Sense yourself being
supported and sustained. Breathe deeply and relax.

SPIRIT: *Hold a piece of hematite*
Dense, black hematite grounds nervous energy and helps you stay
centered. Rub a smooth, tumbled piece of it to stabilize your energy
and balance body, mind, and spirit. It also slows down frenetic
thoughts and improves your memory. Wear or carry hematite in your
pocket to shield you from other people's vibrations, too.

"SEX IS THE SEED, LOVE IS THE FLOWER, COMPASSION IS THE FRAGRANCE." —Osho, *Zen: Zest, Zip, Zap and Zing*

Increase Your Sexual Satisfaction

Sex is more than a brief indulgence in sensory pleasure. Satisfying sex nourishes us on every level and, as research has shown, it contributes to health and happiness. Today, consider ways to enhance the experience of intimacy in your life.

MIND: *Accept yourself sexually*
We all have different sexual desires and appetites. What one person enjoys may be a complete turnoff for another. Allow yourself to explore your own sexual self-interests, without judging yourself, and see what turns you on. Once you open yourself to the pleasure of touch in its many forms, you'll be more comfortable and be able to give and receive pleasure more fully.

BODY: *Experiment with something new*
Are you intrigued by a particular sexual practice, but have avoided it because you thought it was too kinky? Give yourself permission to experiment with new possibilities. However consenting adults choose to find pleasure is okay. Knowing what feels good to you and enjoying it is important to your own happiness, as well as that of a partner.

SPIRIT: *Acquire a Shiva Lingam stone*
This phallic-shaped stone, which often features rings of a contrasting color, is considered sacred in the Hindu tradition. It represents the union of male and female in what's known as the "alchemical marriage." Place one on your nightstand to enhance your environment with sacred sexual energy.

"HEALING THE UNIVERSE IS AN INSIDE JOB."   —*Mindwalk*

Do Yoga to Promote Healing

For 5,000 years people in the East have been doing yoga for physical, mental, and spiritual healing. By practicing yoga you can rejuvenate, care for, and nurture yourself at the deepest levels, which has a positive impact on your relationships. Most importantly, you will develop a better relationship with yourself.

MIND: *Practice dharana*

Stilling the restless mind is a goal in yoga and meditation. A practice known as *dharana* involves focusing on a single object in order to still your mind. Choose a particular object, either something living or something inorganic. When your mind is still, you can be single-minded in your explorations on the path of healing.

BODY: *Stay fit*

Yoga is a wonderful way to get into shape. The practice of forward bends, back bends, lateral poses, twists, and inversions balances and works every muscle, bone, joint, and organ in the body. Weight-bearing yoga poses, crucial for healthy bones, provide one of the best exercise systems known to humankind. Flexibility and strength of the muscles and range of motion in the joints greatly increase. Stamina and endurance also improve.

SPIRIT: *Practice bhakti yoga*

Bhakti yoga is yoga of devotion, devotion to the divine. When you practice this type of yoga, you are opening your heart chakra. One way to practice bhakti yoga is to chant. In bhakti yoga, typically you will choose an element or incarnation of the divine to honor, and focus on it for your highest good and development.

"HE WHO ANGERS YOU CONQUERS YOU." —Elizabeth Kenny

Keep Your Cool

Chill out today. Instead of letting little things eat at you like fire ants, try to keep your perspective. A study of nearly 13,000 people, published in *Circulation,* found that angry people are more at risk for coronary artery disease and heart attacks. Try these tips to keep your cool.

MIND: *Imagine swimming in cool water*
The next time you start to lose your temper, don't blow your top like a fiery volcano. Instead, close your eyes and imagine diving into a deep pool of cool, clear water. Envision yourself swimming peacefully, letting the water keep you afloat. Keep swimming until you feel your anger subside, replaced by a sense of serenity.

BODY: *Take the heat out with aloe*
The soothing juice of the aloe vera plant, a type of succulent that grows in hot, dry climates, makes a wonderful tonic for burns. Slather the gel on sunburn to take the heat out. Rub it on minor burns to relieve pain and reduce the chance of blistering. Drink aloe juice to calm an acid stomach or to help cool the burning sensation of an ulcer.

SPIRIT: *Wear blue*
To help you chill out or stay calm under stress, wear blue clothing. We equate blue with water and cold, red with fire and heat. Studies have shown that heart rate and respiration even slow down when you sit in a blue room.

"THE BEAST IS ALWAYS THE DARK FACE OF THE HANDSOME PRINCE." —Liz Greene, *Saturn: A New Look at an Old Devil*

Make Friends with Your Dark Side

Today, explore your hidden side. Myths and fairy tales often illustrate the search for union and acceptance of the rejected part that resides within us. As Wilhelm Reich, Carl Jung, and other noted psychoanalysts have explained, denying things we don't like about ourselves can cause mental, physical, and social dysfunction. Bringing them into consciousness awakens power.

MIND: *Read a fairy tale or myth*

The fairy tale *Beauty and the Beast* is an allegory about self-acceptance and union. Each of us has a side we don't fully accept and may try to hide from others—even from ourselves. However, when we reject parts of ourselves, we may attract people to us who will act out those qualities. Only by making friends with your *bête noire* can you be at peace with yourself.

BODY: *Consider Rolfing therapy*

Consider getting Rolfed. Rolfing is a form of bodywork that involves deep muscle massage and connective tissue massage to provide structural integration. Developed by Dr. Ida Rolf, this technique works to harmonize the entire body. In the process, deeply held emotions that have become trapped in the body's musculature may be released.

SPIRIT: *Face your dream monsters*

Dream researchers say monsters in your nightmares represent parts of you that scare you or that you don't like. Next time you find yourself being chased by a beast in a dream, turn around and face it. You may discover it isn't as scary as it seemed.

"IF YOU ARE GOING TO LEARN, YOU NEED TO FORGET
WHAT YOU KNOW." —Christopher Moore, *Coyote Blue*

Question Conventional Wisdom

Don't believe everything you hear today. Throughout history, experts have made proclamations of "facts" that later turned out to be false. If something doesn't seem right to you, investigate it further. Trust your instincts, rather than simply accepting what you've been told to believe.

MIND: *Meditate daily*
Until the 1960s, most Westerners had never heard of meditation and many of those who had thought it was weird. Today more than twenty million Americans meditate. Hundreds of scientific studies have shown meditation can aid a panoply of mental, physical, and emotional ills, including coronary problems, cancer, and depression.

BODY: *Drink coffee for your health*
For years we were told coffee was bad for us, but new research shows coffee offers many health benefits. Dr. Frank Hu, professor at the Harvard School of Public Health, and a team of researchers found that coffee drinkers are less likely to suffer from diabetes than nondrinkers. Drinking coffee may also aid Parkinson's disease, dementia, certain cancers, heart rhythm problems, and strokes.

SPIRIT: *Explore various religions*
You may have been raised in a particular religious belief, but whether or not you still follow that faith, you can learn by studying other spiritual traditions. Reading about the concepts and practices of people in other cultures may increase your understanding and tolerance. You might also discover similarities between the different belief systems.

"KEEP KNOCKING, AND THE JOY INSIDE WILL EVENTUALLY
OPEN A WINDOW AND LOOK OUT TO SEE WHO'S THERE."

—Rumi

Connect with Joy

Today, connect with the joy that is your natural birthright. Joy is something that comes from within, from the core of your being, not as a result of external stimuli. True joy is more than delight at receiving something you desire. It is an inextinguishable flame, a spark of Spirit, that constantly warms you; it can be hidden, but never destroyed.

MIND: *Thoughts direct emotions*

Pay attention to how your thoughts trigger your emotions. Think, read, or discuss something unpleasant and notice how you react. Do you become tense? Do you sense your guard going up? Do you feel disempowered? Now shift to thinking or talking about something pleasant. Notice how your feelings change. Do you feel more relaxed, comfortable, powerful?

BODY: *Lift your spirits with aromatherapy*

According to the science and art of aromatherapy, certain scents lift our spirits and make us feel happier. Bergamot, borage, frankincense, orange blossom, vanilla, and ylang-ylang are some fragrances that when inhaled have uplifting effects on the brain. Put water in a spray bottle, add a few drops of one of these essential oils, and shake it vigorously. Then mist a room with the pleasing scent.

SPIRIT: *Reflect on tarot images*

The tarot deck contains numerous cards that depict joyful images, including The Sun, The Star, the Three of Cups, the Nine of Cups, and the Four of Wands. Sift through a deck and choose a card that makes you feel happy when you look at it. Meditate with it or display it where you'll see it often.

"THE QUEST FOR MEANING ALWAYS TAKES US INTO THE UNKNOWN." —F. Aster Barnwell, *The Pilgrim's Companion*

Journey into Unfamiliar Territory

Today, find ways to stretch yourself beyond what's familiar. Stimulate your mind, body, and spirit by going outside your comfort zone—you may be pleasantly surprised. Consider the following suggestions, but don't limit yourself to these.

MIND: *Read about an unfamiliar subject*
One way to keep your mind healthy is to exercise it. A study published in *Neurology* in 2007 found that people who read books tended to be healthier than nonreaders. Book reading also helped protect against cognitive damage and memory loss. Indulge your curiosity and strengthen your mental skills by reading books about topics that are new to you.

BODY: *Travel to a place you've never been*
You don't have to journey to a foreign land; you can go to a spot in your own town where you've never been before. Go with an open mind and a spirit of discovery. Walk about the area slowly. Engage all your senses: listen to sounds; smell the smells that are unique to this place; touch the plants, rocks, buildings, or other features you encounter.

SPIRIT: *Take a shamanic journey*
Shamans in many cultures journey between the different planes of existence. They often do this to gain knowledge that can benefit people here on earth. Shamanic journeying is usually done in a meditative or trancelike state. Using visualization techniques, you travel to other realms and connect with the resident entities. Read about it before trying it yourself.

"A PESSIMIST SEES THE DIFFICULTY IN EVERY OPPORTUNITY;
AN OPTIMIST SEES THE OPPORTUNITY IN EVERY DIFFICULTY."
—Winston Churchill

Be Positive

Look on the bright side today and make a point of enjoying your life, rather than bemoaning it. According to the tenets of Hinduism, thoughts are as powerful as spoken words and produce reactions, either good or bad, according to what you think about. It's a good reason to be positive in your thoughts, words, and deeds.

MIND: *Monitor negative thoughts*

Negative thoughts have a way of multiplying, and if you let them they'll drag you down into the dumps. Start monitoring your thoughts. Every time you catch yourself thinking about something unpleasant, immediately shift to something positive. Keep a few feel-good thoughts handy and go to them whenever you need to dispel negativity.

BODY: *Enjoy sex often*

Orgasm is the most pleasurable sensation most people ever experience. But orgasm offers benefits beyond immediate gratification. During orgasm, blood flows into the prefrontal cortex of the right brain—the site of joy, imagination, and creativity. It gives you a sense of profound gratification. Regular sex can also ease depression because orgasm releases endorphins, the hormones that improve mood and increase optimism.

SPIRIT: *Believe in a loving deity*

Choose to believe in a loving deity—it could help you be healthier. A study published in the AMA's *Archives of Internal Medicine* in 2001 found that older medical patients who felt God was punishing them or had abandoned them had poorer recovery rates from illness and a higher mortality.

"EVERY PLACE IS UNDER THE STARS, EVERY

PLACE IS THE CENTER OF THE WORLD."

—John Burroughs

Be at Peace in Your World

Today, seek peace and comfort in your world. Know that peace is both an inner and an outer state. Even in the midst of activity, you can retreat to your inner sanctuary.

MIND: *What do the stars say about you?*

An ancient axiom states "As above, so below," which means what occurs on earth reflects what happens in the heavens. Astrologers believe the positions of the celestial bodies at the moment of your birth reveal your mental, emotional, and physical attributes. To learn more about your place in the world and how the cosmos influences you, have a qualified astrologer calculate your natal horoscope.

BODY: *Build a personal sanctuary*

Set aside a space in your home or yard where you can retreat from the hectic pace of your daily life, relax, and turn within. Arrange and decorate this personal space in a way that pleases you. Include only objects that make you feel happy or at peace. Spend time in your sanctuary every day, meditating, doing yoga or tai chi, dancing, or whatever makes you feel joyful and serene.

SPIRIT: *Bring harmony to your home with feng shui*

The ancient Chinese art of feng shui aims to create balance in your environment. Combine light and dark, bright colors and cool ones, angular shapes and rounded ones, activity and rest, in order to balance yin and yang energies in your home.

> "HAVE THE COURAGE TO FOLLOW YOUR HEART AND INTUITION. THEY SOMEHOW ALREADY KNOW WHAT YOU TRULY WANT TO BECOME. EVERYTHING ELSE IS SECONDARY."
>
> —Steve Jobs

Follow Your Bliss

Pursue opportunities that seem right to you, even if other people think you're nuts. What if J. K. Rowling had not followed her inspiration to write about the adolescent magician Harry Potter? Or if Ralph Lauren had been afraid to use his tie designs to found his own company? Let your heart be your guide.

MIND: *Start a wish book*

Writing down what you seek in life brings your dreams one step closer to reality. Create a wish book, in which you write what you intend to materialize in terms of career, relationships, health, and so on. Read through your wish book every day and update it regularly.

BODY: *Tap into the energy of Mars*

Since antiquity, herbalists have linked plants with planetary influences and prescribed herbal remedies that contained the energies of the planets. Mars is the planet of courage, vitality, and assertiveness. According to some herbalists, you can tap the energy of Mars by ingesting herbs and plants with Martian qualities, especially spiciness: cayenne pepper, hot mustard, salsa, horseradish, and curry.

SPIRIT: *Wear a bloodstone*

Roman soldiers carried this opaque green jasper, flecked with red (formed by iron oxide), with them when they went into battle. The early Gnostics believed the stone conferred courage to its wearer, and the ancient Greeks thought it would bring endurance and success in competition. Wear a bloodstone to help you achieve your goal.

"WHEN YOU COME TO THE END OF YOUR ROPE,

TIE A KNOT AND HANG ON." —Franklin D. Roosevelt

Hang in There

Many spiritual teachers espouse the benefits of focusing on the present and letting the future come about as it will. What you do today lays the foundation for what will evolve into the future. Therefore, by giving this day, this moment, the proper attention, you take care of tomorrow.

MIND: *Live one day at a time*

Trying to look too far ahead into the future can add stress to an already difficult situation. When you are facing a challenge, try to focus only on what you have to do today. Adopt the saying from Alcoholics Anonymous: *One day at a time.* Do the things that are absolutely essential and let the rest go until a later date.

BODY: *Gain vitality from iron-rich foods*

Iron creates healthy red blood cells that carry oxygen to your body's tissues, creating energy. Meat, fish, eggs, and green vegetables such as Swiss chard, broccoli, asparagus, parsley, and Brussels sprouts contain iron. Close to eighteen million Americans suffer from iron-deficiency anemia, which can cause fatigue. The problem is more common in women than men, but can be remedied by adding iron-rich or iron-fortified foods to your diet.

SPIRIT: *Consult the I Ching*

The 3,000-year-old oracle known as the *I Ching* offers wise counsel when you need answers. Also known as the *Book of Changes*, it contains sixty-four hexagrams (six-lined patterns) that represent different approaches to problem-solving.

"KINDNESS IS THE LANGUAGE WHICH THE DEAF CAN HEAR
AND THE BLIND CAN SEE." —Mark Twain

Perform Random Acts of Kindness

Today, voluntarily do something compassionate, generous, or charitable for someone else. Charitable acts benefit the giver at least as much as they do the recipient. In his book *The Healing Power of Doing Good*, Allan Luks, former executive director of Big Brothers/Big Sisters of New York City, concluded that "helping contributes to the maintenance of good health, and it can diminish the effect of diseases and disorders both serious and minor, psychological and physical."

MIND: *Read to someone*
Go to a nursing home, hospital, prison, or other facility where the residents aren't able to read for themselves. If you prefer, read to someone who is blind or to children who haven't learned to read yet. Choose an uplifting story or one that has a positive message to share. Discuss it afterward.

BODY: *Smile*
Sometimes doing something as simple as smiling at someone can make that person's day. Smiling makes you feel good, too. Make a point of smiling often, at family members, friends, coworkers, neighbors, store clerks, and perfect strangers. Chances are, they'll smile back.

SPIRIT: *Silently bless others*
Sending good thoughts and blessings to others is an act of kindness. Thoughts and feelings resonate energy, and that energy affects you as well as everyone else. Even if someone angers you—*especially* if someone angers you—bless that person instead of cursing him or her. Kindness begets kindness.

"DON'T CONFUSE THE MARKERS WITH THE GAME."

—Tom Robbins

Put Things in Perspective

Today, start assessing what's important to you and why. Where did your ideas and values originate? Are they serving you now or hindering you?

MIND: *Evaluate your need for possessions*

In our consumer-oriented society, we often spend so much time in the pursuit of wealth and possessions that we don't have time to enjoy the things we have. Instead of purchasing the latest and greatest devices—especially expensive technology—ask yourself if you really need it. If not, wait until the second or third version comes out. Usually you'll only have to wait a few months, and the later versions will be cheaper and perhaps more reliable.

BODY: *Stand on your head*

Seeing things from a different perspective—literally—can alter the way you interpret them. Many inverted yoga postures are intended to shift your awareness by shifting your position. When you stand on your head, blood flows into your brain and affects its functioning. Being upside down also rearranges your relationship to the world and how you usually interact with it.

SPIRIT: *Acknowledge the transient nature of existence*

See the inevitable ebb and flow of all things. Problems (and their solutions) are transient: They come and go like the rising and falling tides. Difficulties that seemed insurmountable in the past may now seem like just a bump in the road of life. When you acknowledge this rhythm in life, you'll be better able to put problems in perspective.

"SYMBOLS ARE THE IMAGINATIVE SIGNPOSTS OF LIFE."
—Margot Asquith

The Power of Symbols

Symbols, both natural and man-made, abound in our world. In modern society, businesses use symbols called logos to express a company's intention. Today, consider some well-known symbols and notice what impressions they evoke in you.

MIND: *Symbols can alter and expand consciousness*
All cultures throughout the world use symbols to convey concepts directly to the subconscious. Some symbols have the power to expand consciousness, and many religious and spiritual symbols are utilized for that purpose. Consider the Hindu symbol for AUM—it is believed to be the sound of the universe's vibration. Gazing at the symbol aligns your awareness with the sound.

BODY: *Focus on a symbol to promote healing*
In Jungian therapy, patients are encouraged to focus on symbols that embody special meaning for them in order to promote healing. Choose a symbol that you associate with the condition you want to attract (not the ailment itself). For instance, a yin/yang symbol connotes balance. Therefore, it might be a good one to consider if your digestive system is out of balance. Look at the symbol often to reinforce your intention to heal.

SPIRIT: *Choose a personal symbol*
Choose a symbol that holds cultural or spiritual significance for you. This symbol can serve as a touchstone and provide a sense of connection or comfort. Draw it on paper, carve it in wood, or have a jeweler craft it in silver or gold. Whenever you see or touch your symbol, you'll feel an inner connection to something larger than yourself.

"WHEN YOU CHANGE THE WAY YOU LOOK AT THINGS,

THE THINGS YOU LOOK AT CHANGE." —Dr. Wayne Dyer

Invite Positive Change into Your Life

We tend to get locked into routines that can block opportunities for new experiences. When our attitudes, behaviors, and actions become fixed, we become dulled to the joys of discovery. Change is the nature of life, the only thing we can be sure of. Nothing remains the same forever. Embrace it today.

MIND: *Use the right language*

The language you use can have a profound impact on whether you manifest a positive or negative outcome for yourself. If you're about to give a speech, you may experience some butterflies. Instead of thinking, *I'm so nervous, I'm going to forget what I'm saying*, tell yourself, *Hey, this is pretty exciting. I get to share my ideas with all these people.*

BODY: *Change your regimen*

Walk to a place you go frequently—but this time, take a different route than usual. Observe how the terrain looks when seen from a new direction. Notice how it feels to cover familiar territory in an unfamiliar way. Pay attention to your body's signals—how do you react when you shift your predictable regimen? Do you find it stimulating? Uncomfortable?

SPIRIT: *Make changes slowly*

Be gentle with yourself as you undertake changes. Go slow, and make small changes to see how you react to them. Think of yourself as a plant being transplanted. Give yourself time to adjust before making major shifts.

"SOMETIMES, THE BEST WAY TO SEE IS TO

CLOSE YOUR EYES." —Erroll J. Bailey

Increase Your Intuition

Western society tends to favor rational, logical, left-brain thinking over intuitive, right-brain functioning. Both are important, however. Today, practice using your intuition. Try these techniques for strengthening the right side of your brain and the connections between the two hemispheres.

MIND: *Use Zener cards to enhance ESP*
Developed in the 1930s by Karl Zener, this deck contains twenty-five cards printed with five simple symbols: circle, cross, square, star, and wavy lines. Ask a friend to draw a card and mentally send it to you, while you try to mentally see the symbol. Then switch places. Send while your friend receives the image. Practicing this technique can help strengthen your intuition.

BODY: *Activate your "third eye" with acupressure*
The acupressure point known as "third eye," located between the eyebrows (where the bridge of your nose intersects with your forehead) is linked with mental clarity and intuition. Gently press this point with your fingertip for a minute or so to open yourself to new insights and ideas.

SPIRIT: *Pay attention to hunches*
We all get hunches, but usually ignore them. Often hunches are your intuition speaking to you, giving you helpful information your rational mind might not be able to provide. Start paying attention to these hunches—you may find them to be very useful. Write down impressions, feelings, and insights, and learn to recognize your own personal signals.

"HAPPINESS IS THE MEANING AND THE PURPOSE OF LIFE,

THE WHOLE AIM AND END OF HUMAN EXISTENCE."

—Aristotle

Have a Happy Day

What gives you happiness? What provides you with a sense of purpose? Those are the things to devote your energy to today, not simply those endeavors that earn you a living or that fulfill your obligations and the needs of others.

MIND: *Journal about what makes you happy*
In a journal, make a list of things that make you happy. It could be spending time with friends, petting your animal companion, taking a walk in nature, or listening to music. As you write, call up memories of doing the things you love. Allow these positive feelings to spread through you.

BODY: *Eat omega-3s to elevate your mood*
Cultures whose diets include high levels of omega-3s suffer less depression than Americans, whose diets are high in omega-6 fatty acids. Because more than 60 percent of your brain is fat, your mental health is affected by your intake of the essential fatty acids. Omega-3 fatty acids not only promote your brain's ability to regulate moods, they are also needed for normal nervous system function.

SPIRIT: *Look at a rainbow*
Rainbows are universal symbols of happiness, especially after a dark or stormy time. Find a picture of a rainbow and post it in a place where you will see it often. Or, go online and download an image of a rainbow onto your computer's monitor. If possible, go outside and see the real thing. Let this beautiful image brighten your day.

"IF WE COULD ALL HEAR ONE ANOTHER'S PRAYERS,
GOD MIGHT BE RELIEVED OF SOME OF HIS BURDENS."
—Ashleigh Brilliant

The Power of Prayer

Prayer is a part of virtually all religious and spiritual traditions. You don't have to belong to a particular religion or spiritual path to pray, however. According to a Gallup poll in 1999, more than 90 percent of Americans engage in prayer.

MIND: *The positive effects of prayer*
Like meditation, prayer has a calming effect on mind and body. Brainwave frequencies slow, as do heart rate and respiration. The production of endorphins in the brain—the proteins that enhance positive feelings—increases. Many sources recommend praying without desperation, believing wholeheartedly that your prayers will be answered.

BODY: *Healing prayers*
In *Prayer Is Good Medicine*, Dr. Larry Dossey described how praying for others—even at a distance and without their knowledge—had a positive impact on people's health. Dr. Mitchell Krucoff of Duke University Medical Center found that cardiac patients who received prayers experienced up to 100 percent fewer side effects from medical procedures as people who were not prayed for. Although research into the efficacy of prayer continues, it can't hurt to send positive energy to those in need and it may very well help.

SPIRIT: *Burn incense to send prayers to the heavens*
According to some spiritual traditions, incense smoke serves as a cosmic FedEx service, carrying prayers to the deities. Light a stick of incense and allow your requests to float up to the heavens on the sweet-scented smoke.

"IF ONE ASPIRES TO REACH THE TAO, ONE SHOULD

PRACTICE WALKING IN A CIRCLE."   —Taoist Canon

Find Comfort and Continuity in Circles

Today, contemplate the age-old symbol of the circle and what it means to you. Even our solar system operates in a circular pattern. Some spiritual traditions think of the year as an annual circle. Try the following suggestions and see how you respond.

MIND: *No beginning, no end*
The circle is one of the oldest symbols, found in cultures and countries throughout the world. It represents unity, wholeness, and continuity. A circle has no beginning and no end, no "head" or "foot"—which is why interior designers use circular tables in boardrooms to encourage cooperation. Experiment with sitting in a circle or around a circular table. Do you feel a greater sense of equality? Sharing? Harmony?

BODY: *Walk a labyrinth*
Contrary to popular belief, a labyrinth is *not* a maze. Labyrinths are circular structures with a single, circuitous path that winds around, moving from the perimeter to the center. Since ancient times, people have walked labyrinths to symbolize the soul's journey. Traversing the many turns in a labyrinth also balances your brain's logical and intuitive parts.

SPIRIT: *Protect yourself with a circle*
Before engaging in any type of ritual, imagine a circle around the space where you and other participants will celebrate; this barrier protects you against "bad vibes." The easiest way is to envision a wall of white light surrounding you. When you've finished your ceremony, visually remove the protective circle.

"MEN ARE NOT PRISONERS OF FATE, BUT PRISONERS OF THEIR OWN MINDS." —Franklin D. Roosevelt

Nourish Your Mind

You only have one brain. Take care of it. Like your body, your mind needs to be exercised to continue working properly. The food you eat will also have an important impact on your brain and your mental functions. Here are some suggestions to help keep your brain healthy.

MIND: *Contemplate a Zen koan*
A koan is a story, question, puzzle, or thought-provoking idea that cannot be analyzed with the logical mind. One well-known koan asks: "What is the sound of one hand clapping?" Zen practitioners use koans to gain insight through intuition. Try contemplating a koan yourself to exercise your mental powers.

BODY: *Slow Alzheimer's with vitamin E*
Consuming high levels of vitamin E delays the progression of Alzheimer's disease by about seven months, suggests a Columbia University study. Vitamin E is present in a number of superfoods, but only sweet potatoes provide vitamin E without the fat and calories. In fact, the sweet potato ranked highest in nutritional value according to a study by the Center for Science in the Public Interest.

SPIRIT: *Energize your mind with gemstones*
Crystal workers often suggest using clear gemstones, such as diamonds, aquamarines, and amethysts, to support mental functioning. Sapphires are said to aid intuition. Either wear one or more of these gems, or lie down and place one near the top of your head for about fifteen minutes to receive its energy.

"THE WORLD IS NOT TO BE PUT IN ORDER; THE WORLD IS ORDER, INCARNATE. IT IS FOR US TO HARMONIZE WITH THIS ORDER." —Henry Miller

Bring Balance to Your Life

Today, pay attention to areas in your life that may have become imbalanced. Do you work too much and play too little? Do you spend too much time with people and not enough time alone? Consider ways to promote harmony in mind, body, and spirit.

MIND: *Notice recurring incidences*
Do certain occurrences keep repeating in your life? It could be a signal from your subconscious to pay attention. The appearance of symbols and patterns that mean something to you may also be messages from the intuitive part of your brain. Attuning your awareness can help you balance your intuitive brain with your logical brain.

BODY: *Get a chiropractic adjustment*
When your body is out of alignment, you may feel out of sync with life in general. Getting your spine in line not only improves your physical well-being, but your emotions and mental state as well. When pain diminishes, you may relate to other people better and be more productive at work.

SPIRIT: *Celebrate the Wheel of the Year*
Since ancient times, people have marked the cycles of the earth and heavens with festivities. Many earth-honoring spiritual traditions still celebrate eight holidays in what's known as the Wheel of the Year. These dates include the two equinoxes and the two solstices, as well as the cross-quarter dates that fall halfway between the other four. Following the Wheel helps you align yourself with nature and the cosmos.

"ALWAYS CHOOSE LOVE OVER SAFETY IF YOU CAN TELL

THE DIFFERENCE." —Josephine Humphreys, *Dreams of Sleep*

Dare to Love

Today, open yourself to the healing power of love. Many of us, having been hurt in love before, put up barriers to love. If this is true of you, try removing the bricks in your inner fortress one by one.

MIND: *Reveal your feelings*

Often we don't express our feelings because we fear our loved ones may not respond in the way we'd like. Today, take a risk and reveal to your beloved something you've been holding inside. It may be something you admire about that person, something he or she has done that hurt you, or something you'd like him or her to do.

BODY: *Eat garlic and onions*

Research published in the *Journal of the National Cancer Institute* in 2002 made an interesting case for reducing men's risk of prostate cancer with a diet rich in garlic and onions. The researchers found that men who ate more than one-third ounce of onions, garlic, chives, or scallions daily were less likely to get cancer of the prostate. Of course, it's a good idea for your partner to eat these odoriferous veggies, too!

SPIRIT: *Invite love into your life*

Use a ballpoint pen, nail file, or nail to carve the word LOVE on a red or pink candle. Put the candle in a window (away from drapery or other flammable objects). Light the candle. As it burns, imagine the candlelight shining the way so a lover can find you.

"EACH DAY COMES BEARING ITS GIFTS.

UNTIE THE RIBBONS." —Ruth Ann Schabacker

Seize the Day

Decide to make the most of today. We never know how long we have on the planet or what lies ahead. Therefore, it makes sense to enjoy each day to the fullest, and to take advantage of the opportunities that come your way.

MIND: *Start your day in the right frame of mind*
The first thoughts you have upon awakening can set the tone for the rest of the day. Focus on positive things for a few moments before getting out of bed. You may wish to make a list of things you're thankful for and recite it to yourself as soon as you wake up.

BODY: *Do the "Sun Salutation" each morning*
Performing a series of yoga postures known as the "Sun Salutation" is a great way to begin the day. Stand facing east as you go through these movements, greeting the sun as it rises. The exercise stimulates circulation and breathing, loosens the kinks in your muscles, and aligns you with the energy of the day. Do this every morning and you'll feel refreshed and rejuvenated, ready to face whatever comes your way.

SPIRIT: *Chart your power days*
Astrologers say you have at least twelve days each year that are especially auspicious. Known as "power days," they fall each month on the same date as your birthday. If you were born on the eighteen of a month, the eighteenth day of every month is a power day for you. Take advantage of these fortunate dates.

"MISTAKES ARE THE USUAL BRIDGES BETWEEN INEXPERIENCE AND WISDOM." —Phyllis Theroux

Give Yourself a Break

Self-recrimination and guilt can have adverse effects mentally, physically, and spiritually. At a conference of the British Psychological Society in Winchester in 2000, researchers from the University of Hull explained that guilt can interfere with the immune system's ability to protect against colds, flu, and other illnesses.

MIND: *Forgive yourself*

Stop beating yourself up about a mistake you made in the past. Even if the consequences were hurtful, you can't undo them now. Instead, focus on the learning experiences that have come as a result of the error you made. In certain ways, you are probably a better person now because of the experience.

BODY: *Eat parsley to rejuvenate your body*

If poor eating habits have left your body in less than optimal condition, eating parsley can help treat internal inflammation and protect against free-radical damage. That's because parsley is high in vitamin C, a potent blood cleanser. Free radicals in the body contribute to a variety of diseases that have been linked to poor diet, including diabetes, colon cancer, and atherosclerosis.

SPIRIT: *Practice open-heart meditation*

Listen to what your heart wants to communicate to you. Relax, close your eyes, and breathe deeply as you visualize your heart opening. Smile to your heart and feel it respond. Ask the Source of All to remove jealousy, arrogance, grief, anger, and other negative feelings from your heart. If you wish, you can download a guided meditation from *www.HeartSanctuary.org*.

"IF YOU FOCUS UPON WHATEVER YOU WANT, YOU WILL

ATTRACT WHATEVER YOU WANT. IF YOU FOCUS UPON

THE LACK OF WHATEVER YOU WANT, YOU WILL ATTRACT

MORE OF THE LACK."

—Esther and Jerry Hicks, *The Law of Attraction*

Mind over Matter

Today, view your mind as a powerful magnet that can attract any-thing you desire. Make a conscious effort to keep your thoughts on things you want to draw with your mental magnet. Like attracts like.

MIND: *Manage your thoughts*
What you think about you draw to you, say the contributors to the bestselling book *The Secret.* Your thoughts project energy into the universe, and those thoughts act as a magnet to attract people and circumstances that are in sync with your thoughts. To attract positive conditions, keep your thoughts on positive things.

BODY: *Drink green tea to keep your mind sharp*
Dr. Silvia Mandel and her colleagues at Israel's Eve Topf Center for Neurodegenerative Diseases found that when EGCG (found in green tea) was fed to animals, it apparently prevented brain cells from dying. Improvements were also shown in reducing compounds that led to lesions in the brains of animals with Alzheimer's.

SPIRIT: *Imprint water with your intentions*
Words impact the molecular nature of water, according to research done by Japanese scientist Masaru Emoto. Write a word such as *love, peace,* or *health* on a piece of paper and tape it to a bottle of water, with the word facing in. The energy of the word imprints the water with positive vibrations. Drink the water to ingest those good vibes.

"Even when the sky is heavily overcast, the sun hasn't disappeared. It's still there on the other side of the clouds." —Eckhart Tolle, *The Power of Now*

Silver Linings

Today, remember that life is a series of hills and valleys. If things aren't looking bright right now, that is sure to change. During times of adversity, it's especially important to take good care of yourself on every level.

MIND: *Shift your attention away from yourself*
Take the magnifying glass off what is wrong in your life and turn your attention to other people. Who and what bring you joy? How can you build on this joy by giving back to others? When you direct your attention away from your troubles and focus on enriching the lives of others, you boost your own happiness.

BODY: *Eat yogurt to replant your intestines*
Antibiotics and other drugs can destroy the good bacteria in your intestines, making it difficult to extract nutrients from the food you eat. After an injury or illness that required you to take medication, eat yogurt that contains live probiotics. These help replace beneficial microflora in your intestines and restore proper digestion.

SPIRIT: *Divine light appears when it is needed most*
According to Hindu thought, creation expands and contracts in cycles, some light and some dark. When darkness is upon the earth, holy beings such as the Buddha, Mohammed, and Jesus appear as light-bearers to lead humankind out of darkness and back to light. Some people believe that great and holy beings are always present, working for the well-being of all.

"HOPE . . . WHICH WHISPERED FROM PANDORA'S BOX ONLY
AFTER ALL THE OTHER PLAGUES AND SORROWS HAD
ESCAPED, IS THE BEST AND LAST OF ALL THINGS."

—Ian Caldwell and Dustin Thomason, *The Rule of Four*

Hope Springs Eternal

The well-known placebo effect demonstrates how hope for a cure
can actually produce healing. In *The Anatomy of Hope,* Jerome
Groopman explains that a hopeful person's brain produces endorphins, which block pain and give the patient energy to recuperate.
Hope keeps us going in the face of life's challenges, physical or otherwise. Today, see how a hopeful attitude can improve your life.

MIND: *Think about a hope that has been fulfilled*
Remember something you hoped for when you were young—a new
bike, a trip to a fun place, an invitation to a party—that you received.
Expand your thinking to include many more things you'd hoped for
in the past that came about. Enjoy these reminiscences for as long
as you like.

BODY: *Take five deep breaths at regular intervals during the day*
Use this practice to increase the amount of oxygen flowing to your
body and brain. This encourages what's known as the "relaxation
response," which reduces tension and helps you feel more calm,
present, and optimistic about your life. Anytime you start feeling
overwhelmed or discouraged, take five deep, slow breaths.

SPIRIT: *Light a candle*
In many spiritual traditions, candles symbolize hope—a light in the
darkness. Light a candle and enjoy its soft, flickering glow while you
contemplate something you hope for in your life.

"BEYOND TALENT LIE ALL THE USUAL WORDS: *DISCIPLINE,*
LOVE, LUCK—BUT, MOST OF ALL, *ENDURANCE.*"

—James Arthur Baldwin

Build Strength and Endurance

Whether you are writing a thesis or running a marathon, you need
endurance to reach your goal. Today, work on building strength—
mentally, physically, and spiritually. Each fortifies the others. Set
a pace that's comfortable for you; proceeding in a slow and steady
manner may prevent setbacks or burnout.

MIND: *Play mind games*
Games that engage and challenge your mind can keep you mentally sharp, especially as you age. A study published in *Journal of
the American Medical Association* in 2007 recommended playing
Sudoku as one way to exercise and strengthen the mind. Crossword
puzzles, anagrams, jigsaw puzzles, and card games also give your
gray matter a workout. Play mind-building games regularly, alone
or with friends, to pump up those mental muscles.

BODY: *Eat cherries to increase endurance*
Cherries contain an antioxidant called quercetin. According to a
study published in the *International Journal of Sports Nutrition
and Exercise Metabolism,* you may be able to improve your exercise
endurance by eating more cherries. The study found that quercetin
helped college students bike longer.

SPIRIT: *Contemplate the Strength card*
One of the twenty-two cards in the tarot's Major Arcana, "Strength"
usually depicts a young woman holding the jaws of a lion. The card's
message is to gain mastery over your ego and the animal nature
using patience, gentleness, and compassion. Use this card as a meditation aid to gain inner strength.

"THERE IS ONLY ONE SUCCESS—TO BE ABLE

TO SPEND YOUR LIFE IN YOUR OWN WAY."

—Christopher Morley, *Where the Blue Begins*

Do Your Own Thing

It's never too soon (or too late) to be the person you really want to be. The challenge lies in learning to balance your own needs and desires with those of other people, especially the people you love. You may have to set boundaries in order to live your own truth.

MIND: *Examine the voices in your head*

Do you sometimes avoid doing things you might enjoy because a voice in your head says, "You can't do that" or "You shouldn't do that"? When this happens, notice whose voice it is. Often authority figures plant seeds of doubt in our minds when we're too young to decide for ourselves. Start listening to your own inner voice instead.

BODY: *Slow the aging process*

Add foods with antioxidants to your diet to help you enjoy doing the things you want to do. A diet high in antioxidants has a direct correlation to reduced age-related mental and physical degeneration, according to the U.S. Department of Agriculture's Jean Mayer Human Nutrition Research Center on Aging, based at Tufts University. Many fruits and vegetables including berries, broccoli, tomatoes, and spinach contain antioxidants.

SPIRIT: *Consider yourself number one*

In the ancient study of numerology, all numbers have meanings beyond their quantitative values. The number one represents identity and individuality. Put a big red #1 on your mirror as a reminder that you are a unique and important entity.

"No one can make you feel inferior without your consent." —Eleanor Roosevelt

Boost Your Self-Esteem

Many successful people say they have been able to accomplish their dreams because someone believed in them. More important, however, is believing in yourself. The Law of Attraction, a concept popularized in the bestselling books by Esther and Jerry Hicks, and in Rhonda Byrne's *The Secret*, says that to be successful in the world, you must be able to see yourself as successful.

MIND: *Stop judging yourself*
When you look in the mirror, do you see your beauty or your "flaws"? Do you berate yourself when you make a mistake? Do you compare yourself to others and think you are less attractive, intelligent, successful? Start noticing how many times you criticize or find fault with yourself. Then make a decision to stop judging yourself.

BODY: *Activate your self-confidence with acupressure*
Stimulate the acupressure point known as "Center of Power" or CV 12 to increase your self-confidence and calm anxiety. This point is located at your solar plexus, in the center of your body about halfway between your heart and your belly button. Press it firmly, but gently for about a minute, then release. Repeat as needed.

SPIRIT: *Shun perfection*
An attitude of perfectionism doesn't help you grow; it stifles you. We come to earth to learn—if you were already perfect you probably wouldn't be here. Muslims intentionally weave flaws into Persian carpets, because they believe only God is perfect. See the beauty in your own "flaws."

"REAL LOVE DOESN'T MAKE YOU SUFFER."

—Eckhart Tolle, *The Power of Now*

Choose a Loving Relationship

It may not be possible to totally escape heartbreak or unhappiness in your relationships, but love should bring you more happiness than sorrow. If you are suffering more than you should, you may be in an unhealthy relationship. In some cases, it may be helpful to join a twelve-step program or undergo counseling.

MIND: *Assess your relationships*

Consider your closest relationships with your life partner, family members, friends, colleagues, and others. On a scale of one to ten, how happy would you rate these relationships? If some rank lower than five, think about reducing the amount of time you spend with these people. Make more room in your life for the people with whom your interactions rank higher on the happiness scale.

BODY: *Ease lower back pain with acupressure*

Lower back pain can really hamper your sex life. To reduce aches, weakness, and stiffness in the lumbar area, apply light, steady pressure to the acupressure points known as Sea of Vitality for a few minutes. These points are located waist high, about two finger-widths out on either side of your spine.

SPIRIT: *The eyes are the windows of the soul*

Gaze into your loved one's eyes. Don't talk; just look deeply and allow loving feelings to expand within you. Sense the connection between you—you may feel an energetic exchange. Open yourself to the other person's gaze, trying not to hold anything back. Notice any insights that arise into your awareness.

"MAN IS FOND OF COUNTING HIS TROUBLES, BUT HE DOES NOT COUNT HIS JOYS. IF HE COUNTED THEM UP AS HE OUGHT TO, HE WOULD SEE EVERY LOT HAS ENOUGH HAPPINESS PROVIDED FOR IT." —Fyodor Dostoevsky

Look on the Bright Side

Look on the bright side today—it could be one of the best things you can do for yourself. A positive attitude strengthens your immune system, according to a 2010 University of Kentucky study. It can also help you land the job you want, a 2008–2009 University of Missouri study showed.

MIND: *Change your thoughts*

The Law of Attraction says that if you concentrate on what you want, you will attract what you want. But if you focus on what you lack, you will attract more of the lack. So if you aren't happy with the way things in your life are now, shift your thinking to what would make you happier, not what you lack.

BODY: *Stay in shape*

It's easier to enjoy life when you are healthy, and part of being healthy is maintaining the optimum weight. According to the U.S. Department of Health and Human Services, thirty minutes of walking five days a week is the minimal exercise required to maintain your weight. Exercise feels good, and you feel good when you do it.

SPIRIT: *Trust the universe*

Reinforce your intentions with certainty that whatever you need will be provided for you. That doesn't mean do nothing. But doubt limits your ability to attract what you want. Don't predetermine how opportunities will come to you; just remain trusting that they will.

"THE ADVANCEMENT TO WHOLENESS IS THE REAL

OCCUPATION OF HUMAN EXISTENCE." —Marsha Sinetar

Think Holistically

Our emotional, mental, and physical selves are interlinked. We have ample evidence to prove that our psychological health affects our physical health, and vice versa. It's vital to your overall health and your brain's health to think holistically—to view yourself as a whole being, not a collection of parts.

MIND: *Understand your role in staying well*
In her best-selling book *You Can Heal Your Life*, Louise Hay expressed her belief that "We create every so-called illness in our body." If you accept that idea, you can stop feeling like a victim of a disease and realize you have the power to be well. Read books by Bernie Siegel, Deepak Chopra, and others to learn more.

BODY: *Try holistic healing therapies*
The holistic healing field includes a wide range of alternative and complementary therapies. Some of the best-known are chiropractic, massage therapy, acupuncture, Reiki, reflexology, aromatherapy, homeopathy, and herbal medicine. Many are gentler, less invasive, and more pleasant than typical Western medical treatments. All endeavor to heal mind and spirit as well as the body. Experiment with the ones that seem to offer you the benefits you seek.

SPIRIT: *Understand your energy field*
Holistic healers believe your physical body is surrounded by an invisible energy field (sometimes called the etheric body or aura). Energy centers known as chakras (aligned roughly from your tailbone to the top of your head) serve as portals through which life energy flows. Often disease occurs first in these areas before it manifests physically.

> "IF ONE OVERSTEPS THE BOUNDS OF MODERATION,
>
> THE GREATEST PLEASURES CEASE TO PLEASE." —Epictetus

Everything in Moderation

In ancient Greece, the words *Meden Agan* (μηδεν ἀγαν), which mean "nothing in excess," were written on the temple of the sun god Apollo. Many spiritual traditions also encourage moderation in every area of life. That's still good advice today.

MIND: *Avoid chronic stress*

You can't avoid stress entirely, and might not even want to because mild stress can be motivating. Researchers at the James A. Haley Veterans Administration Medical Center, at the University of South Florida and Arizona State University, found that connections in the brains of chronically stressed rats (living in crowded conditions, in close proximity to cats) atrophied. The researchers deduced that stress can interfere with the brain's ability to learn new information.

BODY: *Lose 10 percent of your excess body weight*

Losing just 5 to 10 percent of excess body weight can help to reduce your risk for health problems. This lowers blood pressure, total cholesterol, LDL cholesterol ("bad" cholesterol), triglyceride levels, and blood sugar. Combining a healthy diet with increased physical activity and behavior modification is the most successful strategy for healthy weight loss and weight maintenance.

SPIRIT: *Devote time to spiritual practice*

People who spend some time in spiritual practice often consider themselves to be happier than those who don't. You don't have to belong to an organized religion and attend regular services. An awareness of your connection to something beyond the material world may be all that you need.

"DREAM AS IF YOU'LL LIVE FOREVER.

LIVE AS IF YOU'LL DIE TODAY." —James Dean

Live Life to the Fullest

A good life isn't necessarily a long one; rather, it's one in which you embrace joy every step of the way. Joseph Campbell often recommended, "Follow your bliss." The best way to care for yourself and perhaps live a long, healthy life is to fill your days with meaning on every level. Today, consider the following:

MIND: *Reconsider your priorities*
When you look back on your life, will you be happier knowing you did the things you wanted to do or that you did the things you were supposed to do? In their later years, few people say they regretted not spending more hours at the office. Instead, they wish they'd made more time for friends, family, and hobbies or interests they prized. It's never too late to devote time to the people and things you love—all you have to do is make them a priority.

BODY: *Eat anti-aging foods*
To look and feel your best for as long as possible, eat superfoods that offer lots of healthy benefits. Superfoods are recommended by the U.S. Dietary Guidelines for maintaining optimal health. Among these foods are apples, blueberries, quinoa, garlic, wild salmon, kale, nuts, oats, sweet potatoes, grapefruit, and yogurt.

SPIRIT: *Look at life karmically*
Karma is a concept that proposes every action generates a reaction. That may not occur in this lifetime, but perhaps in another one.

"IF YOU CANNOT FIND PEACE WITHIN YOURSELF, YOU WILL NEVER FIND IT ANYWHERE ELSE." —Marvin Gaye

The Oasis of Silence

Choose to embrace silence today. Withdraw from the noise and activity that characterize your everyday life and devote yourself to twenty-four hours of quiet contemplation. Mahatma Gandhi was silent one day each week because he felt it helped him find inner peace. Because your body rhythms, breathing, and stress levels slow when you stop speaking, silence can also offer health benefits.

MIND: *Stop talking for a day*

Commit to silence for a day. Don't answer the phone—avoid texting and e-mails, too. Let family members and friends know you are taking a day off to be quiet. Turn within and allow your inner voice to communicate insights and information to you that you might not hear ordinarily.

BODY: *Walk in a quiet place*

Find a quiet place where you can walk alone, without encountering or talking to anyone. Try not to let your thoughts run to everyday matters. Allow your senses to appreciate things you might not notice ordinarily—smells, the ground beneath your feet, the wind, sun, or rain on your face. Enjoy the profound peace within and around you.

SPIRIT: *Go on a silent retreat*

Consider going on a silent retreat. Many spiritual traditions emphasize the importance of silence and host silent retreats where you can temporarily withdraw from the busyness of your everyday life to nourish your spirit. Look online for a silent retreat center near you. Some are associated with a particular religion; others are nondenominational.

"THE FUTURE BELONGS TO THOSE WHO BELIEVE IN THE BEAUTY OF THEIR DREAMS." —Eleanor Roosevelt

Dare to Dream

Start dreaming your way to health, wealth, and happiness today. Whether your dreams are of the waking or sleeping variety, they stir your imagination. Imagination precedes manifestation. Everything you see in the material world started in someone's imagination.

MIND: *Spend time daydreaming*
The Law of Attraction tells us that daydreaming is an important step to creating the reality we desire. Before you can bring something into your life, you must first be able to imagine it. Each day, spend time imagining the things, people, and situations you wish to draw to you. The richer and more vivid your daydreams, the more magnetic power they have.

BODY: *Eat cherries to sleep better*
Sleep dysfunction interferes with your dreaming, as well as your productivity when you're awake. Melatonin helps regulate natural sleep patterns and biorhythms. Cherries are one of the few food sources of melatonin. If you aren't sleeping as well as you'd like to, or suffer from jet lag, add cherries to your diet. Sour cherries contain more melatonin than sweet ones.

SPIRIT: *Record your dreams*
Everyone dreams, every night. Dreams are the way your subconscious communicates information to you. Many famous people, including Albert Einstein and Thomas Edison, found answers to problems in their dreams. Start keeping a record of your dreams, and you'll soon notice meaningful symbols, themes, and patterns emerging that can aid you in your waking life.

"AWARENESS REQUIRES A RUPTURE WITH THE WORLD WE TAKE FOR GRANTED." —Shoshana Zuboff

Become More Aware and Alert

Today, sharpen your observation skills in order to understand people and situations more clearly. As eyewitness studies have shown, most of us only partially see what's going on around us. How much do you miss every day? The following tips can help to improve your awareness.

MIND: *Observe body language*

You can discern a lot about someone by how he sits or how she walks. Arms crossed over the chest suggest defensiveness, for example. Start paying attention to people's body language to understand their feelings. These clues can guide you in your interactions with loved ones, coworkers, and strangers.

BODY: *Perk up with peppermint oil*

If you feel your energy and attention flagging, sniff a whiff of peppermint essential oil. The fresh, clean scent immediately impacts the limbic system of your brain and makes you feel more alert. Put a few drops on a handkerchief and smell it whenever you need a quick pick-me-up.

SPIRIT: *Learn to see auras*

Your emotions, mental state, and physical health are reflected in your aura—the subtle energy field that surrounds your physical body. An aura may look like a whitish or colored glow extending about six inches or more out from the body. Although most people don't notice auras, you can gain information about someone by learning to see them. Practice seeing auras—it's easier if the person stands against a plain dark or white background.

"THERE IS A VITALITY, A LIFE FORCE, AN ENERGY, A
QUICKENING, THAT IS TRANSLATED THROUGH YOU INTO
ACTION, AND BECAUSE THERE IS ONLY ONE OF YOU IN ALL
TIME, THIS EXPRESSION IS UNIQUE." —Martha Graham

Increase Your Vitality

Eastern philosophy speaks of a vital force that animates everything
on our planet. The Chinese call this life force *chi* or *qi*; in India it is
referred to as *prana*. Today, explore ways to tap this enlivening force
mentally, physically, and spiritually.

MIND: *Join a reading group*
Reading books improves imagination, reduces stress, strengthens
memory, and may prevent brain deterioration. One study published
in the *New York Times* in 2007 found that reading books even helped
reverse the damaging effects of lead exposure. Participating in a reading group also lets you enjoy a social connection with other people.

BODY: *Stop smoking*
Statistics from the Centers for Disease Control indicate nearly half a
million smoking-related deaths occur annually in the United States.
Smoking increases the risk of stroke because chemicals in cigarette
smoke can make the blood more prone to clotting. Nicotine dam-
ages the interior walls of blood vessels and makes them susceptible
to atherosclerosis. Numerous clinical studies show that the body
begins repairing damage within days of that last cigarette.

SPIRIT: *Turn on the lights*
In the ancient Chinese practice of feng shui, light equals positive
energy. Want to increase your energy? Turn on the lights, especially in the center of your home where you might not have windows
or natural sunlight. The center of your home corresponds to your
health, so illuminating this area boosts energy.

"THERE IS A FOUNTAIN OF YOUTH: IT IS YOUR MIND, YOUR
TALENTS, THE CREATIVITY YOU BRING TO YOUR LIFE AND
THE LIVES OF PEOPLE YOU LOVE. WHEN YOU LEARN TO TAP
THIS SOURCE, YOU WILL TRULY HAVE DEFEATED AGE."

—Sophia Loren

Look and Feel Younger

It's often said that youth isn't just a physical condition, but a state
of mind as well. Today, shuck off tired, worn-out ideas and behaviors that are dragging you down and draining your youthful vitality.
Unveil the part of you that's vibrant, creative, and joyful.

MIND: *Release old hurts*

Don't let old hurts harden your heart and feelings. Whenever you
find yourself slipping into pain and sadness, say a blessing for yourself. Then say a blessing for the person who hurt you. Tell him or her
that you won't carry this old memory around any longer. Keeping
your heart flexible keeps you young.

BODY: *Defy aging skin*

Cabbage is a good source of vitamin C: one cup contains about
54 percent of your daily value. Data from the National Health and
Nutrition Examination Survey suggests that middle-aged women
who consume plenty of foods rich in vitamin C may have a lower
risk of having wrinkled skin or age-related dryness.

SPIRIT: *Recall a happy time from the past*

Think back to a time in your youth when you were totally happy.
Relive that memory—physically if possible, but otherwise in your
mind. Call up the joyful feelings you experienced then. Whenever
you feel down, immerse yourself in this memory from your youth
once again.

"THE HUMAN RACE HAS ONLY ONE REALLY EFFECTIVE
WEAPON, AND THAT'S LAUGHTER." —Mark Twain

Laugh It Up

How often do you laugh? It's been estimated that children laugh
as many as 300 times per day, whereas adults only crack up about
eleven times. If your laugh quota is below par, today turn off the
news and watch funny movies and TV shows instead. Read humorous
books. Share jokes with friends. Remember the saying, "Laugh
and the world laughs with you."

MIND: *Stop complaining*

Take a lighter approach to life. It's easy to slip into a funk if you
participate in griping about the weather, traffic, cost of gasoline, and
so on. Don't let yourself be drawn into conversations of a negative
nature. If someone seems bent on complaining, either change the
subject to an upbeat topic or excuse yourself and walk away.

BODY: *Laugh more*

Laughter is good medicine. In his bestselling book *Anatomy of an Illness,*
Norman Cousins explained how he was diagnosed with a life-
threatening illness and laughed himself well. Laughter boosts the
antibodies in your bloodstream, which helps your body fight infection.
The *Journal of the American Medical Association* acknowledges that
patients with chronic illnesses can benefit from "laughter therapy."

SPIRIT: *Do something childish*

Recall something you enjoyed doing as a child, such as blowing
soap bubbles, flying a kite, or splashing about in mud puddles. Let
the child in you come out and play again. Engage in those youthful
expressions of joy. Don't censor or judge yourself—laugh at yourself
instead. Notice how quickly your spirits lift.

"YOU CANNOT CONTROL WHAT HAPPENS TO YOU, BUT YOU
CAN CONTROL YOUR ATTITUDE TOWARD WHAT HAPPENS
TO YOU, AND IN THAT, YOU WILL BE MASTERING CHANGE
RATHER THAN ALLOWING IT TO MASTER YOU."

—Brian Tracy

Turn over the Reins

Today, let other people shoulder some of the burden. Continual
demands may have you racing to resolve every crisis. You have no
time to relax or do the things you really want to do. Take care of
yourself by balancing rest with activity.

MIND: *Realize when you are creating chaos*
If crisis and chaos always seem to beat a path to your door, it's likely
that you have turned on the light and invited them in. Consider how
you feel when you are in the throes of a crisis and how you feel when
life is peaceful and quiet. What purpose does chaos serve for you?

BODY: *Get more sleep*
Most adults need seven to nine hours of sleep per night for optimum
health. On WebMD, Michael J. Breus, PhD, explains that chronic
sleep deprivation can contribute to heart attack, stroke, obesity,
mental problems, ADD, and injuries from accidents. If you have
trouble sleeping, explore remedies that can help you get enough
quality shut-eye.

SPIRIT: *Meditate on The Chariot card*
From a tarot deck, select The Chariot card. It usually shows a person
driving a chariot drawn by two creatures, one black and one white.
The card represents steering a steady course and constructively handling multiple factors in your life. Meditate on this card to resolve
conflicts and achieve self-mastery.

"In everyone's life, at some time, our inner fire
goes out. It is then burst into flame by an
encounter with another human being.
We should all be thankful for those people
who rekindle the inner spirit."

—Albert Schweitzer

Make Connections

Studies suggest you'll be healthier in mind, body, and spirit if you interact with other people. Despite social networking, e-mail, and cell phones, people today are more isolated than in previous generations. Today, find ways to connect with human beings and other living creatures.

MIND: *Reach out to other people*
Socializing isn't just a matter of having fun. According to studies done by J. T. Cacioppo and L. C. Hawkley of the University of Chicago's Department of Psychology, social isolation can contribute to morbidity and mortality. Get involved in group activities, attend classes, join a club, or volunteer with a local charity.

BODY: *Grow plants to connect with the earth*
Plant a vegetable or herb garden. Even if you live in an apartment building, you can still plant container gardens, either indoors or on a balcony or fire escape. Growing a garden lets you connect with the earth and nature's cycles. If you have kids, growing vegetables is a great way to teach them where their food comes from.

SPIRIT: *Feel your connection with other life forms*
Go to a park, wildlife preserve, or a place in the country. Sit or walk quietly, observing wildlife. Realize that you and all the animals, birds, reptiles, and insects are part of one, great, all-encompassing whole. Sense your connection with all life forms.

"SEX IS EMOTION IN MOTION."   —Mae West

Sensational Sex

Explore your sexuality today. Sex is proven to lower blood pressure, increase immunity, burn calories, decrease prostate cancer risk later in life, boost self-esteem, manage pain, promote sleep, tone muscles, and bust stress. It's also fun!

MIND: *Make a sex wish list*
In an interview with WebMD, sexologist Dr. Ava Cadell recommends creating a wish list of three experiences that would spice up your sex life and sharing them with your partner once a month. As you and your partner exchange lists, you not only learn what the other person desires, but you get your own needs met, too. Research shows that couples who communicate their sexual needs are more satisfied in their relationships than couples who do not.

BODY: *Tune your sacral chakra*
The sacral chakra, located about three finger-widths below your belly button, is an energy center linked with sexuality and the reproductive organs. Sound healers associate the seven notes on the musical scale with the seven main chakras. D is the note linked with the sacral chakra. To tune up this energy center, play a "singing bowl" tuned to that note. You can find singing bowls made of metal or crystal online.

SPIRIT: *View sex as a spiritual act*
Mystical rites, rituals, and ceremonies involving sex have been practiced in numerous cultures, East and West, for longer than anyone can document. Tantric sex, for example, represents the union of the god Shiva and the goddess Shakti. The next time you make love, envision your partner as an embodiment of the Divine and treat him or her with reverence.

"WE ARE EACH GIFTED IN A UNIQUE AND IMPORTANT WAY. IT IS OUR PRIVILEGE AND OUR ADVENTURE TO DISCOVER OUR OWN SPECIAL LIGHT." —Mary Dunbar

Appreciate Yourself

Make a point of appreciating yourself today. Take note of the special qualities you possess: mental, physical, and spiritual. Give yourself credit for what you do well—and for trying, whether you succeed or not. Know that you deserve to be treated with consideration, by others and by yourself.

MIND: *Surround yourself with supportive people*
Spend time with people who recognize your individual gifts and value them. Limit or curtail your associations with people who criticize, judge, or otherwise bum you out—you don't have to allow yourself to be adversely influenced by their negativity. Accept compliments gracefully—instead of brushing them off, just say thanks.

BODY: *Keep your weight in line to boost self-esteem*
Obesity and poor self-esteem often go hand in hand. One way to show appreciation for yourself is to eat more healthfully. In a study published in the *British Journal of Nutrition,* overweight women added 300 calories of almonds to their diet for ten weeks. At the end of the study, the women who'd eaten almonds didn't gain weight. The fiber in almonds blocked some of the fat calories from being absorbed.

SPIRIT: *Clean out your closet*
What you wear affects how you feel about yourself. Only wear clothes that look good on you, increase your self-confidence, and lift your spirits. Get rid of everything that isn't comfortable and flattering—anything too big, too small, out-of-date, or that you just don't particularly like.

"IF YOU ASK WHAT IS THE SINGLE MOST IMPORTANT KEY TO LONGEVITY, I WOULD HAVE TO SAY IT IS AVOIDING WORRY, STRESS, AND TENSION."

—George Burns (who lived to be 100)

Loosen Up

Stress causes us to tighten our muscles, our behavior, and our attitudes. To help beat stress today, choose to loosen up in mind, body, and spirit. See how much better it feels to be flexible instead of tense.

MIND: *Keep an open mind*
Notice how you react to things you read or hear. Do you find yourself quickly taking up a position or coming to a conclusion, based on old programming or conditioned ways of thinking? Today, try to just listen without assessing, judging, or forming an opinion. Don't agree or disagree; simply hear what the other person has to say.

BODY: *Keep your spine supple*
A yoga technique called the free-motion cat stretch exercises your spine and keeps you flexible. Kneel on all fours. Go through the various movements slowly and gently. Arch your spine like an angry cat, then concave your back. Sit back on your calves and lower your head and shoulders, stretching your arms out in front of you. Come back up on all fours and move your hips and shoulders. Shift positions as is comfortable for you, working your body to limber up.

SPIRIT: *Smile inwardly*
Close your eyes and smile. Feel yourself growing more relaxed and at ease. After a few moments, turn the smile inward at yourself. Sense yourself being warmed inside by the love and beauty of your smile. Let go of all stress and rigidity and just *be*.

"YOU ARE AS YOUNG AS YOUR FAITH,

AS OLD AS YOUR DOUBT; AS YOUNG AS YOUR SELF-

CONFIDENCE, AS OLD AS YOUR FEAR;

AS YOUNG AS YOUR HOPE, AS OLD AS YOUR DESPAIR."

—Douglas MacArthur

Recapture the Joys of Youth

You're only as old as you let yourself be. Today, turn back the clock by making a conscious choice to be more youthful in mind, body, and spirit. The fountain of youth is inside you.

MIND: *Be more spontaneous*
Grant yourself permission to enjoy more freedom by living more spontaneously. Instead of endlessly weighing the advantages and disadvantages of an activity or opportunity, let your heart guide you. See happiness as a journey, not a destination. Allow yourself to experience a childlike sense of wonder and joy.

BODY: *Try black currant seed oil*
Black currant seed oil contains an essential anti-inflammatory agent known as gamma-linolenic acid, which can help strengthen your body's immune system. It is rich in essential fatty acids necessary for providing energy, protecting tissue, and regulating metabolism. It can also aid menstrual cramping and mood swings. Try it to maintain youthful vitality. You can find it in capsule form in health food stores.

SPIRIT: *Don't give up things that give you pleasure*
Aging is as much about your spirit as your body. Just because you're older doesn't mean you have to stop doing things that you enjoyed when you were young. Wear your red polka-dot hat. Skip down the sidewalk. Watch cartoons. Don't worry about being perceived as silly.

"TENSION IS WHO YOU THINK YOU SHOULD BE.

RELAXATION IS WHO YOU ARE." —Chinese Proverb

Turn Off Tension

Set this intention for a restful day: Be who you are, not what you do. Give yourself a real break—and just *be*. Here are some ways to release tension, and relax your way back to your True Self.

MIND: *Take a break from the (bad) news*
It's hard to find spiritual sustenance and renewal in a world rocked by violence, crime, and tension. So turn off the television and radio. Don't read the newspaper today either, and stay off the Internet. Stop the daylong bombardment of negativity from virtually every media outlet.

BODY: *Drink a cup of gyokuro tea*
Theanine is an amino acid that increases alpha brainwave activity—and gyokuro tea is chock-full of it. The alpha brain rhythm is slower than your ordinary beta rhythm, and induces a more relaxed state. At the same time, gyokuro tea helps improve focus and concentration. Drink just one cup of this Japanese green tea and you'll be calmer and wiser for up to four hours.

SPIRIT: *Choose a natural talisman*
A talisman is a token chosen to attract something you desire. The term comes from the Greek word *teleo*, meaning "to accomplish." Crystals, stones, feathers—all are natural talismans you can use to attract peace and wellness. Use your favorite to ease anxiety, relieve stress, and put you in touch with who you really are.

"THERE ARE TWO MEANS OF REFUGE FROM THE MISERIES OF LIFE: MUSIC AND CATS." —Albert Schweitzer

Make the Most of Music

You've heard the expression, "Music soothes the savage beast" and that may be true. Today, explore the many other benefits music offers you. Research done by Alfred A. Tomatis demonstrated that listening to Mozart's music could heal a variety of disorders and improve mental ability (described in Don Campbell's book *The Mozart Effect*). Consider implementing the following tips for using music into your self-care program as well.

MIND: *Study music*
Learning to play a musical instrument can increase your cognitive skills. Research indicates that studying music appears to benefit verbal ability. Harvard University's Gottfried Schlaug showed that musical training can also improve motor and auditory abilities in children, as reported on LiveScience in 2009.

BODY: *Tone your body with your favorite tunes*
Your favorite tunes can improve your workout. A 2010 study from Ohio State University found that listening to music while exercising cleared the brain, so that participants found themselves enjoying their workouts rather than worrying about other obligations. Create a playlist for your iPod and hit the treadmill.

SPIRIT: *Accompany meditation with music*
If you find it hard to sit quietly and meditate, try listening to music. Many people find that soothing music aids their meditation practice. Choose music that does not have lyrics, a catchy beat, or a tune you can follow. You'll find lots of good meditation CDs at *www.soundstrue.com*.

"A FRIEND IS ONE OF THE NICEST THINGS YOU CAN HAVE,

AND ONE OF THE BEST THINGS YOU CAN BE."

—Douglas Pagels

Stay in Touch with Friends

Focus on the importance of friendship today. As numerous studies have shown, friendship plays a key role in health and well-being. If you've lost touch with an old friend, consider reconnecting with that person. If you've had a falling-out with someone, see if you can mend the rift.

MIND: *Use telepathy to contact a friend*

Has a friend you haven't been in touch with lately suddenly popped into your mind, shortly before you receive a phone call or e-mail from him or her? Try intentionally connecting with a friend using mental telepathy, instead of the usual methods. Practice this technique with people you know to strengthen your intuitive powers.

BODY: *Treasure your friends*

Think of your friends as your dearest treasures. A study, reported in a 2009 *New York Times* article, found that elderly people who maintained a network of friends were 22 percent less likely to die during the ten-year study than their more solitary peers. Friends support you in times of need, and when you feel you have someone to turn to, you don't have to shoulder all the stress yourself.

SPIRIT: *Contact your angels*

A 2008 *Washington Post* survey showed that a majority of Americans believe angels not only exist, but interact with humans. Do you want to connect with an angel? Some sources say all you have to do is ask your angel to make itself known to you.

"The system of nature, of which man is a part, tends to be self-balancing, self-adjusting, self-cleansing. Not so with technology." —E. F. Schumacher

Clean Up

Make cleanliness part of your regular routine—not only your body, house, and car, but at every level of your being. Our world is becoming increasingly polluted. To maintain good health, it's essential to cleanse yourself of toxins from your food and environment. Even other people's thoughts and emotions can have an effect on your well-being.

MIND: *Cleanse your brain with zinc*
Zinc helps your central nervous system by scrubbing your brain free of lead that enters your body, for example, when you inhale the fumes of gasoline while you're filling your car's tank. In doing so, it helps prevent brain damage. Zinc also produces a calming effect and can aid mental disorders including ADD and dementia.

BODY: *Do an internal cleansing*
Don't just clean your body on the outside; do an internal cleansing as well. When your colon gets clogged, you can't adequately absorb the nutrients you need, nor can you effectively eliminate waste. Numerous safe, natural products are available to detoxify and revitalize your system.

SPIRIT: *Burn sage to cleanse your aura*
Your aura is sensitive to the energies of other people and environments. Any time you are exposed to "bad vibes" either from another person or as a result of a stressful situation, cleanse your aura with the smoke from burning sage. You can purchase sage in bundled wands or loose. Let the smoke waft about you for a few moments to clear away unwanted energies.

"EXPECT YOUR EVERY NEED TO BE MET.

EXPECT THE ANSWER TO EVERY PROBLEM,

EXPECT ABUNDANCE ON EVERY LEVEL." —Eileen Caddy

Attract Abundance

Abundance is more than money and possessions—it's a state of feeling comfortable and content with your life on every level, knowing that you have everything you need. Today, consider where you experience abundance and where you feel a sense of lack. Then take the following steps to fill what you perceive as lack.

MIND: *Write a story about receiving abundance*
In their bestselling books, Esther and Jerry Hicks recommend imagining yourself enjoying all the things money can buy in order to attract prosperity. A good way to engage your imagination is to write a story. Don't worry about grammar and syntax; just describe in detail how you feel as you receive and enjoy the luxuries you desire. As you write, envision those good things coming to you now.

BODY: *Nourish your body abundantly*
All the money in the world won't buy good health. Take care of your body—it's one of your most precious possessions. The USDA has created a food pyramid (*www.choosemyplate.gov*) as a guide for balancing your diet with proper foods. It's a good place to start learning how to put together healthy meals.

SPIRIT: *Attract wealth with an abundance crystal*
An abundance crystal contains inclusions of greenish material called chlorite. The green color symbolizes money and growth (think of healthy green plants). Place this crystal on your desk, in the cash register of your business, or in your purse to attract prosperity.

"LET FOOD BE THY MEDICINE,
THY MEDICINE SHALL BE THY FOOD." —Hippocrates

Supplement Your Diet

According to a National Health and Nutrition Examination Survey, more than half of all adults in the United States take vitamin supplements. If your diet isn't optimal—and whose is?—consider augmenting with supplements. Consult a nutritionist, naturopath, or other professional for guidance. You'll also find plenty of information available online and in books and magazines such as *Women's Health, Men's Health, Better Nutrition, Prevention,* and *Self.*

MIND: *Consult with a nutritionist or naturopath*
Although recommended daily allowances are set for various vitamin and mineral supplements, each person is unique in his or her nutritional needs. Depending on your age, weight, diet, family history, level of activity, and many other factors, you may need more or less of a particular supplement.

BODY: *Take vitamins to fill in nutritional gaps*
Dr. Andrew Weil, director of the integrative medicine program at the University of Arizona in Tucson, recommends taking vitamins to fill in nutritional gaps in your daily diet: 200 milligrams of vitamin C, 400 to 800 IU of natural vitamin E, 200 micrograms of selenium, 15,000 to 20,000 IU of mixed carotenoids, and 30 to 100 milligrams of CoQ10.

SPIRIT: *Dowse your vitamins*
Use a pendulum to "dowse" vitamins. Hold a vitamin tablet in one hand and a pendulum in the other, so the bob is about six inches above your hand. Ask if this tablet is good for you. If the pendulum swings from side to side, the answer is "no." If it swings back and forth, the answer is "yes." (Don't move the pendulum intentionally.)

> "HEAVEN, TO ME, IS THE COMPLETE SYNCHRONIZATION
> WITH HIGHER FREQUENCIES AND VIBRATIONS OF
> CREATION BEING TOTALLY ENTRAINED.
> IN OTHER WORDS, BEING AT-ONE-MENT." —David Hulse

Tap Good Vibrations

We live in a world of resonance. Everything pulses with its own, unique vibration. When your resonance is high, you experience well-being. When your resonance declines, so does your health. Here are some things you can do to keep your mind, body, and spirit vibrating at a healthy rate.

MIND: *Meditate to shift brainwave activity*
Normally, while you are awake and going about your day, your brainwave frequencies are about 13–30 cycles per second (cps). When you meditate, that decreases to about 8–13 cps. Your heart rate and breathing slow down, too. Shifting your vibration to a slower pace calms your mind and body, which can produce healing on many levels.

BODY: *Drum to harmonize your heartbeat*
In some Native American and African traditions, drumming is used as a way to balance and heal the heart. With your hand or a type of beater, strike the drum head, playing a beat that is in sync with the heart's rhythm. If your heart rate is too rapid, you can calm it by playing a rhythm that is slightly slower. Your heart will align itself to the drum's vibration.

SPIRIT: *Visit a sacred shrine*
Regardless of your belief system, you may benefit from visiting a sacred shrine. In India, modern seekers make pilgrimages to places associated with holy beings. They believe the accumulated vibrations from the prayers uttered in such sites charge the space with positive energy.

"THE GREATNESS OF A NATION CAN BE JUDGED BY THE WAY ITS ANIMALS ARE TREATED." —Mahatma Gandhi

Learn from the Animals

Sharing your life with an animal companion can lower blood pressure, ease anxiety, reduce the risk of allergies, and prevent depression. Spend time with an animal companion today. If you don't have a pet of your own, consider taking a friend's dog for a walk. Or visit a petting zoo, animal shelter, or farm.

MIND: *Pay attention to animal appearances*
When you sight an animal, bird, or other creature—especially one that you don't usually see—pay attention. According to some Native American teachings, the creature may have appeared to give you a message. What qualities do you associate with the animal? These may be qualities you need to exercise now.

BODY: *Pet an animal companion*
Pets can provide positive health benefits, according to Blair Justice, PhD, professor at the University of Texas School of Public Health. Studies show people who have suffered heart attacks survive longer if they have pets. If you have a pet, stroke it with focused attention and enjoy the exchange of loving energy between you—you'll enhance your well-being and your pet's.

SPIRIT: *Seek help from your spirit animal*
In shamanic traditions, spirit animals serve as guides and helpers to those of us here on earth. Do you feel an affinity with a particular animal? That may be your spirit animal or totem. When you need assistance with a life challenge or seek guidance, ask your spirit animal to lend you its special characteristics.

"NOBLE DEEDS AND HOT BATHS ARE THE BEST CURES

FOR DEPRESSION." —Dodie Smith

Wash Away Your Troubles

Since ancient times, people have flocked to healing spas and baths to "take the waters." The ancient Greek physician Hippocrates recommended taking an aromatic bath every day to improve health. You, too, can derive healing benefits from taking a relaxing bath today.

MIND: *Wash away stress*
When you feel stressed out after a trying day, take a few minutes to clean and refresh your mind. Sit in a comfortable spot and close your eyes. Imagine you are standing under a beautiful waterfall. Sense the clear, cool water flowing down over your head and body, washing away all the tension, irritation, and cares of the day.

BODY: *Take a relaxing bath*
Hydrotherapy is a holistic healing method that uses water to treat illness and pain. Soaking in hot water soothes tension, relaxes the muscles, and calms the mind. Cold water, on the other hand, stimulates circulation and invigorates the mind. Whirlpool baths give you a gentle, full-body massage. Enjoy whatever type of bathing experience suits your needs—every day if possible.

SPIRIT: *Place amethysts in your bathwater*
Crystal workers say amethysts emit a gentle, relaxing resonance that can calm you on every level. Place several amethysts in your bathwater—they'll imprint the water with their vibrations, allowing you to absorb the healing properties through your skin. Set amethyst chunks at the corners of your tub, too.

"God, grant me the serenity to accept the things I cannot change, courage to change the things I can, and the wisdom to know the difference."

—Reinhold Niebuhr, "The Serenity Prayer"

Control What You Can, Accept What You Can't

You cannot control what others think, say, feel, or do. You can only control yourself and your responses to situations. Accepting that fact can remove a great deal of stress from your life. Today, set down the burden of trying to control others and allow them to take responsibility for themselves.

MIND: *Pick your battles*

Determine which battles are worth fighting and which are a waste of time and energy. Choose to participate only in those you believe are worthwhile and where you have a chance of effecting positive outcomes. If a discussion starts escalating out of control, walk away and perhaps try at another time.

BODY: *Use acupressure to ease motion sickness*

Do you suffer from motion sickness when you are a passenger in a car, boat, or plane, but not when you are at the wheel? If so, your malady is probably linked with feeling out of control. To relieve motion sickness, put two fingertips on the acupressure point P 5, about three finger-widths up from your wrist on the underside of your arm. Hold until queasiness subsides.

SPIRIT: *Surrender to a higher power*

When you feel a situation or problem is beyond your ability to control or handle, turn it over to a higher power. Surrender your own desire to determine an outcome and allow the entity of your choice to resolve matters.

"THE MOST DARING THING IS TO CREATE STABLE
COMMUNITIES IN WHICH THE TERRIBLE DISEASE OF
LONELINESS CAN BE CURED." —Kurt Vonnegut Jr.

Nurture Your Community

Today, do something to enhance your community. In our fast-paced,
transient society, many of us feel a sense of disconnect and isolation
from our communities and our neighbors, as if we are merely pass-
ing through. The following suggestions can help you feel a part of
your own community and enjoy it more.

MIND: *Support local businesses*
Consider buying something you need from a locally owned business,
instead of a superstore. During the past few decades, major chain
operations have put countless small stores out of business, depriv-
ing communities of jobs and sending money overseas, increasing
national debt. When you support local businesses, you invest in your
community and yourself.

BODY: *Eat local produce*
Locally grown fruits and vegetables are likely to be fresher, less processed, and more nutritious. According to some sources, foods that are
native to your area are healthier for you because your body is in harmony with them. Additionally, imported foods may come from countries that have lower standards for chemical fertilizers and pesticides.

SPIRIT: *Make your community a better place*
Do something to beautify your community. Pick up trash along the
roadside. Plant flowers in an empty lot. Start a community garden
project. Help an elderly neighbor by shoveling his or her sidewalk
when it snows. Avoid using chemicals on your lawn. Every little bit
you do helps, and may inspire others to pitch in, too.

"You come to love not by finding the perfect person, but by seeing an imperfect person perfectly."

—Sam Keen

Make Love Last

Focus on improving your primary partnership today. A 2007 University of Virginia study found that although divorce rates in America are declining, between 40 and 50 percent of marriages still end in divorce. The following suggestions can help keep your relationship healthy.

MIND: *Put your relationship first*
Give your primary relationship priority in your life. Often we put the needs of children, parents, or careers ahead of our partners. Or, we may be more interested in our individual needs and desires than in what's best for the relationship. With your partner, discuss ways to strengthen your relationship by making it your number-one interest.

BODY: *Sip an herbal aphrodisiac tea*
Traditionally vervain was used as an aphrodisiac because it eases tension. Damiana stimulates and balances the hormonal system. Put a teaspoon of dried damiana and a teaspoon of dried vervain in a pot with two and a half cups boiling water. Steep for ten minutes. Strain and flavor with licorice, ginger, or honey. Drink two cups of tea a day to boost sexual energy.

SPIRIT: *Clear clutter from your bedroom*
Your bedroom should be a loving retreat for you and your partner. Clear away anything that doesn't pertain to love, sex, romance, and intimacy. If you have a TV or computer in the bedroom, cover it when it's not in use or close it away in a cabinet. Pick up books and clothing, and keep your bedroom clean.

"THE GROVES WERE GOD'S FIRST TEMPLES."

—William Cullen Bryant

Become a Tree-Hugger

Take a walk in a park or wooded area and enjoy trees. Trees are one of our great resources, offering shade from the sun's heat and wood for fires when it's cold. They clear the air and give us nuts and fruit to eat. They provide homes for birds and animals and give us leaves for fertilizer.

MIND: *Care for a tree*

Watering, pruning, or otherwise caring for a tree can give you a chance to relax and commune with nature. Trees also offer us lessons we can apply in our daily lives. A tree's slow, steady growth provides a good example of endurance, patience, and an ability to adapt to its environment. Its rootedness suggests stability and groundedness.

BODY: *Get nutty*

You can reduce your risk of heart disease just by having a serving of nuts five times per week. The high amount of unsaturated fat helps lower the LDL ("bad cholesterol") and increase HDL ("good cholesterol") in your blood. The omega-3 fatty acids are absorbed by the LDL particles, which triggers the liver cells to remove this cholesterol from your blood.

SPIRIT: *Sit under a tree*

Many spiritual traditions say trees are sources of wisdom. The Buddha supposedly received enlightenment while sitting under the Bodhi tree. Norse cosmology says the god Odin (Woden) gained the wisdom of the runes from hanging on the holy tree Yggdrasil. Sit peacefully beneath a tree and try to connect with its energy. What do you experience?

"WHEN LOOKING FOR ADVENTURE IN A DARK AND
DESERTED LANDSCAPE WE SHOULD ASK ONLY FOR THE
LIGHT OF THE MOON. THEN OUR IMAGINATIONS CAN
CREATE MORE EXOTIC EXPLANATIONS FOR THE RUSTLING
IN THE UNDERGROWTH OR THE DARK (BOTTOMLESS?)
VOIDS, WHICH OPEN UP AHEAD OF US." —Steve Roberts

Align with Lunar Energy

Step outside tonight and gaze at the moon. Our ancestors aligned
themselves with lunar cycles for planting, harvesting, breeding live-
stock, and other facets of daily life. You, too, can benefit from connecting with the moon's energy.

MIND: *What's your moon sign?*
You probably know what your sun sign is, but you may not be aware
that you also have a moon sign. Astrologers say the moon represents your emotions, relationships, home, and family matters. Consult with an astrologer or check an online source to learn more about
your moon sign.

BODY: *Notice lunar cycles*
The moon's phases affect the tides and crop growth, so it's no surprise
that many people feel the changes in its cycle, too. You many notice
that you have more energy or experience more stress during the full
moon, and feel less vital a day or two before the new moon. Chart your
reactions to lunar phases and plan your activities accordingly.

SPIRIT: *Celebrate a moon ritual*
Many people who follow nature-oriented spiritual paths consider the
moon to be a representation of the Divine Feminine and celebrate
her cycles. Consider holding a ritual on the full moon and/or the new
one. The full moon represents abundance and culmination; the new
one signifies beginnings.

"IT IS ONLY WHEN YOU HAVE BOTH DIVINE GRACE AND
HUMAN ENDEAVOR THAT YOU CAN EXPERIENCE BLISS."

—Sri Sathya Sai Baba

Be Open to Spiritual Experience

Consider taking part in a spiritual activity today. A growing number of Americans consider themselves spiritual, although they don't belong to a specific religion, according to a *Newsweek* poll in 2005. The poll found that "many Americans are choosing to seek spiritual experiences outside the framework of traditional religions."

MIND: *Share your faith with others*

Sharing your spiritual beliefs with others can provide numerous benefits. Couples who share a spiritual path are less likely to divorce than those who don't. A study published in the *American Journal of Public Health* also found that people who attended regular religious services lived longer. You don't have to go to a church or temple; you can meet informally with others for inspiration and support.

BODY: *Treat your body with reverence*

See your body as a wonderful gift to be cared for with respect. Endeavor to do the things you know are good for you: eat a healthier diet, exercise at least half an hour a day, keep your weight down, get enough sleep. If you consider yourself to be precious, you'll feel more motivated to treat yourself well.

SPIRIT: *Connect with the Source*

Eastern medicine says you connect to the Source through the crown chakra, an energy center located near the top of your head. When it is clear and balanced you are able to receive divine energy more easily. Visualize violet light above and around your head. Breathe deeply as you allow the glow to envelop your head.

"STRESS IS THE TRASH OF MODERN LIFE—WE ALL GENERATE IT BUT IF YOU DON'T DISPOSE OF IT PROPERLY, IT WILL PILE UP AND OVERTAKE YOUR LIFE." —Danzae Pace

Nip Stress in the Bud

Today, start implementing some easy practices to reduce the stress you experience. Stress is a factor in many illnesses because it spurs the fight-or-flight response, which over time impairs the immune system. Stressors are omnipresent in modern life, but you can choose how you react to them.

MIND: *Read inspirational literature*

Start your day by reading something inspirational and upbeat. It could be a passage from a religious or spiritual text, a poem, or news about something positive in your community. When you begin the morning on a positive note, it helps you put things in perspective later on when tension begins to build.

BODY: *Set out lavender*

Lavender has been shown to have calming and soothing effects on the body. A group of Australian researchers and another in Miami found that breathing in the scent of lavender can make you more relaxed, less anxious, and less depressed—it can also induce sleepiness. Put a few sprigs on your pillow to help you sleep better or on your desk to calm stress.

SPIRIT: *Remove computer stress with tourmaline*

Place a piece of black tourmaline beside your computer. This crystal is a powerful energy balancer. It helps protect you from the adverse effects of electromagnetic stress that can come from computers, WiFi, cell phones, and other electronic equipment. It blocks "bad vibes" and strengthens your aura.

"CATS ARE CONNOISSEURS OF COMFORT."   —James Herriot

Get Comfortable

Give yourself permission to be comfortable today. Snuggle up in a cushy chair with a good book and a cup of herbal tea. Put your feet up. Take it easy.

MIND: *Avoid discussing unpleasant subjects*
Engage in pleasant discourse that focuses on upbeat subjects. Steer clear of topics you know may raise controversy or discomfort, unless absolutely necessary. Unless you can do something to improve a situation, arguing or whining about it won't accomplish anything positive—it will only cause animosity. Choose to discuss matters that give you a lift and connect you with other people.

BODY: *Shun uncomfortable garments*
Kick off those stiletto heels. Loosen your tie. Unfetter yourself and wear clothes that don't bind, itch, or irritate you in any way. Even if you work in the corporate world, you can dress in a way that doesn't constrict you. Tight clothing interferes with healthy breathing and movement. High heels and uncomfortable shoes can throw your body's alignment out of whack. Opt for comfort, not high style.

SPIRIT: *Arrange your furniture in comfortable configurations*
Feng shui, the ancient Chinese art of placement, emphasizes comfort, ease, and harmony. One way to accomplish this is to arrange the seating in your living areas so that people can converse without having to shout. Position chairs and sofas in conversation groups so that no one will be seated more than about eight to ten feet away from anyone else.

"IF YOU SEE IT IN YOUR MIND, YOU'RE GOING TO

HOLD IT IN YOUR HAND." —Bob Proctor, *The Secret*

Improve Your Vision

For most of us, seeing is our dominant sense. But even though our eyes may be taking in stimuli and our brains may be recording what we've observed in the subconscious, we don't maximize our seeing ability. Try these tips to enhance your physical sight and your second sight.

MIND: *What you see is what you get*

According to some philosophies, what you see is what you get. By changing your ideas and expectations, you can change the situations you experience. Notice the dominant thoughts you hold today. Those are the things you are drawing to you right now. If that's not what you want, change your thinking.

BODY: *Look away from your computer periodically*

You can ease eyestrain by looking away from your computer screen at regular intervals throughout the day. According to optometrist Dr. Marc Grossman, more than half of all computer users suffer from eyestrain, blurred vision, headaches, and other visual complaints. Every half hour or so, spend a few minutes focusing on something at least ten feet away to help relieve computer-related eye problems.

SPIRIT: *Gaze at a candle flame*

Try this clairvoyant technique to expand your vision. Light a candle and gaze at the flickering flame, allowing your vision to soften and your mind to relax. As you look at the flame and the smoke rising from it, allow yourself to see images forming there. What insights do they offer you?

> "MONEY IS NEITHER MY GOD NOR MY DEVIL. IT IS A FORM
> OF ENERGY THAT TENDS TO MAKE US MORE OF WHO WE
> ALREADY ARE, WHETHER IT'S GREEDY OR LOVING."
>
> —Dan Millman

Encourage Financial Health

Are you feeling the pinch of economic woes? Perhaps it's time to look at more than just the recommendations of financial gurus. You may want to consider other factors that affect your fiscal well-being.

MIND: *Pay yourself first*
Before you pay your bills, pay yourself. This form of savings lets you acknowledge your worthiness and helps you value yourself more. As your nest egg grows, you'll also feel proud of yourself for managing to put away money on a steady basis.

BODY: *Eat breakfast like a king*
Start the day with a healthy breakfast that includes protein, whole grains, dairy products, and fruit. Breakfast should be your biggest and most nutritious meal—it has to revive you after many hours of fasting and fuel you throughout the day. A hearty and well-balanced breakfast will give you the physical vitality and mental clarity you need to function productively.

SPIRIT: *Drop coins in a jar*
Remind yourself of your intention to increase your wealth. Set a jar beside your front door. Each time you enter or leave your home, drop a coin in the jar. As you do, affirm that every day you are growing more prosperous. When you have filled the jar, deposit the coins in the bank and begin again. At the end of the year, you may be surprised at how much you've saved.

"ALWAYS BE A FIRST-RATE VERSION OF YOURSELF, INSTEAD OF A SECOND-RATE VERSION OF SOMEBODY ELSE."

—Judy Garland

Be Your Own Best Friend

Give yourself a pat on the back today. You are special, unique in all the world. You can shine and be seen, heard, and appreciated. You are worthy of loving and being loved. Self-love precedes love of others, so develop a loving relationship with yourself.

MIND: *Become your own admirer*

We're often too quick to find fault with ourselves and not quick enough to pat ourselves on the back. Today and every day find something to admire about yourself. It might be your new hairstyle, a great meal you cooked, or the way you handled a problem. List things you like and value about yourself, and read your list regularly.

BODY: *Be in harmony with your body*

You won't reap the positive benefits of exercise if you resent having to do it and are fuming the whole time you are walking, swimming, or cycling. Choose an exercise you enjoy doing. Accept and appreciate your body. Consider it your friend and ally. Be thankful for all the wonderful things it does for you every day.

SPIRIT: *Get in touch with your Higher Self*

You could think of your Higher Self as a higher resonance of your physical self, the part that connects you to the Divine. It is always there, but you may not be aware of its presence. During meditation, invite it to make itself known to you. You may sense a loving force near you or permeating you. Embrace it.

"MEMORY IS A COMPLICATED THING, A RELATIVE TO
TRUTH, BUT NOT ITS TWIN." —Barbara Kingsolver

Be Kind to Your Memory

Don't overtax your memory today. As we age, we notice our memories and recall aren't as sharp as they used to be. That might be because we're trying to do too much and put undue stress on our brains. Relax and stop trying to force recollections to the forefront of your mind—and try these memory aids.

MIND: *Make lists*

Studies have shown that even the best of us can't remember more than seven things—and trying to do so causes frustration and stress. To reduce the need to hold copious details in your brain, make lots of lists. Carry a small notepad in your purse or pocket; keep one beside your bed. Once you write something down, you can stop wasting brainpower thinking about it and move on to other, more important pursuits.

BODY: *Use acupressure to stimulate memory*

When you want to recall something, activate what are known in acupressure as the Sun Points. These two points are located on your temples. Press your fingers gently, but firmly, to these points and hold for about a minute to ease mental stress, clear your head, and improve your memory.

SPIRIT: *Use calcite to reconnect with memories*

Black calcite can help you get in touch with old memories that you may have suppressed because they were painful to deal with. Hold this crystal in your hand during meditation to bring those memories into consciousness so that you can gently release them.

"LAUGHTER AND ORGASM ARE GREAT BEDFELLOWS."

—John Callahan

Increase Sexual Satisfaction

Is your sex life as good as you'd like it to be? According to the 2010 Durex Sexual Wellbeing Global Survey, only 44 percent of people are satisfied with their sex lives. Stress, boredom, and just being too tired are common reasons for dissatisfaction. Take steps today to improve your sexual fulfillment.

MIND: *Shut off electronics at bedtime*
Leave your electronics behind when you go to bed. A survey reported in *The 30-Day Sex Solution* by Victoria and John Wilson found that "37 percent of Americans take their laptops to bed with them, and 30 percent interrupt sex to answer their cell phones." If you want to improve your sex life, set priorities.

BODY: *Give your libido a boost*
A foot massage feels great, but it can also boost your libido. With your thumbs, rub the ankles above and below the anklebones, and across the tops of the feet where they bend. Spend several minutes massaging the feet. This technique activates reflexology points in the feet that are energetically linked with the reproductive organs.

SPIRIT: *Tie a red ribbon on your bedroom doorknob*
You've heard of tying a string around your finger to remind you of something. This tip uses the same idea. Tie a big red ribbon on the doorknob to your bedroom to remind you to focus on loving thoughts. Every time you see it, you'll instantly think of love, romance, and passion—and because the mind is where sexual satisfaction begins, your thoughts can boost your sex life.

"DON'T DRINK BY THE WATER'S EDGE.
THROW YOURSELF IN! BECOME THE WATER.
ONLY THEN WILL YOUR THIRST END." —Jeanette Berson

The Healing Power of Water

The fountain of youth may indeed be water. Our bodies are about 60 percent water, so it's no surprise that water offers lots of benefits. Many sources show that bathing, swimming, and just sitting beside a lake can generate healing effects. Immerse yourself in the power of water today.

MIND: *Let water refresh your mind*
Austrian scientist Wilhelm Reich believed life energy, which he called orgone, was concentrated near bodies of water. That's why sitting near the ocean or a waterfall causes you to feel relaxed and refreshed. Sit by a body of water today and try to see the gently swirling orgone hovering just above the water. Allow this life-enhancing energy to soothe and balance your mind.

BODY: *Go for a swim*
Swimming is the best exercise to engage in if you want to live longer, according to a study published in *Medical News Today* in 2009. The University of South Carolina study found that swimming slowed the aging process by as much as 20 percent. Swimming puts less stress on your body than running, lifting weights, or aerobics. It also blends exertion and relaxation.

SPIRIT: *Make crystal-infused water*
Place a piece of rose quartz or amethyst—or both—in a clear glass bowl and fill the bowl with spring water. Place the bowl in the sunlight. Allow the stones to sit for twenty-four hours in order for their vibrations to infuse the water. Drink the water to calm stress and generate a sense of peace.

"MOST OF THE SHADOWS OF THIS LIFE ARE CAUSED BY STANDING IN ONE'S OWN SUNSHINE."

—Ralph Waldo Emerson

Get Out of Your Own Way

Today, observe how you may be limiting yourself mentally, physically, or spiritually. Perhaps feelings of inadequacy or fear of someone else's disapproval are keeping you from doing what you want to do. Begin to let your light shine, a little at a time.

MIND: *Nourish a hidden talent*

Have you always wanted to draw or write poetry, but were afraid you weren't good enough? Unless you try, you'll never know. Many people erroneously believe they don't have talent because they expect instant success. But like anything else, you have to practice to become good. Put your expectations on hold and just experiment. Having fun is the first step.

BODY: *Take the first step toward eliminating a bad habit*

Habits build up over a period of time, and sometimes it takes time to undo them. Today, just focus on taking the first step. If you want to stop smoking, for instance, maybe you can cut down a few cigarettes at a time if going cold turkey seems too hard. It's important to keep the end result in sight, but don't let the enormity of your goal overwhelm you and cause you to give up.

SPIRIT: *Observe sunlight and shadow*

As the sun climbs higher in the sky, watch the shadows grow smaller. See this as a metaphor for yourself. As you let your own light open up and ascend, notice how the darkness and fears diminish.

"IT IS THE SWEET, SIMPLE THINGS OF LIFE WHICH

ARE THE REAL ONES AFTER ALL." —Laura Ingalls Wilder

Skimp on Sugar

In the United States, we have a love affair with sugar. However, it's not a healthy relationship for most of us. A 2011 National Health and Nutrition Survey found that teenagers consume about three times the recommended calories from sugars. If you get more than 150 calories a day from sugars, consider cutting back.

MIND: *Examine your relationship with sweets*

If you eat too many sweets, examine what they mean to you. Were you given sweets as a reward when you were young? Do your fond memories involve sweets? Do you use them as a substitute for love? If so, evaluate why you desire sugar and start looking for ways to find "sweetness" in other areas of your life.

BODY: *Cut down on sugar*

You may think sugar gives you a quick energy boost, but the opposite is true. Sugar gets into your bloodstream quickly, but just as quickly it dumps you into the doldrums. This addictive, mood-altering substance is linked with all sorts of mental and physical ills, ranging from depression to diabetes. The average American consumes about 140 pounds of sugar annually—start reducing your intake today.

SPIRIT: *Use honey instead of sugar*

Honey's benefits have been known for millennia. Its antibacterial properties heal wounds, aid physical stamina, and strengthen the immune system. Honey also symbolizes eternal life because it never spoils. The ancient Egyptians placed it in their tombs and it was still edible when discovered after thousands of years.

"EACH AND EVERY COMPONENT THAT MAKES UP YOUR
LIFE EXPERIENCE IS DRAWN TO YOU BY THE POWERFUL
LAW OF ATTRACTION'S RESPONSE TO THE THOUGHTS
YOU THINK." —Esther and Jerry Hicks, *Money and the Law of Attraction*

Thinking Makes It So

Your mind is the body's command center. Therefore your mental state and the thoughts you think will have an impact on every area of your life. Today, pay attention to your thoughts and how they affect your emotions and your physical well-being.

MIND: *Pay attention to what you are attracting*

Are the people around you angry or glum? Are bills piling up faster than you can pay them? In their bestselling books, Esther and Jerry Hicks explain that you can see clearly what sort of ideas you hold—perhaps unconsciously—by looking at the circumstances in your life. If you don't like what you see, change your attitudes.

BODY: *Choose holistic healing methods*

Holistic healers do not separate the body from the mind, emotions, and spirit. Instead, they consider all to be connected—and in order to be healthy, all levels must be functioning well. Research Ayurveda, acupuncture, homeopathy, herbal therapy, and other holistic methods to determine which one(s) may be right for you.

SPIRIT: *Make a talisman*

Talismans are good-luck charms you make to attract something you want. In a drawstring pouch, place several small items that symbolize whatever it is you wish to attract. These things should all hold positive significance for you. When you've finished, affirm to yourself that what you desire is coming to you now.

"YOU CAN CLUTCH THE PAST SO TIGHTLY TO YOUR
CHEST THAT IT LEAVES YOUR ARMS TOO FULL TO
EMBRACE THE PRESENT." —Jan Glidewell

Appreciate Your Life Now

Today, be conscious of the things you tend to take for granted and be grateful for living at this time. When you take a shower, for example, think of what it would be like to haul water from a stream and heat it on the stove for a bath. Although we like to reminisce about the good old days, in reality our ancestors' lives were more difficult in many ways than ours are today.

MIND: *Read about an earlier time period*
When you read about the hardships of earlier times, you can better appreciate the advantages you enjoy now. Virtually every aspect of life in previous centuries was more grueling and less comfortable than it is today. Enjoy the pleasures of the present.

BODY: *Appreciate a medical treatment*
Although few of us enjoy going to the dentist or undergoing other types of medical treatment, it may be easier to endure if you remember what medicine was like 100 years ago. If you have a tooth filled, be grateful for Novocain. If you have an infection, give thanks for antibiotics.

SPIRIT: *Value religious freedom*
Today, exercise your right to practice your beliefs. Although religious persecution still exists, in many parts of today's world people enjoy greater religious freedom than in previous centuries. The U.S. military now recognizes Wicca as a religion. In many places, ideas that once would have been punished by execution are now common.

"THE MIND IS LIKE AN ICEBERG, IT FLOATS WITH
ONE-SEVENTH OF ITS BULK ABOVE WATER."

—Sigmund Freud

Give Your Gray Matter a Boost

Today, set an intention to begin using your gray matter more fully. Although science suggests we use only a small percentage of our brains, studies have shown that we have many methods available to us for improving brain power. Diet, exercise, meditation, and many other practices—including the tips listed below—can improve mental function.

MIND: *Improve your vocabulary*
One way to keep your mind sharp and perhaps prevent age-related deterioration is to give it plenty of exercise. Consider improving your vocabulary by learning a new word every day. The English language is constantly evolving and now contains one million words. When you run out of those, start adding words from other languages.

BODY: *Boost brain function*
Have you ever noticed that a walnut looks a little like a human brain, with a left and right hemisphere? Even the wrinkles or folds in the nut resemble the brain's neocortex. It may not be a coincidence. Research shows that eating walnuts helps to develop more than three dozen neurotransmitters for brain function.

SPIRIT: *Tap into the Akashic Records*
Many spiritual traditions mention the Akashic Records (in Sanskrit, *akashic* means "sky"). This record is an account of all knowledge and experience that has ever existed. Some call it the Universe's DNA. In meditation, attempt to connect with this body of cosmic wisdom. Don't push it; just allow insights to gently emerge into your awareness.

"WHEN WE GET TOO CAUGHT UP IN THE BUSYNESS OF THE WORLD, WE LOSE CONNECTION WITH ONE ANOTHER—AND OURSELVES." —Jack Kornfield

Make Human Contact

Get up close and personal today. As electronic media become more popular, many of us have lost the personal touch. However, Facebook and text messages are no substitute for real human contact. Try these suggestions:

MIND: *Mean what you say*

Show genuine interest in the people you encounter. When you say, "Have a nice day," look the person in the eye and mean it. When you ask, "How are you?" say it with sincerity and listen to the person's response. Often we use these phrases as throwaways, but notice what happens when you invest the words with real caring.

BODY: *Reach out and touch someone*

Touch friends and family members frequently. According to the Touch Research Institute at the University of Miami School of Medicine, touch can ease pain, reduce stress, boost immunity, help premature babies thrive, help wounds heal faster, and aid a range of diseases from diabetes to cancer. Even a stranger's friendly touch, such as brushing a cashier's finger when you receive change, can have positive effects.

SPIRIT: *Send blessings to others*

Prayer circles, such as the one at Unity Village that operates 24/7, can help loved ones and strangers alike. Buddhists hang flags with prayers written on them outside their homes and temples. The work of Dr. Larry Dossey and others has shown that prayers can produce healing benefits, even when the person being prayed for doesn't know about it.

"AIM FOR THE MOON. IF YOU MISS, YOU MAY HIT A STAR."

—W. Clement Stone

Let the Stars Guide You

Six thousand years ago, stargazers began identifying constellations and assigning meanings to them. The ancients believed the planets and stars were the homes of gods and goddesses, who guided earthly affairs. Stars have long been symbols of hope. Today, let them guide and inspire you, too.

MIND: *Look at the stars*

Go outside on a clear night and gaze up at the stars—just as people have done for millennia. Enjoy the tranquil beauty of the sky overhead. Allow yourself to appreciate the vastness of the Universe. Feel your connection with this vastness, knowing that you are a part of all that is.

BODY: *Clear congestion with star anise*

The star-shaped seedpod of the star anise tree has many aromatherapy properties. To clear the congestion of a cold, put a few drops of star anise essential oil in a vaporizer. Or, add the essential oil to a bowl of hot water and lean over it, inhaling the fragrant scent. The stimulating aroma can also aid a cough or sinus problems.

SPIRIT: *Wish on a shooting star*

When you see a shooting star, make a wish. The idea may not be just a childlike amusement. Wishes are the first step to bringing something you desire into your life—unless you know what you want, you're not likely to get it. Believe your wish can come true, then do whatever is necessary to make your wish a reality.

"IT IS HORRIFYING THAT WE HAVE TO FIGHT OUR OWN
GOVERNMENT TO SAVE THE ENVIRONMENT."

—Ansel Adams

Care for Our Planet

If we don't care for our environment, it can't take care of us. Our quality of life depends on the quality of our planet; our health depends on its health. Today, be aware of how your actions impact the earth and do your part to lessen the burden. Even little things count, such as the following suggestions.

MIND: *Shop at resale stores*

Shopping at resale stores provides lots of advantages. You save money. You recycle goods rather than throwing them away or using energy to produce more goods. And, if you buy from shops whose profits go to support charities, you contribute to worthy causes. Donate things you no longer use to resale stores, too.

BODY: *Pick up trash when you walk*

Combine environmental consciousness with exercise. When you go for a walk, take a bag with you and pick up trash along the way. If you walk every day and fill a bag at a time, you'll soon see a notice-able improvement. All that bending over helps work your waistline and stretch out your hamstrings, too.

SPIRIT: *Think kind thoughts*

Negative thoughts are a form of pollution. We may not be able to see them, but they have a harmful impact on our psyches and on our interactions with others. Kind, compassionate, peaceful thoughts, on the other hand, seed the cosmos with kindness, compassion, and peace.

> "HAPPINESS IS NOT A MATTER OF INTENSITY BUT OF
> BALANCE, ORDER, RHYTHM AND HARMONY."
>
> —Thomas Merton

Balance Your Chi

In Eastern philosophy, *chi* or *qi* (pronounced *chee*) is the life force that flows through everything—the earth, the cosmos, our bodies, our environments. Chinese medicine, feng shui, martial arts, and other practices seek to harmonize the movement of chi through your body, your home, and your life. By balancing your personal chi, you can enjoy a happier, healthier existence.

MIND: *Believe in your success*

Your mind is an important factor in directing chi through your body or your environment. Acupuncture uses needles, and feng shui uses mirrors, crystals, and other tools, to balance chi. But these implements are only part of the healing process. Your belief in the success of the practices you employ is essential.

BODY: *Do tai chi*

This ancient martial art combines breathing with flowing movements to ease stress and anxiety. According to the Mayo Clinic, tai chi (pronounced *tie-chee*) may also aid balance, flexibility, sleep dysfunction, blood pressure, muscle strength, fatigue, and chronic pain. Because it is a gentle mind-body exercise, tai chi is ideal for older people or those who have moderate levels of physical ability.

SPIRIT: *Invite chi into your home*

Feng shui, the ancient Chinese art of placement, emphasizes the importance of attracting positive chi into your home to achieve health, wealth, and happiness. One way to do this is to paint your front door a cheerful color, preferably red or purple, which are considered lucky colors in China.

"When we long for life without difficulties,
remind us that oaks grow strong in contrary
winds and diamonds are made under pressure."

—Peter Marshall

Get Stoned

Seek the wisdom of stones today. Stones are among the most ancient substances on earth and have many stories to tell. They teach geologists about the past and reveal the future to seers. Look into ways they can help you.

MIND: *Learn about crystals*

Explore the fascinating world of crystals and gemstones. Crystal workers attribute healing properties to various stones and use them to aid mental, physical, emotional, and spiritual conditions. Originally, birthstones were worn to attract desirable qualities and ameliorate unwanted ones. Consult a good book, such as Judy Hall's *Crystal Bible*, to see which crystals might benefit you.

BODY: *Enjoy a hot stone massage*

Soothe body and soul by treating yourself to this ancient form of massage, which has recently become popular in the United States. Smooth stones made of iron-rich basalt are placed on your back, hands, and feet. The soothing heat relaxes muscles, eases tension, and stimulates circulation. If you suffer from arthritis, stiffness, or back pain, you may be a good candidate for a hot stone massage.

SPIRIT: *Get a rune reading*

Consult the runes to get answers to questions. This system derives from old Norse alphabets and equates each letter symbol with a meaning. Casting runes is a form of divination. Early rune symbols were carved on stones, bones, and wood. Today they may be imprinted in gemstones, glass, plastic, clay, or other substances.

"THE WORD 'REALITY' MUST ALWAYS BE
USED WITH QUOTATIONS." —Vladimir Nabokov

Get Real

Separating reality from illusion can be a challenge, especially in these days of sophisticated media, electronic technology, synthetic fabrics, and engineered food. Today, consider getting back to basics. You may find you gain more satisfaction from taking a simpler, more wholesome approach to living.

MIND: *Interact with other people*
Instead of spending time on the computer doing social networking, make real contact with real human beings. Schedule an outing with friends. Visit a family member you haven't seen in a while. Join a group of people with whom you share an interest. Online interactions may be convenient and easy, but they're no substitute for genuine human contact.

BODY: *Stop comparing yourself to supermodels*
Appreciate your body just as it is. We may know that magazine images don't reflect reality, yet they influence our opinions of ourselves nonetheless. A 1995 study found that after women looked at fashion magazines for just three minutes, nearly three-quarters of them felt depressed and ashamed of their own appearances. Realize this is one image of beauty, but not the only one.

SPIRIT: *The world of illusion*
In Buddhist philosophy, the material world is an illusion based on our inability to see the truth. Consider this possibility when you start to give too much importance to a minor problem or worry about what you see happening around you. You may not be aware of the big picture.

> "An ounce of prevention is worth a pound of cure."
>
> —Benjamin Franklin

Protect Yourself

Today, evaluate your protection strategies and notice if there are any holes in your umbrella. You may not be able to ward off danger at every corner, but some commonsense practices can make you and your loved ones more secure. It's better to be safe than sorry, as the old saying goes.

MIND: *Update your insurance*

Are your home and auto insurance policies up-to-date? Review your insurance policies and make sure your coverage is adequate. Consider getting replacement insurance for your home—other forms of insurance will only give you pennies on the dollar for your possessions in case of damage. Look into an umbrella policy, too. Remember to read the fine print.

BODY: *Wear your seat belt*

Buckle up today. According to the U.S. National Highway Traffic Safety Administration, seat belts have saved more than 72,000 lives between 2005 and 2009. Sixty percent of people killed in auto accidents weren't wearing seat belts. Although 85 percent of U.S. motorists now use seat belts, many people still risk serious injury or death by not complying. Don't become a statistic!

SPIRIT: *Hang a star on your door*

Some spiritual traditions, including Wicca, consider stars as symbols of protection. The Texas Rangers, and some other lawmen, wear star-shaped badges on their chests, which may offer metaphysical protection. To safeguard your home, hang a star on it. Dangle one from your car's rearview mirror to offer protection while driving.

"DO ALL THE GOOD YOU CAN, IN ALL THE WAYS YOU CAN,

TO ALL THE SOULS YOU CAN, IN EVERY PLACE YOU CAN,

AT ALL THE TIMES YOU CAN, WITH ALL THE ZEAL YOU CAN,

AS LONG AS EVER YOU CAN." —John Wesley

Be a Do-Gooder

Get proactive about making your own life and the world better. If you want to improve conditions outside yourself, first devote yourself to improving conditions inside. Consider the following tips for shifting the scale to the good side.

MIND: *Discuss feel-good topics*
Do you find discussions with friends often turn into gripe sessions? If so, introduce subjects that make you feel good. "Feel good" doesn't mean fluffy or superficial. It means conversing about topics that are uplifting, pleasant, and constructive. Focus on what's good in the world, not on what's bad. Share inspiring stories. Encourage people to talk about their successes or what makes them happy.

BODY: *Do something good for your body*
Avoid high-fructose corn syrup (HFCS). This chemical compound is used as an inexpensive alternative to sugar. In 2010, Princeton University researchers revealed that rats fed a diet of HFCS gained 48 percent more weight than those fed regular table sugar. Studies show that HFCS can also cause insulin resistance, leading to type 2 diabetes.

SPIRIT: *Give your life meaning through good works*
Many organizations are working to alleviate hunger and sickness in underdeveloped countries. Make a contribution to a global mission. Become involved in a humanitarian program, especially one that respects the indigenous cultures of the people they seek to help.

"WORRY NEVER ROBS TOMORROW OF ITS SORROW,

IT ONLY SAPS TODAY OF ITS JOY."

—Leo Buscaglia

Ease Anxiety

Everyone experiences anxiety at times in response to stress. Anxiety can cause heart palpitations, sleeplessness, dizziness, headaches, and many other conditions. Often, anxiety is rooted in worrying about things that may never happen. Instead of turning to drugs to ease the symptoms of mild, temporary anxiety, try the following tips.

MIND: *Find solace in the past*

Recall a place that holds positive memories for you. It may be a childhood hideout, a vacation getaway, or a country you've visited. Recall as many details as possible: the weather, environmental features, the architecture. Choose a familiar spot in this scenario, and place yourself in it, as you are now. See what happens.

BODY: *Take Rescue Remedy to stay calm*

In the 1930s, Dr. Edward Bach developed a series of flower essences that work to heal the body, emotions, and spirit gently and naturally. The best-known is a blend of five different flowers, known as Rescue Remedy, which calms anxiety, restlessness, and irritability. Put a few drops in water or under your tongue for quick relief.

SPIRIT: *Talk to your angels*

A Baylor University Institute for Studies of Religion poll in 2008 found that a majority of Americans believe they are aided by angels. If you feel the need for some heavenly assistance, try calling upon your guardian angel for help with a problem. You may feel a greater sense of peace and comfort.

"I SEE HUMANITY NOW AS ONE VAST PLANT, NEEDING FOR
ITS HIGHEST FULFILLMENT ONLY LOVE, THE NATURAL
BLESSINGS OF THE GREAT OUTDOORS, AND INTELLIGENT
CROSSING AND SELECTION." —Luther Burbank

Spend More Time Outdoors

Today, make a point of getting outdoors. A 2008 study reported in
the *Seattle Times* found that American adults spend 25 percent less
time outdoors in parks and other natural environments than they did
in 1987. The health benefits of spending time outside are myriad.
Here are a few.

MIND: *Find peace of mind outside*
In modern society, we spend most of our days inside in artificial
environments. Spending time outdoors, however, improves your
mental well-being, according to research published in *Environmental Science and Technology* in 2011. Subjects reported that they felt
less tense, confused, angry, and depressed when they were outside
in natural settings.

BODY: *Exercise outdoors for better results*
A team of researchers at the Peninsula College of Medicine and
Dentistry found that people who exercised outdoors felt more energized and revitalized than those who worked out in a gym or other
indoor setting. The study of more than 800 adults also noted that
those who exercised outside enjoyed their exercise program more
and were more likely to continue doing it.

SPIRIT: *Commune with the devas*
The Sanskrit word *deva* means deity, but today the term usually
refers to the spirit beings who guard and nurture plants and animals.
When you are outside, try to connect with the devas in nature. You
may sense their presence around trees, flowers, and other plants.

"GREAT THINGS ARE DONE BY A SERIES OF SMALL THINGS BROUGHT TOGETHER."

—Vincent van Gogh

Break Down Your Day

You may be able to accomplish more today if you take it little by little, instead of letting the enormity of the day's demands overwhelm you. Stress and boredom often result from trying to handle too much. Try breaking up your day into manageable portions.

MIND: *Set an intention for each period of your day*

From the time you wake up until you fall asleep at night, set intentions for yourself—one at a time. As you eat breakfast, for instance, affirm that the food you eat will nourish your body optimally. As you drive to work, intend to have a safe and pleasant trip. Setting goals in this way helps you stay on track and accomplish what you set out to do.

BODY: *Break up your workout into small parts*

If you tend to get bored or tired during a long workout, try doing smaller amounts of exercise several times a day. Take a short walk before work. Take the stairs rather than the elevator. Do some yoga in the evening to release the stress of the day. Plan a routine that works best for you.

SPIRIT: *Turn within to find peace*

Every hour or so throughout the day, take a few moments to turn within and connect with the peace that lies there. Close your eyes, relax your mind and body, and breathe slowly, deeply. Feel a sense of calm and serenity seep in to ease the busyness of your day.

"LET US BE GRATEFUL TO PEOPLE WHO MAKE US HAPPY,
THEY ARE THE CHARMING GARDENERS WHO MAKE OUR
SOULS BLOSSOM." —Marcel Proust

Value Your Relationship

If you are in an intimate relationship, focus on the good things it offers you today. Married people live longer and enjoy better health, according to a 2007 study by the British Office of National Statistics. Having someone to go through life with can support mental, physical, and spiritual well-being. As a Swedish proverb says, shared joy is a double joy; shared sorrow is half a sorrow.

MIND: *Give your partner a compliment*
It doesn't matter how many times you've told your partner she has pretty eyes or he's a great cook. We all enjoy being appreciated, especially by our loved ones. See something good in your partner and express it with genuine enthusiasm.

BODY: *Do couples yoga*
A type of *hatha* yoga strengthens bonds between couples. Couples yoga involves poses that require partners to support one another physically, which translates into feelings of being emotionally supported as well. Yoga teacher Mishabae Mahoney, author of *Lovers' Knot*, says working with a partner can also help you move beyond your self-limiting ideas about what you can and can't do.

SPIRIT: *Learn fidelity from swans*
Some shamanic traditions say you have a particular spirit animal or totem for life, but other animals may assist in guiding you from time to time. Swans, which mate for life, can teach you the value of fidelity. Invite these animal guides to help you appreciate your mate and your relationship.

"ONE OF THE VERY NICEST THINGS ABOUT LIFE IS THE WAY WE MUST REGULARLY STOP WHATEVER IT IS WE ARE DOING AND DEVOTE OUR ATTENTION TO EATING."

—Luciano Pavarotti

Enjoy Mealtime More

Make the most of your meals today. Studies such as one by the National Center on Addiction and Substance Abuse have shown that kids who eat dinner with their families tend to be healthier mentally, emotionally, and physically. Whether you eat alone or with loved ones, try the following tips to make mealtime more enjoyable.

MIND: *Keep mealtime conversation positive*
Discuss pleasant topics while eating. Arguing or bringing up disturbing subjects causes stress that can interfere with digestion. Dr. Kenneth Koch, professor of medicine at Wake Forest University, explains that stress can increase acid in your stomach, cause spasms in your esophagus, and other types of discomfort.

BODY: *Eat slowly*
One of the easiest ways to lose weight is to eat more slowly. It takes about twenty minutes for your digestive system to send signals to your brain that you're full. Therefore, if you bolt down your food, you may end up eating more than you need. Chewing each bite slowly also lets you savor your food more, aids digestion, and may help you eat less.

SPIRIT: *Say grace before meals*
Before you eat, give thanks for the plants, animals, and people whose efforts brought you the food on your plate. Being aware of how interdependent we all are can give you a stronger sense of belonging. Fostering peaceful, positive thoughts before meals may also improve your digestion.

"EVERY CLOSED EYE IS NOT SLEEPING,

AND EVERY OPEN EYE IS NOT SEEING." —Bill Cosby

Open Your Eyes

The conceptions we form of the world may prevent us from seeing things that don't coincide with our established ideas. Studies conducted by researcher Nikolai Axmacher of the University of Bonn, Germany, confirmed that we may psychologically suppress material that we can't immediately understand and pigeonhole. Today, strengthen your perceptual abilities by employing the following suggestions.

MIND: *Notice something new in your neighborhood*
Drive or take a walk around your neighborhood. Go slow and observe with care the things you've come to take for granted. Your objective is to notice something new today. It might be a plant just bursting into bloom, a neighbor's new porch furniture, or a stone in the road. Practice seeing familiar things in a new way.

BODY: *Protect your eyes*
Eat your veggies. Broccoli provides you with the carotenoid antioxidants lutein and zeaxanthin, which, along with vitamin C, are highly beneficial for the lens and retina of the eye—to the point of protecting your eyes from free-radical damage that ultraviolet light can cause.

SPIRIT: *Practice visualization*
Many meditations involve visualization techniques that can help you relax. Close your physical eyes and call up an image of a soothing scene—waves gently breaking on the beach, for instance. Enrich the vision by bringing in other senses: smell, sound, and so on. Allow the scene to unfold and enjoy the sense of serenity that accompanies your visualization.

"WE DON'T STOP PLAYING BECAUSE WE GROW OLD;
WE GROW OLD BECAUSE WE STOP PLAYING."

—George Bernard Shaw

Take Time to Play

Schedule playtime into your day—no matter what age you are. When you are engaged in a playful activity, you are in a near-meditative state, which can have physical, psychological, and spiritual benefits. For kids, unsupervised play with peers teaches them to cooperate, solve problems, and be creative. For adults, play reduces stress and keeps your mind and body active.

MIND: *Play well with others*
Playing with other people, whether it's bridge or softball, lets you make quick social connections by sharing your enjoyment of a mutually pleasurable activity. Play gives you a break from work and responsibilities, and eases loneliness, depression, and worrying. Playing games can also sharpen your learning capacity, memory, and decision-making skills.

BODY: *Go play outside*
Playing physically active games outdoors can be a fun way to get exercise and shed unwanted pounds. Obesity is a growing national health problem; according to the Centers for Disease Control, one-third of adult Americans are obese. Obesity among children is escalating, too, due to less physical play and more time spent using electronic devices. If you have kids, play together today.

SPIRIT: *Make contact with angels*
According to some angel researchers, angels are fun-loving, light-hearted beings. If you want to attract angels to you, they suggest, be playful. Laugh. Do things that make you happy. Lighten up a little. Invite your angels to share in festive occasions with you.

"A ROCK PILE CEASES TO BE A ROCK PILE THE MOMENT A
SINGLE MAN CONTEMPLATES IT, BEARING WITHIN HIM
THE IMAGE OF A CATHEDRAL." —Antoine de Saint-Exupéry

Connect with Your Creativity

Express your creativity today. Research published in the *Washington Post* in 2008 found that older adults who engaged in creative pursuits had increased neural activity and less depression; creativity may even lower the risk of Alzheimer's. Don't wait until you're old to be creative. Try these suggestions to engage your creativity.

MIND: *Write haiku*

Haiku, a Japanese poetic form, traditionally uses three lines and seventeen syllables. Many haiku poems depict subjects from nature. Try your hand at writing one. The exercise not only taps your creativity, it gives you an opportunity to find beauty in the world around you. See "Haiku for People" at *www.toyomasu.com/haiku* for more information.

BODY: *Play in the mud*

Remember how much fun it was to make mud pies when you were a kid? Playing with mud is still fun. Take a pottery class—this tactile experience can be very therapeutic. Throwing on a potter's wheel requires centering yourself and focusing in the moment, so it becomes a physical meditation. It's a great way to get in touch—literally—with your creativity.

SPIRIT: *Energize your sacral chakra*

The sacral chakra, located just below your navel, is associated with creativity. To energize it, close your eyes, breathe in, and envision the breath flowing into your lower belly. Hold the breath for a moment, picturing an orange glow there. Exhale slowly as you imagine negativity leaving the body through your nose.

"A RUFFLED MIND MAKES A RESTLESS PILLOW."

—Charlotte Brontë

Get More Sleep

It's estimated that one in four Americans and half of all seniors experience sleep problems. Even occasional insomnia weakens your immune system and makes it more difficult for you to function in everyday life. If you have trouble getting a good night's sleep, consider the following suggestions.

MIND: *Calm your mind with meditation*

When your mind doesn't shut down after you've shut your eyes, you may find it hard to get to sleep or to stay asleep. A study done at the University of Calgary, Alberta, found that meditation enabled participants to improve their overall quality of sleep. For best results, meditate for about fifteen minutes in the morning and again for fifteen minutes in the evening.

BODY: *Take kava kava before bed*

If you've had a stressful day, take kava kava before going to bed. This herb, which is native to the Pacific Islands, is said to bring "oneness of body and mind." Brew a cup of kava kava tea at bedtime to promote restful sleep. The herb is also available in capsule form and can be beneficial as a mild sedative and tension reliever.

SPIRIT: *Paint your bedroom a restful color*

Blue and green have a calming effect on us. Studies have shown that when people sit in a blue room their heart rate and breathing slow down. To create a restful, relaxing environment that's conducive to sleep, decorate your bedroom with cool, calming colors: blue, green, teal, or indigo.

> "A KISS IS A LOVELY TRICK DESIGNED BY NATURE TO
> STOP SPEECH WHEN WORDS BECOME SUPERFLUOUS."
>
> —Ingrid Bergman

Enhance Your Romance

Today, set an intention to break out of a romantic rut. Boredom is what often ruins an otherwise good relationship. You don't have to succumb to dull routine or take your relationship for granted. Seize opportunities to show your partner you care. Often it's the little things that mean a lot.

MIND: *Appreciate your partner*
Tell your partner something you appreciate about him or her. It could be her parenting skills, his ability to stay cool under pressure, her smile, his abs. It might be something you've said before or something you've never shared. Express your appreciation every day. We never grow tired of being complimented and valued by our loved ones.

BODY: *Do your kegels*
Kegel exercises (named after the doctor who invented them) are used to strengthen the vaginal muscles. Doing kegels improves orgasms because toned vaginal muscles improve the arousal communication between your body and brain. To perform a kegel, pretend you are urinating and need to hold it for a moment. The muscle you feel tightening is the pelvic muscle you're trying to exercise. Squeeze and release ten times; increase repetitions over time.

SPIRIT: *Place two red roses on your nightstand*
We associate roses with love and link the color red with passion. Two is the number of a couple. To enhance romance, combine these symbolic elements. Set a vase of fragrant roses beside your bed to set the stage for love.

"No journey carries one far unless, as it extends into the world around us, it goes an equal distance into the world within." —Lillian Smith

Bon Voyage

In recent years, travel has become more stressful than ever. High costs, delays, security checks, and crowds can diminish the joys of a journey—if you let them. Whether you're going to a foreign land or taking a day trip, see traveling as a chance to expand your horizons, literally and figuratively.

MIND: *Don't be undone by uncertainty*
One of the worst—and best—parts of traveling is uncertainty. Strange language, customs, and terrain can throw unseasoned travelers into high anxiety. However, the unfamiliarity that may cause trepidation also provides learning opportunities. Plan what you must, but allow for serendipity.

BODY: *Take melatonin to reduce jet lag*
According to Dr. Robert Sack, psychiatry professor at Oregon Health and Science University, melatonin has been extensively studied and found helpful in treating symptoms of jet lag. Melatonin is sold as a nutritional supplement, so you don't need a prescription. A dose of 0.5 to 3 milligrams is usually enough to ease jet lag, with few side effects.

SPIRIT: *Pack a travel altar*
When you travel, bring sacred items with you to create a portable altar that will help you feel serene wherever you are. Pack a few items in a padded cosmetic bag: a small candle, a cone of your favorite incense, a quartz crystal, a figurine of a beloved deity. Wrap them up in a pretty scarf that can double as an altar cloth. When you get to your motel, conduct a settling-in ritual.

"BE YOURSELF. THERE IS SOMETHING THAT YOU CAN DO BETTER THAN ANY OTHER. LISTEN TO THE INWARD VOICE AND BRAVELY OBEY THAT." —Anonymous

Nurture Your Self-Image

Today, put your best foot forward. Your self-image is both a magnet and a shield. It attracts people who can assist you and protects you from those who might wish you ill. Even if you have to "fake it 'til you make it," each small victory will strengthen your self-confidence and personal power.

MIND: *See yourself as you want to be seen*

If you think you're worthy, chances are other people will perceive you that way, too. If you think you're a loser, you'll project that image. Find something you value about yourself and focus on that admirable quality. If someone tries to diminish or intimidate you, bring that quality to the forefront of your mind and let it illuminate you like a spotlight.

BODY: *Stand up straight*

You can't change some things about your body, but one thing you can do right now to improve your image is to stand up straight. Hold your head high, your shoulders back, your tummy tucked in and you'll instantly feel more self-confident. Other people will see you that way, too. Good posture also enables you to breathe more deeply and eases neck and shoulder tension.

SPIRIT: *Wear yellow topaz for confidence*

Crystal workers link this golden gemstone with self-confidence and leadership. To overcome self-doubt or uncertainty, wear yellow topaz. It helps you express your inner power, tap your personal resources, and attract fortunate opportunities.

"THE BEST PLACE TO SEEK GOD IS IN A GARDEN."

—George Bernard Shaw

Find Peace Among Plants

The garden is a symbol of peace, comfort, and happiness—an oasis from toil and trouble. If you live in an apartment, you may not have room for a garden, but you can still cultivate houseplants. Houseplants improve air quality, ease stress, and can reduce the frequency of colds, according to a University of Agriculture in Norway study.

MIND: *Talk to your plants*

If you think this sounds weird, consider studies done by polygraph expert Cleve Backster, reported in the bestselling book *The Secret Life of Plants*. When Backster attached sensors to plants, he discovered they responded not only to spoken words but also to thoughts. Speak encouraging words to your plants and watch them flourish.

BODY: *Cultivate native plants*

Plant native flowers, grasses, and trees on your property. They're easier to grow and harmonize with the natural environment. If you live in an arid area, opt for drought-resistant species that don't need much water. Don't aim for a golf-course green lawn if you live in west Texas, for example. A lush lawn may rely on harmful chemicals and require more upkeep than native grasses, ground covers, or wildflowers.

SPIRIT: *Position plants for growth*

Feng shui, the ancient Chinese art of placement, links plants with well-being. If you want to improve your health, set a healthy plant in the central part of your home. This space relates to health, according to the tenets of feng shui. As you care for the plant, you symbolically nurture yourself.

"ONLY LOVE CAN BREAK A HEART.

ONLY LOVE CAN MEND IT AGAIN."

—Gene Pitney

Heal a Broken Heart

When a relationship ends, grief is normal. But the end of a relationship isn't the end of the world. Instead of languishing in misery, take positive steps to heal the pain and embrace new possibilities. Let go of the past and look forward to the future.

MIND: *Buy new underwear and sheets*
After a breakup, consider making a clean sweep. Get rid of intimate articles that remind you of your former love. Go shopping as a physical affirmation that you are inviting new love to come your way. Purchase sexy new undergarments and pretty sheets that make you feel luscious (get rid of the old ones).

BODY: *Massage your sole to soothe your soul*
Reflexology, a type of bodywork that connects sensitive spots on the feet with parts of the body, associates the ball of your left sole with the heart. To ease the pain of heartache, massage the bottom of your left foot from the center outward. Use your thumb or knuckles to apply pressure. Rubbing the area in a circular motion soothes your heart.

SPIRIT: *Wear ruby in zoisite*
Crystal workers say this merger of two stones provides grief relief. The red ruby, associated with passion, and the green zoisite, linked with temperance, balance one another. Wear the gem near your heart to bring painful emotions to the surface where they can be healed. This stone helps you understand the meaning behind losses and lets you evolve beyond suffering.

"It is the eye of ignorance that assigns a fixed and unchangeable color to every object; beware of this stumbling block." —Paul Gauguin

Color Yourself Beautiful

Today, notice the role color plays in your life. Even our language equates color with feelings. Are you in the pink? Feeling blue? Red hot? Color can also be used to promote well-being on every level. Here are a few suggestions:

MIND: *Get your colors done*
This beauty system, popularized in Carole Jackson's book *Color Me Beautiful*, examines which colors look best on you. It suggests that wearing certain colors enhances your hair, skin, and eyes. The method lets you choose clothing that flatters your natural coloring and compliments your features. Once you determine your best palette, you can improve your appearance and streamline your wardrobe.

BODY: *Heal with chromatherapy*
This form of vibrational healing, also called color therapy, directs colored light onto the body to promote well-being. Your cells respond to light and color; therefore, exposing your body to certain colors can have a therapeutic effect. Blue light, for instance, can calm heart rate and respiration. Red light stimulates circulation. Chromatherapy can help to balance your energy and support healing.

SPIRIT: *Color symbolism*
We respond to colors emotionally and psychologically. For centuries, artists have used colors to convey messages symbolically. In general, red represents vitality and passion; orange equates with optimism and expansion; yellow symbolizes joy and creativity; green relates to healing and growth; blue suggests peace; purple inspires wisdom and spirituality. Experiment with colors to see how they affect you.

"THE BASIS OF ALL ANIMAL RIGHTS SHOULD BE THE
GOLDEN RULE: WE SHOULD TREAT THEM AS WE WOULD
WISH THEM TO TREAT US, WERE ANY OTHER SPECIES IN
OUR DOMINANT POSITION." —Christine Stevens

Appreciate Animals

Today, appreciate how animals contribute to your happiness, well-being, and quality of life. An earthquake in Kobe, Japan, in 1995 put this notion into perspective. Dr. Gen Kato, president of the Japanese Animal Hospital Association, observed that people who had pets coped better with the crisis.

MIND: *Support animal welfare*
As human beings continue to encroach on animals' territory, it's up to us to provide for their welfare. Donate money, time, or both to organizations that protect wildlife, domestic and farm animals, and creatures of all kinds. Treat all animals with kindness and respect.

BODY: *Play with your pet*
Toss a ball for your dog. Wiggle a string for your cat. Playing with animal companions takes your mind off troubles and inspires joy. It also encourages healing. A study at City Hospital in New York found that patients with pets lived longer after being discharged than pet-less people. Playing with your pet can lower blood pressure, relieve depression, and reduce the risk of heart attack.

SPIRIT: *Connect with your spirit animal*
According to some shamanic traditions, spirit animals aid us in many facets of our daily lives. You may feel an affinity with a certain animal, which could be your totem. You can also solicit a spirit animal's assistance by setting a picture of that animal in a place of honor in your home.

"E-MAIL, INSTANT MESSAGING, AND CELL PHONES GIVE
US FABULOUS COMMUNICATION ABILITY, BUT BECAUSE
WE LIVE AND WORK IN OUR OWN LITTLE WORLDS, THAT
COMMUNICATION IS TOTALLY DISORGANIZED."

—Marilyn vos Savant

Take a Break from Electronics

Minimize your dependence on electronics. Electronic devices emit electromagnetic fields (EMFs), which some sources believe may pose health risks; the National Institute of Health and other organizations are continuing research in this area. Cell phone use causes nearly 3,000 auto deaths and 350,000 injuries annually in the United States. Would you be better off by reducing your use of electronics?

MIND: *Turn off electronic media devices*
Unhook yourself from electronic media today. A study done for the Kaiser Family Foundation found that children and young people between the ages of eight and eighteen spend from eight to twelve hours every day engaged with some type of electronic media. Find other ways to spend your time.

BODY: *Turn off the TV*
Watching TV can be hazardous to your health. According to WebMD News, "sitting in front of the TV for hours on end can raise your risk of early death from heart disease." The U.S. Bureau of Labor Statistics found that in 2009 the average American spent about three hours a day watching TV. Turn yours off today and do something active instead.

SPIRIT: *Enjoy silence*
Once you turn off your electronic devices, you may be amazed at how quiet your life becomes. Take this opportunity to commune with yourself. Talk to your spirit guides and angels. It's easier to hear them when everyday noise has been silenced.

"A VOICE IS A HUMAN GIFT; IT SHOULD BE CHERISHED AND USED, TO UTTER FULLY HUMAN SPEECH AS POSSIBLE. POWERLESSNESS AND SILENCE GO TOGETHER."

—Margaret Atwood

Find Your Voice

Do you have something to say? If so, express it today. Eloquence is not as important as honesty and sincerity. Consider the acronym THINK: Is what you have to say True, Helpful, Intelligent, Necessary, and Kind?

MIND: *Write to your local newspaper*

Newspapers are full of reports about crime, war, and corruption. You can help offset this by writing a letter or opinion piece to your local newspaper about something good in your community. Recognize the efforts of people who are making a difference; commend charitable organizations; alert readers to worthy causes they may want to support. Be the voice of good news.

BODY: *Sing*

Lift up your voice. Singing can heal, whether you sing in the shower, the church choir, or on karaoke night. Singing eases stress, reduces blood pressure, and slows heart rate. A three-year study at the Levine School of Music in Washington, DC, found that seniors who sang in a chorus had fewer doctors' visits, experienced less depression, and needed less medication. A University of Frankfurt study showed that singing improved immunity.

SPIRIT: *Chant*

Chanting plays a role in many spiritual traditions. The rhythmic repetition of sounds balances mind, body, and spirit and shifts you into a trancelike state. A popular chant is *om mani padme hum,* the Buddhist mantra of compassion. To encourage inner harmony, chant this or something else that has meaning for you.

"DON'T MAKE MONEY YOUR GOAL. INSTEAD, PURSUE THE
THINGS YOU LOVE DOING, AND THEN DO THEM SO WELL
THAT PEOPLE CAN'T TAKE THEIR EYES OFF YOU."
—Maya Angelou

Have a Healthy Relationship with Money

The best things in life may be free, but money makes everything else easier. Today, focus improving your finances. Jack Canfield, bestselling author of *Chicken Soup for the Soul*, says that focusing on prosperity and believing you can have it is the first step to attracting wealth.

MIND: *Pay bills promptly*
Pay your bills as soon as they arrive. Once you've put the checks in the mail, you can stop worrying about them, which will help to reduce stress. You'll also avoid late charges or interest payments, which are equivalent to just throwing money away and may damage your credit rating.

BODY: *Activate your solar plexus chakra with acupressure*
Eastern medicine connects the solar plexus chakra with self-confidence and personal power. This energy center is located about halfway between your heart and your belly button, in the center of your midriff. Press your fingers to this chakra in order to stimulate confidence in your ability to attract prosperity of all kinds.

SPIRIT: *Put the toilet lid down*
This may sound odd, but the ancient Chinese art of feng shui says that chi (the creative force in the universe) and money flow down toilets and drains. The best way to prevent this from happening is to keep the toilet lid down and the shower curtain closed. Chi (and money) will stay in your home instead of draining away.

"TEA IS DRUNK TO FORGET THE DIN OF THE WORLD."

—Tien Yiheng

Take Time for Tea

Enjoy a cup of tea today. For thousands of years, people in Asia have drunk tea for social, health, and spiritual purposes. Medicinal teas have been used throughout the world for many centuries, and still are. A 2010 Alzheimer's Association study found that seniors who drank tea experienced better cognitive function than those who didn't.

MIND: *Have a tea party with friends*
History credits Anna Maria Stanhope, the Duchess of Bedford, with establishing the ritual of afternoon tea. No matter what your age, having a tea party with girlfriends can be a fun way to spend an afternoon. Dress up in flowered dresses, gloves, and picture hats. Serve tea and little sandwiches on Grandma's china.

BODY: *Take a tea break*
The English have long enjoyed the custom of afternoon tea. Taking a break in the late afternoon can be a wonderful way to unwind and perhaps get a second wind if it's not possible to stop working yet. Sip a soothing herbal tea, such as chamomile, vervain, or lavender, to relax. Drink a cup of peppermint or green tea with caffeine if you want a mild pick-me-up.

SPIRIT: *Observe a tea ceremony*
The Japanese tea ceremony, also known as the Way of Tea or the Tao of Tea, is an ancient ritual, influenced by Zen Buddhism. In addition to making and serving tea, it may involve arts such as calligraphy and flower arranging, and can take hours to perform. Observing the ritual is an aesthetic, sensory, and spiritual experience.

"NATURE IS FUEL FOR THE SOUL."

—Richard Ryan

Let Nature Nurture You

Nature is a tonic for tired minds, bodies, and spirits. After 9/11, more people than ever visited New York's parks and botanical gardens. Today, stroll beside a stream. Walk along the ocean. Hike in the forest. Or just stretch your legs in a city park.

MIND: *Look at pictures of nature*

If you can't get out into the great outdoors, look at pictures of nature. Hang photos or paintings of landscapes on your walls. Choose nature images for your computer's screensaver. According to studies published in 2010 by University of Rochester's psychology professor Richard Ryan, just looking at pictures of nature energized people who viewed them.

BODY: *Go camping*

Take a camping trip in the outdoors to commune with nature. Natural environments have a rejuvenating effect on the body, mind, and spirit, providing fresh air and exercise. People who live near a park or woodland live longer, healthier lives, according to a British study published in 2008. You'll defeat the purpose, however, if you drive your RV to a crowded campsite and spend your time watching TV.

SPIRIT: *Create an inner landscape*

In their book *The Best Mediations on the Planet,* Dr. Martin Hart and Skye Alexander recommend creating a safe place inside yourself where you can go to find peace. Close your eyes and visualize a place in nature—one you've been to before or one you imagine. When you need to relax and retreat from the world, you can go to this serene place that is yours alone.

"THE ACT OF PUTTING PEN TO PAPER ENCOURAGES
PAUSE FOR THOUGHT, THIS IN TURN MAKES US THINK
MORE DEEPLY ABOUT LIFE, WHICH HELPS US REGAIN
OUR EQUILIBRIUM." —Norbet Platt

Write It Down

Today, reconnect with the fading art of writing by hand. Most of
us keyboard these days, rather than putting pen to paper, and some
schools no longer consider cursive writing useful. However, handwriting activates acupressure points in your fingers that can encourage creativity and relaxation.

MIND: *Unblock your creativity*

In *The Artist's Way,* author Julia Cameron recommends a writing
exercise called "Morning Pages" to unblock your creativity and connect with your inner knowing. Every morning, fill three pages with
handwriting. Don't worry about grammar, syntax, or even making
sense—be spontaneous. Let your subconscious express what's going
on inside you. You may gain some valuable insights in the process.

BODY: *Write to change character traits*

You can lessen traits you don't like about yourself and strengthen
ones you prefer by intentionally changing your handwriting. Gra-
phology or handwriting analysis is the art of discerning character
by viewing a person's handwriting. Letter strokes, angles, spacing,
and so on all reveal personality traits. For example, crossing your Ts
higher can help you set your sights higher.

SPIRIT: *Write down a request*

Some spiritual traditions suggest writing a request on a slip of paper
and giving it to a deity to materialize. Fold the paper and place it at
the foot of a statue or other likeness of the deity. Make an offering—
incense, flowers, or food—to thank the god or goddess for assistance.

> "HAVING SEX IS LIKE PLAYING BRIDGE. IF YOU DON'T HAVE A GOOD PARTNER, YOU'D BETTER HAVE A GOOD HAND."
>
> —Woody Allen

Spice Up Your Sex Life

How satisfying is your sex life? In the 2010 National Survey of Sexual Health and Behavior, 90 percent of men and 86 percent of women reported having had sex in the past year, with varying degrees of satisfaction. If you'd like your sex life to be more fulfilling, consider the following suggestions.

MIND: *Ask for what you want*

Don't expect your partner to intuit what turns you on. Tell your lover what you want and ask him or her to accommodate your wishes. If you feel comfortable doing it, show him or her. Offer to reciprocate.

BODY: *Masturbate*

No, you won't go blind or insane or grow hair on your palms. In fact, sex therapists recommend masturbation for a variety of reasons— whether or not you have an intimate partner. Orgasm releases endorphins, the hormones that improve mood and increase optimism. It also lets you discover what you like so you can share your preferences with a partner.

SPIRIT: *Send someone a sexy message—psychically*

Try sending sexy signals to your partner over a distance, using only your mind. Close your eyes and envision being engaged in a sexual act. Feel yourself becoming aroused. Then imagine projecting that vision to your partner. Note the time when you sent the psychic message. Later, ask your partner if he or she received your thoughts, and if so when?

"WE HAVE FINALLY STARTED TO NOTICE THAT THERE IS
REAL CURATIVE VALUE IN LOCAL HERBS AND REMEDIES
. . . THEY ARE OFTEN MORE EFFECTIVE THAN WESTERN
MEDICINE."   —Dr. Anne Wilson Schaef

Bring on the Basil

Look to the plant kingdom today for healing on all levels. Although
of ancient origins, herbal remedies are still the most widely used
form of medicine in much of the world. But herbs offer more than
relief from physical ills, they nurture the mind and spirit as well.

MIND: *Plant basil*

Consider planting basil, an herb with myriad culinary, medicinal,
and mystical properties. Countless studies have shown the therapeutic benefits of cultivating plants, including stress reduction and
decreased depression. Growing a plant is an act of creativity that
connects you with the forces of nature.

BODY: *Eat basil to prevent free-radical damage*

Fragrant basil not only enhances the flavor of your food, it can reduce
inflammation associated with rheumatoid arthritis. Rich in antiox-
idants, the herb protects against damage caused by free radicals.
Basil's antibacterial properties make it useful in treating wounds.
When eaten or taken as an herbal supplement, it aids colds and flu.
Fresh basil is more potent than dried leaves.

SPIRIT: *Make a basil amulet*

Metaphysicians prize basil for its protective properties. Dry fresh
basil leaves (or purchase dried basil in a supermarket) and place
them in a cloth pouch. On a piece of paper, write the affirmation: "I
am safe at all times and in all situations" and add this to the pouch.
Carry this amulet in your pocket to keep you safe.

> "THERE ARE TWO WAYS OF SPREADING LIGHT;
>
> TO BE THE CANDLE OR THE MIRROR THAT REFLECTS IT."
>
> —Edith Wharton

Let There Be Light

Today, improve the quality of light in your home and workplace. Poor light can lead to eyestrain, fatigue, and diminished enthusiasm. Notice how sunlight illuminates nature, sometimes brightly and sometimes filtered through foliage. Opt to replicate that indoors.

MIND: *See your home as your stage*

Illuminate your home as though it were your stage. Choose lighting that flatters you. Incandescent bulbs that emphasize the warm end of the spectrum enhance most skin tones and are usually preferable to fluorescents. Select various types of lighting, instead of simply relying on overhead fixtures. Install dimmers that let you adjust the levels of light to your preference.

BODY: *Use full-spectrum lights to beat SAD*

Seasonal affective disorder, or SAD, is a form of depression that occurs when you don't get enough sunlight. The problem impacts up to 10 percent of people seasonally, especially those who live in northern climates or areas with minimal sunlight. If you suffer from SAD, install full-spectrum lights in your home and workplace. These contain the infrared and ultraviolet ends of the spectrum and may help improve your moods.

SPIRIT: *Light your entryway*

Attract positive energy to your home by putting a light above your front door. According to feng shui, the ancient art of placement, light enhances chi, the enlivening force in the universe. To make sure chi can find its way to your home, turn on the light.

"Luxury lies not in richness and ornateness but in the absence of vulgarity." —Coco Chanel

Treat Yourself to Little Luxuries

Be good to yourself today. Too often we deny ourselves little luxuries because we think they're extravagances. Many small treats don't cost much, however, and they provide a great deal of pleasure. Go ahead and splurge a little—you're worth it!

MIND: *Buy fresh flowers*

Fresh flowers brighten your room and your mood. During the winter months, fresh flowers remind you of brighter days ahead and increase optimism. During the summer, you may want to fill a vase with wildflowers. Treat yourself to a bouquet of blooms—don't wait for a special occasion. Flowers are an ideal gift to share with friends, too.

BODY: *Use scented soap*

Any kind of soap will clean your body, but aromatherapy soap heightens your senses, influences your mood, and adds a touch of elegance to your daily bathing ritual. Buy hand-milled soaps made from natural ingredients and scented with pure essential oils. To perk up body and mind in the morning, wash with mint-scented soap. To relax in the evening, bathe with lavender-scented soap.

SPIRIT: *Get a tarot reading*

For centuries, people have consulted the oracle known as the tarot for guidance in every area of life. Treat yourself to a tarot reading. It can give you answers to questions about love, money, work, health, and more. A reading is usually good for about three months. Many New Age stores can steer you toward a knowledgeable tarot reader.

"A FISH IS THE MOVEMENT OF WATER EMBODIED,

GIVEN SHAPE." —Doris Lessing

Something Fishy

Although you may not feel as closely connected to our finny neighbors as our furry ones, fish enrich our lives in many ways. In China, goldfish (koi) are considered good luck. And of course, many doctors now tout the health benefits of fish oil in your diet.

MIND: *Take the kids fishing*

Whether or not you keep the fish you catch—or even if you don't catch anything at all—a family fishing trip is a great way to bond by sharing a pleasant outing together while enjoying the beauty of nature. Sunshine gives you vitamin D, and the moderate amount of exercise can benefit all ages.

BODY: *Eat more fish*

The omega-3 fatty acids in fish, especially wild salmon, tuna, and mackerel, are potent anti-inflammatory agents that also aid autoimmune diseases such as rheumatoid arthritis. An Italian study found that people who ate fish once a week had a 20 to 30 percent lower risk of some cancers, too. Try to eat fish three times a week to get your healthy omega-3s.

SPIRIT: *Enjoy an aquarium*

Sit in front of an aquarium and watch the rainbow-colored fish slowly glide by. It's a lovely way to unwind and let go of your worries for a little while. Gazing at an aquarium may be more than just a soul-soothing pastime. The Chinese believe aquariums bring good luck, so you may want to install one in your home or workplace.

"IT'S NOT WHAT YOU LOOK AT THAT MATTERS,

IT'S WHAT YOU SEE." —Henry David Thoreau

The Power of Vision

From an early age, we are trained to see things in a particular way. Your training, however, can sometimes inhibit your ability to see outside the box. Could your life be more joyous and juicy? Today, use your power of vision to open new possibilities.

MIND: *Envision the life you desire*
Do you see the world as a safe or dangerous place? Do you see people as kind and friendly or surly and annoying? According to the Law of Attraction, a concept that suggests you attract what you envision, you can create the reality you desire by visualizing your life as you want it to be. See the end result, not the steps required to get there.

BODY: *Eat eggs to protect your eyes*
The yolk of an egg gets its coloring from yellow-orange plant pigments called lutein and zeaxanthin, which come from the hen's corn-rich diet. Lutein and zeaxanthin are betacarotoids, and have been shown to reduce the risk of cataracts and age-related macular degeneration. Scientists believe high levels of these betacarotoids may protect your eyes from damage due to oxidation.

SPIRIT: *Gaze into a crystal ball*
A practice known as scrying involves seeing beyond your normal range of perception by gazing into a crystal ball. Relax your mind and don't try too hard. Allow your vision to soften as your eyes fall upon the wisps, inclusions, and shapes within the crystal ball. Perhaps you can gaze even into the past or future.

"PEOPLE ARE LIKE STAINED-GLASS WINDOWS.
THEY SPARKLE AND SHINE WHEN THE SUN IS OUT, BUT
WHEN THE DARKNESS SETS IN, THEIR TRUE BEAUTY IS
REVEALED ONLY IF THERE IS A LIGHT FROM WITHIN."

—Elisabeth Kubler-Ross

A Touch of Glass

There may be more to glass than meets the eye. Not only is it beautiful and functional, glass may provide healing as well. Today, look more carefully at the potential benefits of glass.

MIND: *Appreciate stained glass*

The stained-glass rose windows in Chartres, Reims, and other cathedrals aren't just beautiful, they have mystical and healing properties. These windows, created according to the principles of sacred geometry, symbolize the cosmos, sun, eternity, the soul, and the power of love. Standing in the light that shines through the windows has healing properties for mind, body, and spirit.

BODY: *Switch to glass containers*

Plastic containers may increase your chances of getting certain types of cancer, according to the Canadian group Environmental Defence and acknowledged by the U.S. National Toxicology Program. A toxic chemical compound called Bisphenol A (BPA), used in many plastics, can leech into food. Switch to glass bottles and storage containers for food, and don't heat plastic in the microwave.

SPIRIT: *Hang glass balls*

Glass balls are one of the most popular tools in the ancient Chinese art of feng shui. They capture and reflect light, which feng shui practitioners say increases positive energy known as chi. Hang a small faceted glass ball in a dark corner of your home or workplace to symbolically enhance light and chi in your space.

"WARMTH IS THE VITAL ELEMENT FOR THE GROWING

PLANT AND FOR THE SOUL OF THE CHILD." —Carl Jung

Warm Up

You don't hear about many people retiring and moving to a cold climate. There's a reason for this. A 2004 University of Michigan study showed that warm, sunny weather improved both mood and cognition. Researchers also found that 72 degrees Fahrenheit is the temperature people find most comfortable.

MIND: *How do you respond to warmth?*

How do you respond to affectionate gestures and generosity from other people? Do you blossom like a flower turning to the sun, or put up protective barriers against the warmth? If you feel uncomfortable with closeness or with letting others give to you, it may be rooted in a need to be in control. Examine your motivations.

BODY: *Take a sauna*

A popular pastime in Scandinavia, taking a sauna (dry heat) eliminates toxins, relaxes tension, soothes sore muscles, and can ease you into a happier mood. Taking a sauna also makes your skin glow. Traditional saunas use hot rocks to produce heat. Many modern saunas, however, are heated electrically. Drink lots of water to replace what you lose.

SPIRIT: *Sit by a fire*

Sit by a fire and gaze into the dancing flames. Let it warm your spirit as well as your body. Since ancient times, fire has not only served practical purposes, but spiritual ones as well. Notice how many holiday festivities include candles, for example. Fire is one of the four elements, the fundamental components of our universe. It symbolizes vitality, optimism, and enthusiasm.

> "PERHAPS IMAGINATION IS ONLY INTELLIGENCE HAVING FUN."
> —George Scialabba

Free Up Your Imagination

Children use their imaginations all the time—they love creating imaginary worlds and playmates. Play with your imagination today. Allow this rich resource within you to express itself fully.

MIND: *Write a wish list*

Let your imagination come up with possibilities to accomplish what you would like to do or have in your life. Write a wish list on a sheet of paper. On another piece of paper, write down all the thoughts that come up, telling you reasons why you cannot have or do those things—get them out of your system. Now, on the back of your wish list, write down how you could literally make your wishes happen. When a negative thought comes up, write that on the other piece of paper. At the end of this exercise, burn the negative thoughts and re-read the wish list.

BODY: *Unblock your third-eye chakra*

The third-eye chakra, located between your eyebrows, is the center of imagination. Sit quietly, close your eyes, and breathe slowly and deeply. As you inhale, imagine the breath flowing into the third-eye chakra, energizing it. As you exhale, imagine any blockages flowing out of the chakra and leaving your body.

SPIRIT: *Watch clouds*

Lie on your back and watch the clouds drift by overhead. Relax and let go of preconceptions. Let your imagination run free. What do you see in the shapes as the clouds form, break up, and reform? Do the images have meaning for you on a deeper level or provide any insights?

"LOVE IS THE ANSWER, BUT WHILE YOU ARE WAITING FOR
THE ANSWER, SEX RAISES SOME PRETTY GOOD QUESTIONS."
—Woody Allen

Be Sexier

Take steps to improve your sex life today. Many health professionals
now recommend having sex often as a way to improve your overall well-
being. Sex relieves stress, boosts immunity, burns calories, improves
cardiovascular health, and releases "feel-good" chemicals in your brain.

MIND: *Try it, you might like it*

It's been said that erotica is something you find sexually stimulating,
whereas pornography is something another person finds stimulating
but you find disgusting. Examine your ideas about sexual practices.
Are taboos preventing you from exploring activities you might enjoy?
Give yourself permission to try a range of sensual pleasures—without
judgment or guilt.

BODY: *Eat dark chocolate*

It's no accident that we give chocolates on Valentine's Day. In the
mid-1990s, researchers at the University of Michigan found that eating dark chocolate causes the brain to release endorphins, the chemicals that make us feel good—like being in love. Share a few pieces
of rich, dark chocolate with your partner as a prelude to sex. Use
your imagination and come up with interesting ways to incorporate
chocolate into your foreplay.

SPIRIT: *Use The Lovers card to enhance your sex life*

Among the twenty-two cards in the tarot's Major Arcana you'll find
The Lovers. This card symbolizes the union of male and female, and
some decks such as *The Gilded Tarot* depict beautiful erotic imagery. Place the card on your bedside table or another place in your
bedroom where you'll see it often.

"THE CURE FOR ANYTHING IS SALT WATER:

SWEAT, TEARS OR THE SEA." —Isak Dinesen

Season with Salt

Today, consider how you use salt—and how much. Although most Americans consume too much, salt is essential for good health—at least 500 mg per day, according to the National Academy of Sciences. This essential mineral has a colorful history, too; it influenced the development of cities and played a role in wars.

MIND: *Your brain likes salt*

Your brain is largely made up of water. Dehydration and pH imbalance in the brain can lead to a range of cognitive difficulties, including memory problems and dementia. Research shows that sea salt is good for your brain. According to retired nurse Jean Perrins, "If you have fuzzy thinking or you can't find your glasses so you can find your car keys, drink more water and sprinkle a little unrefined sea salt on your food."

BODY: *Exfoliate with sea salt*

Regular exfoliation produces healthier-looking skin and aids the development of new collagen. Make an exfoliating scrub using sea salt. Combine one part oil (such as sweet almond) and two parts sea salt to form a somewhat thick mixture. Thin it more if you like. You can also add honey as a softening agent.

SPIRIT: *Clear unwanted energies with salt*

When you move into a new home or after an unpleasant experience, clear bad vibes with salt. Sprinkle a little sea salt in the corners of every room to energetically cleanse your space.

"WHEN THE BEE COMES TO YOUR HOUSE, LET HER HAVE
BEER; YOU MAY WANT TO VISIT THE BEE'S HOUSE SOMEDAY."

—Congo Proverb

Reduce Irritations

Focus on reducing the irritations in your life today. Often we let little things bother us disproportionately. Before you let a petty matter stress you out, ask yourself if you will even remember it in a month.

MIND: *What's bugging you?*

Mental stress can cause itching, rashes, hives, and eczema. Stress and anxiety can also exacerbate existing conditions. Although medications may improve skin irritations such as these, if the root cause is stress, you might have to deal with the mental aspects of the problem to alleviate the physical ones. Meditation and other stress-busting practices can help.

BODY: *Treat insect bites with aloe*

Aloe vera is a succulent plant that contains a sappy liquid or gel that is an effective topical treatment for insect bites. Grow an aloe in your home, or outside if you live in a warm climate. Snip off a piece of a leaf and apply the sappy end to bites to ease the stinging and itching. You can also purchase aloe vera gel in a bottle.

SPIRIT: *Insect dreams*

Do you dream about insects? If so, the bugs may be symbols of little annoyances in your waking life that are "bugging" you. Consider the characteristics of the particular insect to determine the dream's meaning. If ants are biting you in your dreams, it might suggest irritations at work. Ticks could mean something is sucking your energy.

"WE CAN ONLY BE SAID TO BE ALIVE IN THOSE MOMENTS
WHEN OUR HEARTS ARE CONSCIOUS OF OUR TREASURES."

—Thornton Wilder

Enjoy Your Treasures

Stop saving your best things for a special occasion—enjoy them
today. Don't leave your best dress in the closet until it's out of style.
Using your best possessions tells your subconscious that you are
worth it.

MIND: *Use your good dishes*

What's the point of keeping your good china and silverware packed
away where no one can enjoy it? Invite a few friends over for lunch
or dinner and serve the meal on your best dishes. Allow yourself and
your friends to appreciate this touch of unexpected beauty and let it
brighten your day.

BODY: *Wear your nicest underwear*

Wear your prettiest undies today. Even if no one else sees them,
you'll know you have them on and that will make you feel prettier
all day long. When you feel better about yourself, you are likely to
have more energy, treat other people with more kindness, and even
be more productive at work.

SPIRIT: *Cherish a meaningful symbol*

Symbols reach us at deep levels, often bypassing the conscious mind
and speaking to the soul directly. A symbol can guide you to a place
of inner peace and restore a sense of harmony in your life. A symbol
needn't be associated with a particular religion; it can be anything
that holds special meaning for you. Hold or gaze at your symbol and
let it work its wonders for you today.

> "SINCE THERE IS NOTHING SO WELL WORTH HAVING AS
> FRIENDS, NEVER LOSE A CHANCE TO MAKE THEM."
>
> —Francesco Guicciardini

Be Sociable

Human beings are social creatures. Without the companionship of others, we fail to thrive. A University of Chicago study found that isolation even contributes to health risks, especially among the elderly. Today, focus on enhancing your relationships with other people.

MIND: *Seek unity with others*

Have disappointments in the past led you to go it alone? Although self-reliance may be a worthwhile trait, isolation can cause unhappiness. Cultivate a rapport with those around you. No matter how different or unfamiliar the territory, discover the essential qualities you have in common with others. You may be surprised to find you are more alike than disparate at your cores.

BODY: *Activate your heart chakra*

In Eastern philosophy and medicine, the heart chakra is the locus of relationships. Located in the vicinity of your physical heart, this energy center is affected by love, joy, grief, and other emotions. When the heart chakra is blocked or devitalized, you may suffer from coronary problems. Energize your heart chakra by meditating and imagining green light glowing in the center of your chest.

SPIRIT: *Let love flow through you*

Open yourself to the inflowing love from the Source of your being. When you block giving or receiving love, you thwart your opportunity to be nourished by the heart of the Divine. Permit this love to spiritually renew you. Then let it flow from you into your relationships with others and outward into the world.

"QUIETUDE, WHICH SOME MEN CANNOT ABIDE BECAUSE
IT REVEALS THEIR INWARD POVERTY, IS AS A PALACE OF
CEDAR TO THE WISE." —Charles H. Spurgeon

Three Cheers for Cedar

The cedar tree has a long and mystical history; its value is described
in religious texts and poetry. The Arabs believed the cedars of Leb-
anon embodied a power that made them live forever. The ancient
Egyptians used cedar resin in the process of mummification. Various cultures and spiritual traditions use cedar in rituals and ceremonies. Today, see how this aromatic tree can benefit you.

MIND: *Store winter clothes in cedar*
Pack winter clothes, blankets, and other woolen items in cedar to
protect them from moth damage. Mothballs may repel insects, but
they contain toxic chemicals that can be poisonous if eaten, handled,
or even inhaled. Cedar is safer and smells nicer, too.

BODY: *Treat your skin with cedar essential oil*
Aromatic cedar oil can aid oily skin, psoriasis, acne, and other skin
conditions. Blend a few drops in a carrier oil such as grape seed,
jojoba, or olive oil and apply it to improve skin quality. You can also
use it as a massage oil—its warming quality can ease arthritic joints.

SPIRIT: *Clear the air with cedar*
In parts of Asia and the Southwestern United States, cedar is burned
to purify the air before a ceremony or during meditation. Before
beginning a ritual, light cedar incense or small chips of cedar wood
and waft the smoke around the area to cleanse your sacred space of
unwanted energies.

"I AM THANKFUL FOR THE PILES OF LAUNDRY AND IRONING
BECAUSE IT MEANS MY LOVED ONES ARE NEARBY."

—Nancie J. Carmody

Come Clean

Whether or not you believe cleanliness is next to godliness, getting
clean physically, mentally, and spiritually can help you feel better.
Set your intention today to clean up certain areas of your life. Notice
how much lighter and calmer you feel as a result.

MIND: *Clear your mind of a problem*
Bring to mind one problem that you can't do anything about today,
but which you keep fretting over. Make a point of not worrying
about that particular issue for one whole day. Whenever you catch
yourself thinking about that problem, gently push it out of your mind
and remind yourself *not today*. Clearing your mind of just one matter can reduce stress.

BODY: *Take a bath in oatmeal*
Tie a handful of oatmeal into a piece of cheesecloth. Run hot water
into the bathtub and hold the oatmeal under the faucet. When the
tub is full, put the bag of oats in the water with you and squeeze it
periodically to release the oatmeal's milkiness. Use the bag to scrub,
clean, and soften your skin.

SPIRIT: *Clean out a closet*
Choose one closet to clean up today. Closets symbolize the hidden
parts of yourself, things you may not want to face. Instead of jam-
ming more stuff into a closet, clear out anything you don't use or
need. You may experience some inner clarity as you do this. Organize what's left in a neat and orderly fashion.

"YOU WERE MADE FOR ENJOYMENT AND THE WORLD WAS FILLED WITH THINGS WHICH YOU WILL ENJOY."

—John Ruskin

Pamper Yourself

When was the last time you devoted a day or even an hour to pampering yourself? Maybe you can't even remember. If you haven't indulged yourself in a while, today is the day to give yourself a treat.

MIND: *Go out to lunch with a friend*

Spending time with friends can be one of the best ways to support your well-being. In 2010, *O: The Oprah Magazine* reported, "Studies have also shown that social support can lower blood pressure, protect against dementia, and reduce the risk of depression." Make a date to have lunch with a friend, at least once a week. Choose a different restaurant each time. Or, pack a lunch and eat in the park.

BODY: *Get a pedicure*

Your feet have a hard job—they have to support all your weight, often on hard pavement in uncomfortable shoes. Treat them to a pedicure. This little luxury will soothe and comfort not only your feet, but the rest of you as well. Guys, don't overlook this part of your grooming. Dirt under your nails isn't "manly"; it's a turnoff for a lot of women.

SPIRIT: *Love yourself*

Self-care begins with self-acceptance and self-love. Learn to love yourself as though you were showing love to your children, your spouse or lover, or your pet. Spend a few moments bringing up those warm feelings that you experience when you are with a beloved being. Turn those powerful feelings inward.

"FOR WOMEN THE BEST APHRODISIACS ARE WORDS.
THE G-SPOT IS IN THE EARS. HE WHO LOOKS FOR IT
BELOW THERE IS WASTING HIS TIME." —Isabel Allende

Turn Up the Heat

Make a commitment to enjoy your sex life more today. As repeated studies have shown, sex is good for you mentally, physically, and spiritually. People in committed, loving relationships report having more fulfilling sex than people who aren't in love with their partners.

MIND: *Talk dirty*

The mind has been called the most sensitive erogenous zone. Entice it with sexy sayings. Become the narrator in your own X-rated movie. Tell your lover what you find desirable about him or her. Explain what you want to do with your partner and how it makes you feel. Be explicit. Eschew textbook terms and get down to the nitty-gritty.

BODY: *Eat oysters together*

Maybe the true road to love is through the stomach. Raw oysters are high in zinc, which may improve sperm in men and testosterone production in both sexes. Testosterone is known to increase sex drive and arousal. Have fun slurping down these tasty shellfish, which resemble the female genitalia—it might lead to other kinds of excitement.

SPIRIT: *Decorate your bedroom with love gods and goddesses*

Among the pantheons of deities in many cultures you'll find a number of lusty gods and goddesses. Choose a few whom you find especially appealing: Aphrodite, Venus, Freya, Isis, Cybele, Aengus, Green Man, Pan. Acquire pictures or figurines of these deities and place them in your bedroom to bless your sex life.

"Sometimes the most important thing in a whole day is the rest we take between two deep breaths."

—Etty Hillesum

Slow and Steady Does It

Remember Aesop's fable about the tortoise and the hare? In our fast-paced society, we tend to rush toward our goals in a helter-skelter fashion, creating stress and chaos along the way. However, the tortoise's way—slow and steady—may be more healthy and long-lasting in the end. Today, work gradually to achieve long-lasting results.

MIND: *Engage in a long-term project*

Our society seeks immediate gratification. However, taking on a long-term project anchors you in the here-and-now, even as you strive for future satisfaction. Make a quilt. Plant a garden. Write a book. Remodel your kitchen. Each step of the project moves you gradually toward a greater sense of achievement and self-knowledge.

BODY: *Practice Pilates*

Developed by Joseph Pilates in the early 1900s, this form of exercise helps you develop flexibility, balance, and better posture. Like yoga, Pilates is not a high-intensity aerobic exercise. Instead, it puts you in tune with your body as you focus on doing each movement slowly. That doesn't mean it's easy, however! These graceful motions gradually tone your core and burn calories.

SPIRIT: *Take part in a ritual*

Regardless of your spiritual views, you can benefit from the relaxing aspects of ritual. The carefully choreographed steps and the slow, methodical pace of many rituals calm and center you. Rituals also take you out of your mundane world and into the mystical realm.

"COLOR IS LIKE FOOD FOR THE SPIRIT—PLUS IT'S NOT
ADDICTIVE OR FATTENING." —Issac Mizarani

Living Color

Today, explore how color influences you. A study published in the journal *Science* in 2009 found that colors affect behavior and can alter your mood and performance. Red, researchers discovered, increased focus. Blue helped children be more creative. How can you use color to brighten your life?

MIND: *Wear pink for self-confidence*
The next time you have an important meeting or public appearance, wear pink. Psychologically, bright pink inspires self-love and cooperation. It's less provocative than red, and encourages others to see you in a positive light. Hot pink also lets you connect with your personal power in a nonassertive way.

BODY: *Heal throat problems with blue*
Eastern medicine links each of the body's seven major chakras, or energy centers, with one of the seven rainbow colors. The throat chakra, located near the hollow at the base of your neck where your collarbones come together, corresponds to the color blue. If you have a sore throat, laryngitis, or other throat ailment, envision clear blue light glowing at this chakra.

SPIRIT: *See colors in auras*
Your physical body is surrounded by a subtle energy body called your aura. The colors in your aura reflect emotional and physical conditions. Try to see your own or someone else's aura—it's easier if you stand in front of a plain white or black background. Bright colors signify health and vitality; dull or dark colors may indicate low energy, depression. or other problems.

"WE CAN DO NO GREAT THINGS, ONLY SMALL THINGS

WITH GREAT LOVE." —Mother Teresa

Make Someone's Day

Today, focus on other people instead of yourself. Doing something for others not only makes you feel good inside, it can actually benefit your mental, physical, and spiritual well-being, as numerous studies have shown. People who offer assistance to those in need often report being happier and healthier, which comes from having a sense of purpose in life.

MIND: *Surprise someone with a thank-you note*
Let someone know you appreciate him or her by writing an unexpected thank-you note. Thank your mother for bringing you into the world. Thank your neighbor for growing a flower garden you enjoy. Thank a teacher for inspiring you. Countless people have contributed to your well-being over the years. Today, let them know they mattered.

BODY: *Help yourself by helping someone else*
Do something to assist another person today. Help an elderly person cross the street. Hold a door for someone whose hands are full. Volunteer to work for a local charity. According to a study conducted by Paul Arnstein of Boston College, people with chronic pain who volunteered to help others experienced improvements in their own physical and mental health.

SPIRIT: *Thank your angels*
Do you believe in angels? A majority of people say they do, and they think their guardian angels are always on the job, helping out. Thank your angels today for guiding you and keeping you safe. Thank them for watching over your loved ones. You may hear them say, "Our pleasure."

"And in today already walks tomorrow."
—Samuel Taylor Coleridge

Plan for the Future

In today lie the seeds of tomorrow. Start doing what's necessary to bring about the future you desire. Save money for retirement. Start eating a healthier diet. Begin an exercise program. Decide what you want and take steps to achieve it.

MIND: *Create your future now*

The Law of Attraction, an ancient concept popularized recently in the books of Esther and Jerry Hicks, says that what you think today influences your future. If you want to know how your future will turn out, examine what you are thinking and feeling right now. If you want the future to be different from the present, change your thoughts.

BODY: *Take milk thistle for your liver*

Take milk thistle capsules to promote a longer, healthier life. The liver is the only organ in your body that can rejuvenate itself. Because the liver is your main source of detoxification, keep it healthy. The use of milk thistle to treat liver disease goes back two millennia. Almost everyone can benefit from improving liver function, especially as our environments become more toxic.

SPIRIT: *Brighten your future*

According to the ancient Chinese art of feng shui, the center back section of your home (when viewed from your front door) is linked with your future. You can enhance your future prospects by illuminating this area. Make sure this part of your home has plenty of light—if it doesn't, add a lamp, hanging fixture, or light candles there. This shows your intention to brighten your future.

"LIFE IS LIKE RIDING A BICYCLE. TO KEEP YOUR BALANCE,
YOU MUST KEEP MOVING."

—Albert Einstein

Attune Yourself to Harmony

Today, set an intention to be in harmony with yourself, other people, and the world around you. Steer your ship away from rough waters and seek calm seas, within and without. Find ways to express love, peace, and harmony in all you do.

MIND: *Avoid arguments*

An argument requires the participation of two or more people. If someone becomes confrontational today, walk away instead of responding. If you're not there, it's unlikely that person will continue arguing. Confrontations can end the minute one person shifts the paradigm. Leave the room, go outside, get in your car, or whatever it takes.

BODY: *Walk in balance*

Pay attention to each step as you walk. As your left foot meets the ground, focus on what you are receiving in life. As your right foot meets the ground, consider what you can give to others. Giving and receiving are two parts of a whole, and both are necessary to achieve balance.

SPIRIT: *Balance your aura*

Your aura is an energy field around your body that is usually invisible to most people. You can feel it, however. Hold your palms open a few inches away from your head. If you're feeling stressed, your aura may feel prickly or staticky. Close your eyes and imagine soft, blue-green light surrounding your head. Keep doing this until your aura feels smooth and balanced.

"THERE IS NO SECURITY ON THIS EARTH.

ONLY OPPORTUNITY." —Douglas MacArthur

Feel More Secure

A sense of real security comes from within. It's not about money, possessions, or other people. It's the belief that you have the right to be alive, that you are worthy of loving and being loved. It stems from the recognition that your life isn't an accident or a mistake. You can shine and be seen, heard, and appreciated.

MIND: *Envision your connection to the earth*

Stand and close your eyes (hold on to a chair if necessary). Imagine your legs have roots growing deep into the earth. Know you are rooted and connected. Imagine energy coming down from your head, down your spine, and out through your root chakra at the base of your spine, into the earth. For several minutes, envision this energy connection with the earth.

BODY: *Take regular activity breaks*

When you are anxious, your energy is predominantly up in your mind. Doing something physical will bring energy down from the mind into your body. Take regular physical movement breaks. Literally move your body. Taking a five- or ten-minute break every hour or two during your day will not slow you down; it will help you be calmer and more productive.

SPIRIT: *Feel connected to a divine Source*

A true sense of security comes from feeling connected to your Source. Focus on your breathing, and know that each breath of air is a spark of Spirit. You don't have to do or be anything other than you are to receive this life-giving breath.

"GIVE YOUR STRESS WINGS AND LET IT FLY AWAY."

—Carin Hartness

Untie Your Inner Knots

Does stress have you tied up in knots? Chronic stress can wreak havoc with your entire system, eventually leading to illness. Herbert Benson, MD, founding president of the Mind/Body Medical Institute, says that stress increases your risk of heart attack, stroke, depression, infertility, and a host of other problems. Instead of letting stress get the better of you, try the following tips to loosen those inner knots.

MIND: *Envision a day at the beach*

Close your eyes and cup your hands over your ears. Can you hear a faint roaring sound that reminds you of the ocean? As you listen to your inner ocean, imagine you are sitting on the beach on a beautiful, sunny day, relaxing and watching the waves. Feel your mind relaxing. Enjoy this visualization for as long as you like.

BODY: *Take chondroitin to improve joint flexibility*

Osteoarthritis occurs when the cartilage that cushions the ends of bone joints breaks down, resulting in stiff joints and pain. Studies suggest that taking chondroitin supplements is an effective treatment for osteoarthritis. Chondroitin is thought to give cartilage elasticity and increase the lubricating fluid in the joints, which may improve joint function.

SPIRIT: *Repeat a Zen mantra*

A mantra is a word or phrase that has special meaning for you. Zen master Thich Nhat Hanh recommends repeating this mantra to untie the kinks in your body, mind, and Spirit: "Breathing in I am calm. Breathing out I smile." Do this for a minute or so to relax.

"THE BEST CAR SAFETY DEVICE IS A REAR-VIEW MIRROR
WITH A COP IN IT." —Dudley Moore

Be a Better Driver

Become more conscious of your driving today. One of the most
dangerous things you can do is drive a car. Although auto fatalities
are declining in the United States, more than 30,000 people died in
2009 on the roadways. Set an intention to be a safer and more cour-
teous driver.

MIND: *Don't drive and text*

The use of cell phones and especially texting while driving is
extremely dangerous—you are six times more likely to have an accident if you are texting, according to the Injury Board. Yet nearly 60
percent of U.S. drivers admit to doing it. Play it safe. Pull off the
road if you're going to use your cell phone for talking or texting.

BODY: *Mist your car with lavender*

Driving in city traffic can be stressful, but aromatherapy can help
you stay calm. Put water in a spray bottle and add a few drops of lavender essential oil. Shake the bottle and mist the inside of your car
with the fragrant blend. If you like, add some lemon or mint essential oil to perk you up.

SPIRIT: *Protect yourself with amber*

For centuries, amber has been linked with protection. Use this hard-
ened resin to safeguard yourself while driving. Purchase a few amber
beads and string them on a piece of jeweler's wire. Then attach the
beads to the rearview mirror inside your car. Or keep a chunk of
amber in your glove compartment or console.

"FORGET NOT THAT THE EARTH DELIGHTS TO FEEL
YOUR BARE FEET AND THE WINDS LONG TO PLAY
WITH YOUR HAIR." —Kahlil Gibran

Go Outside and Play

Regardless of your age, playing outdoors is one of the best things
you can do for yourself, mentally, physically, and spiritually. Most
of us spend too much time sitting indoors at our computers and TVs.
Make a point of going outside today and having fun.

MIND: *Go hunting—with your camera*
Take a walk in a park, the woods, or your own neighborhood and
stalk wildlife. Observe their beauty, antics, and skills through the
lens of your camera. Connecting with nature and animals affords
numerous health benefits, and taking pictures focuses your mind in
the present. You'll be noticeably calmer when you've finished—and
you'll have the photos to enjoy later.

BODY: *Go outdoors to play*
Most of us spend entirely too much time indoors. According to
researchers at the University of Michigan, today's children play
outdoors in an unstructured way for less than seven minutes a
day on average. No matter how old you are, spending time outside increases the amount of vitamin D your body receives, which
helps your body absorb calcium for strong bones. Playing—like you
did in childhood—reduces stress, inspires creativity, and boosts
vitality.

SPIRIT: *Listen to birds singing*
Go outside and listen to the birds singing. Try to imagine what the
birds might be saying and feeling. Do they seem happy? Are they
courting mates? Claiming their territory? Feel a connection with the
birds and let their songs lift your spirits.

"MUSIC WASHES AWAY FROM THE SOUL THE DUST OF

EVERYDAY LIFE." —Berthold Auerbach

Make Music Part of Your Day

Music influences us on many levels, soothing, enlivening, and inspiring us. It aids medical conditions and eases pain. A 2009 study at Cleveland Clinic found music eased patient anxiety during surgery. Can music make your day better? Try it and see.

MIND: *Include music in your daily activities*
Listen to music while doing household chores, exercising, driving, shopping, or working. Classical music, in particular, eases stress, such as when you're waiting in the dentist's office or studying for a test. Use your MP3 player or other portable device with earphones to shut out the stressors in your environment.

BODY: *Get up and dance*
Dancing keeps you flexible. It tones your muscles. It improves your balance. It provides cardiovascular benefits. It stimulates circulation and breathing. But most of all, it's fun. Dancing is also a social activity, and relating to other people in a pleasurable way can help you live longer and healthier. Play some old rock 'n' roll. Try a Texas two-step. Enjoy ballroom dancing with a partner.

SPIRIT: *Wake up to music*
Chuck that noisy alarm clock and let music ease you into the morning. Your first few moments upon waking set the tone for the rest of the day. When you gently awake to peaceful music, you are more likely to feel embraced than jarred by the transition from one stage of consciousness to another.

"THE WHOLE OF NATURE, AS HAS BEEN SAID,

IS A CONJUGATION OF THE VERB TO EAT,

IN THE ACTIVE AND IN THE PASSIVE." —William Ralph Inge

Eat to Live

Do you eat to live or live to eat? Today, make a decision to eat better in every way. Eat more healthfully. Enjoy what you eat more. Share your meal with others. Be grateful for the food you have and all who contributed to making it possible.

MIND: *Donate canned goods to a food bank*

While obesity is increasing in the Western world, ironically hunger is, too. Donate canned and packaged food to a food bank in your community. The Salvation Army and many churches collect and distribute food donations to needy families. If your community doesn't have a food bank, consider starting one.

BODY: *Eat less*

Obesity is rampant in Western society. In the United States, about one-third of adults are obese—and the more overweight you are, the more likely you are to experience health problems such as diabetes, coronary disease, and stroke. Serve yourself smaller portions on a smaller plate. Avoid "all you can eat" restaurants. Drink a glass of water before eating. Eat slowly. Eat less!

SPIRIT: *Feed your soul*

Our souls and spirits need nourishment, just as our bodies do. Jack Canfield's *Chicken Soup for the Soul* books succeeded because they connected with this need in us. What feeds your soul? What makes your spirit sing? How would you like to be nourished spiritually, as well as physically? Make this a priority in your life.

"I CONSIDER THAT A MAN'S BRAIN ORIGINALLY IS LIKE A LITTLE EMPTY ATTIC, AND YOU HAVE TO STOCK IT WITH SUCH FURNITURE AS YOU CHOOSE." —Sir Arthur Conan Doyle

Keep Your Brain Healthy

Take steps today to nourish your brain. Your brain, like your body, must be exercised regularly and fed properly to keep it functioning optimally. University of California, Los Angeles professor of neuro-surgery Fernando Gómez-Pinilla says what you eat not only affects your brain health, it can also impact your grandchildren's brains.

MIND: *Take an online course*
Whether you want to get a college degree or just take a course for the sheer pleasure of learning, you'll find lots of opportunities online. Many universities now offer degree programs online. Brush up your skills or get certified in a special area. Some schools even allow you to design your own curriculum.

BODY: *Limit high-fat foods*
A Canadian study published in 2008 on ScienceDirect.com linked a high-fat diet to brain changes akin to those seen in Alzheimer's disease. The study suggested that food choices affect your brain's health, as well as your body's. Cut down on high-fat foods to ensure that you can continue enjoying optimum brain and body health.

SPIRIT: *Quiet your mind before beginning your day*
Before you get out of bed, take a few minutes to enjoy the morning. Notice the sounds, smells, and golden morning light. Can you hear birds singing? Is a loved one lying peacefully next to you? Even if it's going to be a busy day, starting off in a peaceful, meditative state will make everything easier.

"THE FAMILY—THAT DEAR OCTOPUS FROM WHOSE
TENTACLES WE NEVER QUITE ESCAPE, NOR, IN OUR
INMOST HEARTS, EVER QUITE WISH TO." —Dodie Smith

Strengthen Family Ties

Studies show that both children and adults are happier and healthier
when they enjoy more time together. However, a study published
in *Canadian Social Trends* in 2007 found that people are spending
more time at work and less time with family. Here are some ways
you can enhance your connection with family members.

MIND: *Look through family photo albums*
Take a trip down memory lane by looking at family albums with
your loved ones. Relive pleasant times together by sharing experiences. Introduce kids to their ancestors by showing them photos of
their relatives. Acquaint them with bygone days and explain their
heritage. You may wish to post some photos online to connect with
relatives who live faraway.

BODY: *Join a fitness club together*
Many fitness centers offer special rates if you join as a family. And
virtually all offer a wide range of activities for people of all ages;
some may be adults only, some for kids, and some that the whole
family can enjoy such as bowling or swimming. Plan regular family
fitness dates and go to the club together.

SPIRIT: *Honor a family ritual*
All families have personal ways of celebrating holidays and special
occasions. Often these involve rituals of some kind, religious or secular or both. Honor a family tradition and pass it down to your children. Cherishing a family ritual provides a sense of connectedness
and continuity that transcends time.

> "A WISE MAN ADAPTS HIMSELF TO CIRCUMSTANCES AS
> WATER SHAPES ITSELF TO THE VESSEL THAT CONTAINS IT."
> —Chinese Proverb

Put Your Own Oxygen Mask on First

Caregivers are probably the people most in need of self-care, yet they may be the last to give themselves the care they need. You can't nurture others optimally unless you are nourished yourself. Make self-care a priority today in every way.

MIND: *Ask for help*

There comes a time when you simply can't do it all yourself—and you don't have to. Friends, relatives, and neighbors are usually glad to help out in a pinch. You can return the favor at a later date. If necessary, hire the help you need: home health care services, lawn maintenance, house-cleaning, or whatever. Set priorities, and let others handle the rest.

BODY: *Add protein to your diet*

Quinoa is an excellent vegetarian protein source to add to your diet—but you don't have to be a vegetarian to enjoy it. Considered a complete protein, quinoa provides ten essential amino acids and is packed with minerals, B vitamins, and fiber. Extra-high amounts of the amino acid lysine, which is essential for tissue growth and repair, lifts quinoa to the status of a superfood.

SPIRIT: *Join a caregivers' support group*

Caregiving can take a toll on the giver, which only those who are in similar situations can understand. Confiding in other people like yourself can make the load easier to bear and may prevent burnout. Support groups offer a confidential place to express yourself, and offer tools for coping.

"EVEN AFTER ALL THIS TIME THE SUN NEVER SAYS TO THE EARTH, 'YOU OWE ME.' LOOK WHAT HAPPENS WITH A LOVE LIKE THAT, IT LIGHTS THE WHOLE SKY." —Hafiz, *The Gift*

Welcome the Sun

Today, appreciate the sun, the center around which our solar system revolves. Nothing we know would exist without it. Early people revered the sun as a god. Welcome the essential role the sun plays in your life.

MIND: *Watch the sunset*

Unwind at the end of the day by watching the sunset. Enjoy the wash of colors, the slow ebb from day into night. Each day we are treated to this miraculous visual display, and it's absolutely free. Cherish this wondrous natural event today, and as often as possible.

BODY: *Shun the sunscreen*

Although sunscreen may protect you from getting burned at the beach, it also prevents vitamin D from being absorbed by your body. Brief periods of sun exposure may have more benefits than drawbacks. Additionally, many sunscreens contain chemicals that when converted to free radicals could actually lead to cell damage. Check out the Environmental Working Group's website for a list of name-brand sunscreens and their ingredients (*www.ewg.org*) and limit yourself to about fifteen minutes of sun at a time.

SPIRIT: *Learn about your sun sign*

When someone asks, "What's your sign?" he or she means what part of the zodiac was the sun in when you were born. For thousands of years, astrologers have studied the relationship between the positions of the heavenly bodies and events on earth. Consult an astrologer or read books on the subject to learn more about your strengths, weaknesses, and possibilities.

"IF SKIN IS A FENCE THAT DIVIDES PEOPLE, SEX IS THE
GATE THAT OPENS YOUR BODY TO THE OTHER PERSON."

—Andrew Davidsonid

Make Intimate Contact

People who have sex regularly live longer than those who don't, a
twenty-five-year-long Duke University study first reported in 1982.
Since then, numerous studies have shown that sex aids virtually
everything from cardiovascular health to memory. Sex also burns
as many calories per half hour as weight training or walking. Which
would you rather do today?

MIND: *Gaze into your partner's eyes*

It's been said that the eyes are the windows of the soul, but some
people find it threatening if you look deeply into them. It can be a
way to make a strong, intimate connection, however. Sit facing one
another and gaze into each other's eyes for a few minutes. After the
time is up, share your experiences.

BODY: *Shop for sex toys together*

Sex toys aren't just for people who don't have partners. Sex toys can
add a new dimension to your sexual pleasure with your partner. Shop
for sex toys together, either online or at an adult store. You may be
surprised at the amazing array of gadgets available. Then have fun
playing with your new toys.

SPIRIT: *Wear a carnelian to increase passion*

Carnelian is a reddish-orange stone whose name comes from the
Latin *carnis*, meaning flesh. No surprise, then, that crystal workers
connect it with sexuality. Prized since antiquity for its high-energy
vibrations, it can enhance your vitality and libido. Wear a carnelian
to help your inner fire burn hotter.

"Our smallest judgment adds to war, and our smallest forgiveness adds to peace."
—Marianne Williamson, *The Gift of Change*

Find Peace Through Acceptance

Today, try to erase the boundaries between you and other people by focusing on your commonality rather than your differences. You can acknowledge differences without letting them stand between you. Fear, isolation, and prejudice have a detrimental effect on us as individuals and societies.

MIND: *Notice when you judge others*
Today, monitor the judgments you make about other people as you go through the day. Every time you make a judgment about someone— her hair, his car, their political views—you create a gap between you and the other person. Judgment causes you to feel separate and isolated from others, rather than connected. Simply being aware of how you judge others will help you become more accepting.

BODY: *Love your body*
Come to love and accept your body. Finding fault with your physical appearance is an act of unkindness toward yourself. Throughout time, images of beauty have varied widely. Look at Renaissance paintings. Check out the Venus of Willendorf. Find something you like about your body and let your appreciation for it grow from there.

SPIRIT: *Practice nonviolence*
Practicing nonviolence is an act of strength, not weakness. Nonviolence is much more than not harming another person physically. It means monitoring your thoughts and feelings, too. Thinking hateful thoughts can have a destructive effect, and so can venting angry emotions. You may want to buy products from companies that support peace efforts, too, rather than those that profit from war.

"THE TIME TO RELAX IS WHEN YOU DON'T HAVE TIME

FOR IT." —Jim Goodwin and Sydney J. Harris

Make It Easy on Yourself

Surveys by many researchers indicate that stress-related conditions account for the majority of visits to doctors. If that's the case, finding ways to reduce stress—or change your reaction to it—may be the best thing you can do for yourself. Today, notice the things that cause stress for you, and look for ways to make things easier.

MIND: *Determine your stressors*
Make a list of the things that are causing stress for you now. Rank them from one to ten. Make two columns: one for things you can do to alleviate stress now, and one for things you can do in the future. Read through your list: This is your action plan. You have taken the first step toward mastering your stress.

BODY: *Stomp your feet*
Stomping your feet is a great way to release tension. If you stomp outside, you leave the energy out there. Let it go. You can even stomp your feet outside each day after work, before entering your home. Even if you love your job, this will allow you not to bring work stress into the house.

SPIRIT: *Explore the benefits of spirituality*
Forty years' worth of studies at Harvard Medical School have shown that prayer and prayerlike states of consciousness can reduce the effects of stress. More than 100 schools, including Harvard, now offer courses in the relationship between spirituality and health. Consider investigating the benefits of spiritual practice on stress.

"IT TAKES HANDS TO BUILD A HOUSE, BUT ONLY HEARTS CAN BUILD A HOME." —Anonymous

Take Care of Your Home

Caring for your home is a factor in caring for yourself. Your home is your castle, even if it's only a tiny apartment. Take pride in your home today by doing something to make it more beautiful or comfortable.

MIND: *Make repairs around the house*
A leaky faucet, a door that sticks, and other malfunctioning items around the house can add small amounts of annoyance and stress to your life. Don't keep putting off repairs. Set aside time to fix these little irritations. You'll feel a sense of satisfaction and relief knowing you've taken care of these problems. You may even save money in the long run by catching small problems before they become bigger ones.

BODY: *Do yard work*
Raking leaves, pruning shrubs, planting flowers or vegetables, and other yard work provide great opportunities for getting exercise and fresh air. You'll also see the satisfying results of your labors at the end of the day—something you don't get from working out at the gym. Do yard work on a sunny day and you'll soak up your quotient of vitamin D as well.

SPIRIT: *Wash windows*
Wash your home's windows—it will instantly look more cheerful. According to the ancient philosophy of feng shui, the life energy known as chi enters your home through the doors and windows. If your windows are clean, more of this life-giving force can stream into your home to enhance your health, wealth, and happiness.

"THE ONLY WAY A RELATIONSHIP WILL LAST IS IF YOU SEE
YOUR RELATIONSHIP AS A PLACE THAT YOU GO TO GIVE, AND
NOT A PLACE THAT YOU GO TO TAKE." —Anthony Robbins

Build a Better Relationship

Good relationships don't just happen; they require work and dedication. In your job, you must continue to put forth effort if you want to succeed. The same holds true in your personal relationships. Today, start building a better relationship.

MIND: *Take a class together*

Share an interest with your partner by taking a class together. Many colleges offer continuing education courses. So do YMCAs/YWCAs, senior centers, and other organizations. Learning a new subject or skill or expanding your knowledge of a current hobby can let the two of you grow closer together.

BODY: *Work out together*

Make a commitment to get healthier by working out together. If you or your partner—or both of you—could stand to lose a little weight, exercising together offers support and reinforces your intention. Because exercise increases production of the "feel good" chemicals dopamine and serotonin, you're likely to feel better about yourself and your relationship if you work out together.

SPIRIT: *Show respect for each other*

Often it's the little things that count in creating a happy, fulfilling relationship. Showing constant and genuine respect for one another is like watering a plant—it nourishes your relationship and makes your connection stronger. When your partner feels valued and loved by you, he or she is more likely to be healthier and feel more fulfilled in life.

"ART WASHES AWAY THE DUST OF EVERYDAY LIFE."
—Pablo Picasso

Get Cultured

Art isn't mere decoration, nor is it simply for the elite. Art engages the part of your brain that is associated with creativity and intuition—whether you observe it or do it yourself. It can encourage problem-solving by helping you think outside the box. Today, expose yourself to art in one form or another.

MIND: *Attend an art opening*

If you don't know much about art, an art opening is a great way to learn. Many small galleries, art associations, philanthropic groups, and educational centers host openings—events that showcase an artist's (or artists') work. In a small venue like this, you don't feel over-whelmed. Often the artists are present to talk about their work and respond to questions.

BODY: *Attend a concert*

Numerous studies have demonstrated the healing properties of music. Mitchell Gaynor, MD, explains in *Sounds of Healing*, "Music can have a powerful salutary effect on our cardiovascular, immune, and nervous systems, not to mention our emotional and spiritual selves." Listening to classical or Baroque music has been shown to lower blood cortisol levels, an indicator of stress.

SPIRIT: *Visit a cathedral*

Throughout much of history, churches were the main patrons of the arts. The great cathedrals of Europe and some in the United States house diverse art treasures by some of the world's greatest artists. In Asia and the Middle East, you'll find beautiful temples and mosques that feature exquisite sculpture, mosaics, and more. Even small missions in the American Southwest are adorned with artwork.

"GARDENING IS ABOUT ENJOYING THE SMELL OF THINGS GROWING IN THE SOIL, GETTING DIRTY WITHOUT FEELING GUILTY, AND GENERALLY TAKING THE TIME TO SOAK UP A LITTLE PEACE AND SERENITY." —Lindley Karstens

Establish an Ongoing Rapport with Nature

The benefits of nature on human health have been well-documented by numerous clinical studies. Chicago cardiologist Bruno Cortis even found that hospital patients got better faster when they could look through a window at a garden. Today, strengthen your connection to nature and enjoy its healing properties.

MIND: *Put up a birdhouse*

Invite your feathered friends to visit your home by putting up a birdhouse. Watching birds and listening to their songs can be a pleasant, educational, and relaxing experience for your family. Educate yourself about the species you'd like to attract, then provide the type of home and food they like best.

BODY: *Plant organic veggies*

Grow your own organic vegetables in a home garden plot, or with other people in your community. Chemical pesticides may pose health risks including nerve damage, cancer, birth defects, and other problems. Although the EPA regulates pesticide use in the United States, other countries may not follow the same standards. Avoid the risks by growing fresh, healthy veggies yourself.

SPIRIT: *Invite a deity's blessing*

Invite a deity to bless your property. In your yard or garden, place a statue of your favorite spiritual figure, such as the Buddha, the Virgin Mary, Green Man, or a guardian angel. Or, set one by your front door to welcome family members and visitors to your home.

"SLOW DOWN AND EVERYTHING YOU ARE CHASING WILL

COME AROUND AND CATCH YOU."

—John De Paola

Time Out

Give yourself a break today. You can only push yourself so hard for so long, and then it's time to say "stop." Taking time out can enable you to be more productive, healthy, and happy.

MIND: *Take a mental health day*

If you feel like you're dragging yourself through your days or you dread going to work, it's time for a mental health day. On this day off, don't run errands, do housework, or anything else that might be considered work. The purpose is to rest. Sleep late. Lie on the couch. Sit outside. Picnic in the park. Do whatever you need to recharge your brain and body.

BODY: *Take a power nap*

Schedule twenty minutes into your day for a power nap. As we become more sleep deprived, we become less productive and more stressed out. A short nap may not make up for a good night's sleep, but it can help your mind and body rejuvenate. A Harvard School of Public Health study found that taking naps regularly reduced the risk of coronary disease by 37 percent.

SPIRIT: *Let your heart be light*

Can you laugh at the bizarre nature of life? Or do you take everything seriously? Spiritual teachers emphasize the benefits of laughter and childlike joy. Seek levity, even in serious moments. Accept that whatever happens is part of a larger whole, and that by trusting in divine guidance, you allow what is best for all concerned to transpire.

"SING LIKE NO ONE'S LISTENING, LOVE LIKE YOU'VE NEVER
BEEN HURT, DANCE LIKE NO ONE'S WATCHING."

—Various attributions

Let Down Your Guard

When you've been hurt, it's hard to allow yourself to be open and
vulnerable. But it's how you choose to move on that matters. Letting
feelings of anger, resentment, fear, or jealousy take over will prevent
you from accessing the very things you desire. Instead of building
walls, build bridges.

MIND: *Be receptive to new possibilities*
The future needn't be a repeat of the past, unless that's what you
choose. Keep an open mind when you meet new people or encounter new situations. Try not to make comparisons between what hap-
pened in the past and what the present circumstances are. Holding
on to preconceptions can lead you to repeat old patterns.

BODY: *Enjoy active and receptive phases*
In yoga, the moments of relaxation are just as important as the periods of exertion. Those quiet moments between physically demand-
ing postures enable you to appreciate what your body has accomplished, and to enjoy the resulting flow of energy throughout your
system. If you are always active, you won't have a chance to digest
the benefits of your activity.

SPIRIT: *Listen for the call*
Often we are so wrapped up in our daily lives that we don't hear our
inner guidance calling to us. Set aside time each day to turn inward
and listen to the voice within. Tune out all outer-world distractions
and just sit quietly. Invite your angels, spirit guides, higher self, or a
favorite deity to speak to you.

"Put your heart, mind, intellect

and soul even into your smallest acts.

This is the secret of success." —Swami Sivananda

Make the Best of Your Workspace

Many of us spend more hours at our desks than we do in our beds. If your daytime territory is limited to a tiny cubicle, make the best of it. Here are suggestions you can try today.

MIND: *Clear your desk*
Clearing your desk at the end of the day allows you to bring order and resolution to the day's work, and to go home with a sense of peace. When you come in to work the next morning, you won't be faced with an overwhelming to-do list. You can ease into the day, organizing and prioritizing tasks without feeling that you are already behind the eight ball.

BODY: *Do neck rolls at your desk*
Periodically throughout the day, stop what you're doing and release tension in your neck. Drop your head forward loosely, then slowly roll it to the right and back. Continue making a circle with your head, letting it drop toward your back and then to the left. Allow your head to fall forward, so your chin touches your collarbones, then repeat the circle. Do this three times slowly in a clockwise direction. Then reverse and roll in a counterclockwise direction.

SPIRIT: *Be receptive to new opportunities*
Many spiritual traditions associate the east, where the sun rises, with beginnings. Figure out which is the easternmost portion of your desk. Clear this section of clutter to make room for new opportunities to come your way.

"TO ERR ON THE SIDE OF KINDNESS IS SELDOM AN ERROR."

—Liz Armbruster

Give Yourself Some TLC

We can all use a little kindness and TLC. Don't wait for someone else to give it to you today; give it to yourself. Start by banishing self-criticism and lavishing yourself with self-encouragement. Notice how much better you feel, mentally, physically, and spiritually.

MIND: *Acknowledge an accomplishment*

Recognize yourself for achieving a goal or overcoming an obstacle. Often we forget to credit ourselves for accomplishing something small, such as holding your temper in a disagreement or losing two pounds. But each small victory strengthens your confidence and deserves to be celebrated.

BODY: *Give yourself a massage*

Sure, it's nicer if someone else gives you a massage, but when that's not possible, treat your body to the healing touch. Loosen up your muscles and work out the kinks—you'll feel better right away. Rub your feet, your hands and arms, your legs. Ease the stiffness from your neck and shoulders. Use a slow, firm, steady motion. Make it even more pleasant by applying an aromatherapy lotion.

SPIRIT: *Program your dreams*

Before going to sleep, tell yourself that you will have sweet dreams, restful sleep, and awake refreshed. If you like, you can also program your subconscious to work on a particular issue while you sleep. Or, just ask for guidance or insight. Practice doing this every night and you'll soon find you can manage your dreams quite effectively.

"FAMILY FACES ARE MAGIC MIRRORS. LOOKING AT
PEOPLE WHO BELONG TO US, WE SEE THE PAST, PRESENT,
AND FUTURE." —Gail Lumet Buckley

Focus on Family

If your loved ones always seem to be going off in different directions, here are some ways to implement more cooperation and communication among family members. Instead of each person focusing on his or her own interests, focus on the health of the group. Sharing at every level can help your family thrive.

MIND: *Schedule weekly family meetings*
Companies hold regular staff meetings to discuss ideas, problem-solve, and keep one another updated on what's happening. Do the same with your family. Give each person an opportunity to air grievances or concerns, announce upcoming events, and ask questions. Agree to listen and be respectful of one another—no interruptions. Stay calm and don't let the meeting turn into a gripe session or argument.

BODY: *Take turns cooking dinner*
Let family members take turns planning and preparing dinner. The cook can decide what he or she wishes to make (providing it's a healthy and balanced meal). Children may need some assistance from their elders, but allowing them to participate makes them feel grown-up and important. This gives everyone a chance to share the love and responsibility of nurturing one another.

SPIRIT: *Celebrate family rituals*
All cultures have ceremonies to mark important events and rites of passage in their lives. Christenings, Bah Mitzvahs, graduations, and weddings are some familiar ones. Choose occasions that are special to your family and mark them with personal ceremonies.

"A FRIEND IS A PRESENT YOU GIVE TO YOURSELF."

—Robert Louis Stevenson

Make New Friends and Embrace Old Ones

We all need friends—no man is an island, as the saying goes. According to a study conducted by James Fowler of UC San Diego and Nicholas Christakis of Harvard, each happy friend increases your own happiness by about 9 percent. If you've been too busy lately to spend time with friends, rectify that today by connecting with a friend.

MIND: *Make new friends*

If you've been having trouble making friends or want to meet some new people, host a get-together that revolves around an interest of yours. Invite people you know—family, neighbors, coworkers—and ask each to bring someone else along. Everyone will know someone, but each person will also have a chance to meet new people, too.

BODY: *Try out new recipes with friends*

Nothing bonds people like breaking bread together. Try a new recipe and take some of what you've cooked to a friend to enjoy. Encourage your friends' cooking adventures, too. Swap successful recipes. Sharing food is an ancient practice that sometimes results in lifelong friendships.

SPIRIT: *Feel connected through your breath*

No one owns or can contain the air—it belongs to all of us. It is also a link between every creature on earth. As you breathe, feel your connection to everyone else, even those who live on the other side of the world. Know that through your breath you touch them and they touch you. We are all one.

"EVERY TOOTH IN A MAN'S HEAD IS MORE VALUABLE

THAN A DIAMOND." —Miguel de Cervantes

Take a Bite Out of Life

In holistic medicine, physical properties and conditions symbolize psychological states. In her book *You Can Heal Your Life*, Louise Hay associates dental problems with indecisiveness. Are you holding back out of fear, confusion, or laziness? If so, take the bit in your teeth today and take charge of your destiny.

MIND: *Sink your teeth into something you enjoy*
Notice how time flies when you're having fun. Set aside a block of time to do something you enjoy and devote yourself to it fully. Do a crossword puzzle, read a good book, draw a sketch, knit a sweater, play a musical instrument, refinish a piece of furniture—whatever makes your heart sing.

BODY: *Take care of your teeth*
Nobody likes going to the dentist, but if it's been longer than six months since you've had your teeth checked, make an appointment. Catching problems in the early stages can prevent more serious ones from taking hold. To maintain good dental health, brush your teeth with a soft-bristle brush and floss at least twice a day.

SPIRIT: *Bite through obstacles*
The *I Ching*, a three-thousand-year-old body of Chinese wisdom, offers spiritual guidance for everyday living. One section, called "Shih Ho," advises "biting through" obstacles to unity with others by releasing the compulsion to rectify wrongs and allowing the cosmic force to correct matters. By doing so, we "bite through" our own egotism.

"THE BRAIN IS LIKE A MUSCLE. WHEN IT IS IN USE WE FEEL VERY GOOD. UNDERSTANDING IS JOYOUS." —Carl Sagan

Be Good to Your Brain

Your brain is your most important organ, the body's control tower. Its more than 100 billion cells send commands to direct all your other cells. In most people, the brain declines with age; however, you can take steps to slow this process.

MIND: *Balance your brain's hemispheres.*

Use this breathing exercise to encourage the two sides of your brain to work together harmoniously. Hold your left nostril shut and inhale through your right nostril. Hold for a count of ten, then exhale through your mouth. Repeat three times, then switch sides and repeat three times. Once you get the hang of it, you can do this exercise anytime, anywhere.

BODY: *Nourish your memory with herbs*

Professor Elaine Perry of the University of Newcastle-upon-Tyne in northern England found that plant extracts of sage and lemon balm produced promising results in studies to improve memory and behavior in Alzheimer's patients. Use these botanicals in aromatherapy, or take the herbs in tablets, teas, capsules, or extracts to nourish your memory.

SPIRIT: *Pay attention to Mercury retrograde periods*

Astrologers link the planet Mercury with the mind. Every four months, for a period of three weeks at a time, Mercury appears to move backward (or retrograde) in its path around the sun. During these times, your thinking may be less clear than usual, resulting in mistakes or confusion. Check Mercury's position before making important decisions.

"THE GLUE THAT HOLDS ALL RELATIONSHIPS TOGETHER . . .

IS TRUST, AND TRUST IS BASED ON INTEGRITY."

—Brian Tracy

Learn More about Your Partner

No matter how long you've known someone, you can never know everything about him or her—and the mystery is part of the appeal. However, learning to appreciate something about your beloved that you may have overlooked can be a tantalizing experience. Today, open up a bit more to your partner.

MIND: *Share a secret*
Sharing secrets with someone is an act of trust that can strengthen your connection. If revealing yourself makes you uncomfortable, start with something small that would provide your partner with useful insight into you and benefit the relationship. Invite him or her to reveal a secret in exchange. Work up to more significant sharings over time.

BODY: *Create an arousal map on your partner's body*
Notice the areas of your bodies that seem particularly sensitive to sexual arousal. Because each of us is unique, these "passion points" probably won't be the same for everyone. Chart a course that takes you from one stimulation point to another, starting with the least sensitive and ending with the most sensitive.

SPIRIT: *Examine your partner's "heart line"*
A person's hand contains a wealth of information—if you know what to look for. The heart line is the middle line on most people's palms, which runs horizontally from the space between the thumb and index finger toward the outside of the palm. If it's straight, he's a pragmatist; if it dips down toward the wrist, she's a romantic.

> "When the grass looks greener on the other side
> of the fence, it may be that they take better care
> of it there." —Cecil Selig

Treat Yourself Well

Give yourself the consideration and generosity you would offer to your dearest friend. If you tend to overlook yourself and your own needs, while tending to the needs of others, it's time to stop short-changing yourself. Treat yourself to some TLC today.

MIND: *Build treats into your life*

Make a list of ten things you really like and would consider giving to yourself as a reward. These things should make you feel rejuvenated, validated, and supported. Focus on healthy treats with no downsides, instead of junk food or extravagant shopping sprees, such as a manicure, a visit with a friend, or a bubble bath.

BODY: *Eat dark chocolate*

Chocolate is a favorite treat for many, but it's also one that's good for you. It may even help prevent cancer. Pentameric procyanidin, a natural compound found in cocoa, deactivates a number of proteins that likely work in concert to push a cancer cell to continually divide. Chocolate also contains polyphenol antioxidants, a natural protection against cancer. Dark chocolate with a high cocoa percentage (70 percent or better) is healthier than milk chocolate.

SPIRIT: *Get daily inspiration*

Begin each day on a positive note. Sign up to receive inspirational quotes daily by e-mail—you'll find lots of Internet sites that provide this service. Every day when you turn on your computer, you'll be treated to upbeat and heartwarming sayings.

"SUCCESS IS GETTING WHAT YOU WANT.

HAPPINESS IS LIKING WHAT YOU GET."

—H. Jackson Brown Jr.

Attract What You Desire

Start using your thoughts constructively today. The Law of Attraction, an ancient concept that says your thoughts attract people, things, and circumstances, enables you to consciously create whatever you desire. Be aware that you are creating all the time—so focus on what you want.

MIND: *Use an affirmation for three days*
Affirmations are short, positive statements you create in order to produce an effect in your life. Write an affirmation to attract something you want: money, love, a new job, or whatever. State it in the present tense, as if you already have what you desire. Repeat it regularly for three days.

BODY: *Repeat a walking mantra*
A mantra is a word or phrase that has special meaning for you and aids you in some way. Create a short mantra to use while you walk. Say the words to the rhythm of your steps, one word per step. In this way, you incorporate your intention into your body to help activate it. Each step brings you closer to your objective.

SPIRIT: *Use prana to manifest your desires*
Hindu sacred writings speak of life energy as prana, a force that sustains us and cannot be destroyed. When you direct this energy with your mind, it generates an effect. This psychic force has the power to create what your mind conceives. Determine what you wish to manifest, then envision directing this energy toward what you want to bring it to you like a magnet.

"FOR EVERY MINUTE SPENT IN ORGANIZING,

AN HOUR IS EARNED." —Anonymous

Get Organized

If you're like most people, you have more stuff than you need. Today, consider reducing the clutter in your life by getting rid of things you don't use. Organize the rest so you don't waste time looking for what you want. You'll reduce stress and frustration, too.

MIND: *Organize your file cabinet*
Go through your files and weed out all the old paperwork that you no longer need. Getting rid of outdated material will free up room and make it easier to find what you want. Psychologically, you also signal that you are ready to receive new projects. Update files you still want to keep or believe you may need. Organize materials in a filing system that is convenient for you.

BODY: *Organize your medicine cabinet*
Go through your medicine cabinet and check dates on all prescription and nonprescription medications. Medicines that are beyond recommended usage dates may have lost some of their power. Dispose of them and, if necessary, replace them. Organize medications so you can easily find what you need.

SPIRIT: *Clear halls and walkways*
Make sure the halls, doorways, and other passageways in your home are free of obstructions. Clear away clutter. If necessary, reposition furniture to make it easier to move from place to place. Not only will this make your living space more convenient and safer, it encourages chi—the invisible energizing force of the universe—to flow smoothly and enrich your life.

"DON'T BLOW IT—GOOD PLANETS ARE HARD TO FIND."

—Quoted in *Time* magazine

Honor the Earth

More and more people are going green, as our environmental awareness increases. You can, too. Today, choose ways you can take better care of the environment and yourself. The choices you make will have immediate and long-term results.

MIND: *Give friends consumable gifts*
Show respect for the earth by not generating more waste—and help prevent clutter from building up in your loved one's homes. Give gifts that will be consumed: soap, candles, edibles, wine. Choose "green" products and those that are made by companies who donate portions of their profits to worthy causes.

BODY: *Eat organic foods*
Eat organic food or grow your own. Commercial growers use chemical fertilizers and pesticides to increase crop yield. These chemicals pose dangers for you and for the environment. In humans, pesticides have been shown to affect the immune and nervous systems, and increase risks for cancer and other diseases. In nature, pesticides contaminate water, air, and soil. They also kill birds, fish, animals, and helpful insects.

SPIRIT: *Ask nature for forgiveness*
After the 2011 Japanese earthquake, scientist and author Masaru Emoto asked people around the world to pray for the water that had been contaminated by leakage from the Fukushima Nuclear Plant, and to ask the water to forgive us. Humans have done tremendous damage to the earth, yet she continues to support us. Ask nature to forgive us and attempt to be more respectful in the future.

> "VARIETY'S THE VERY SPICE OF LIFE,
>
> THAT GIVES IT ALL ITS FLAVOR." —William Cowper

Add Zing to Your Day

What gives your life meaning? What makes you feel alive, excited, full of zest and zip? If you're feeling lethargic, uninspired, or down-right dull today, try the following suggestions to add a pinch of spice to your life mentally, physically, and spiritually.

MIND: *Listen to salsa*
Download some spicy salsa or merengue music to your portable device and listen to it while communing or at work (if possible). The lively, uplifting beat will stimulate your own inner rhythms and give you an energy boost. Make a playlist of your favorite tunes and listen to it whenever you need a lift. Attend a concert of live music if you get the opportunity.

BODY: *Grab some ginger*
Cook with ginger to stoke those metabolic fires. An Australian study found that this spicy root can temporarily raise metabolic rates as much as 20 percent. It's packed with as many antioxidants as a cup of spinach. Ginger assists with digestion and reduces inflammation. Drink ginger tea or sprinkle fresh ginger on your food. It can help you be more active and lively all day.

SPIRIT: *Burn spicy incense*
Light a stick, coil, or cone of incense and inhale its aroma to quickly shift your spirits to a vibrant place. Choose spicy scents such as clove, cinnamon, cedar, sandalwood, or patchouli to enliven you. Incense made with all-natural ingredients will generate the best results.

"THERE IS NO DEFENSE AGAINST ADVERSE

FORTUNE WHICH IS SO EFFECTUAL AS AN HABITUAL

SENSE OF HUMOR." —Thomas W. Higginson

Reduce Annoyances

You may not be able to eliminate all the annoyances in your life, but you can do something to reduce the toll they take on you. Today, deal with the irritations that you *can* stop and deal with your reactions to the ones you can't. Here are some suggestions you can try.

MIND: *Stop telemarketing calls*
Stop the intrusion of these annoyances. Instead of letting unwanted phone calls disturb you, do something about it. Go online and sign up for the Do Not Call registry at *www.donotcall.gov*. Or, call 1-888-382-1222 from the phone you wish to register. It only takes a few minutes.

BODY: *Step away from your desk during the workday*
Whenever you catch yourself getting tense or annoyed at work, stand up and step away from your workspace. Disperse irritation by walking down the hall or around the block. Go up and down the stairs a few times. Twist from side to side. With each movement, feel stress and anxiety flowing away from your body. Spend at least five minutes before going back to work. You'll feel calmer and recharged.

SPIRIT: *Carry an agate to relax*
Green agates calm and balance you emotionally, physically, and mentally. By balancing yin and yang energies, they help cleanse your system of tension and anger. Green agates also connect you with the grounding, supportive power of nature and the earth. Carry one in your pocket and rub it to soothe body and soul.

"THERE'S NEVER ENOUGH TIME TO DO ALL THE

NOTHING YOU WANT." —Bill Watterson, *Calvin and Hobbes*

Get More R & R

According to the National Sleep Foundation, the average American works forty-six hours per week, and nearly 40 percent work more than fifty hours. Factor in commuting time, housework, and other chores, and there's not much left for relaxation. Today, make a point of getting more R & R.

MIND: *Relax with zazen meditation*
To relax your mind, try this form of Zen meditation, which can be defined as "just sitting." Wear loose clothes and sit on the floor (or a pillow) in a comfortable position. Close your eyes and breathe slowly. Count mentally from one to ten with each breath, to help keep your mind centered and relaxed. Spend ten minutes every day to calm your mind.

BODY: *Do yoga stretches before bed*
To help curb potential stress-related insomnia, do a few easy stretches before you slip between the sheets. Stand with your feet hip-width apart, bend over slowly, and let your body and head go limp. Feel your back and body stretching and relaxing. Then, stand and raise your arms overhead. Gently lean back, arching your back. Repeat three times.

SPIRIT: *Spend time reviewing your dreams*
Instead of popping out of bed like toast from a toaster as soon as your alarm rings, spend five or ten minutes reviewing your dreams. Psychiatrists and dream researchers say your dreams offer guidance for the day, so examining them could provide valuable aid or insight.

"WHEN YOU ARE PREPARED FOR ANYTHING, THE

OPPORTUNITY TO USE IT PRESENTS ITSELF."   —Edgar Cayce

Open the Door for Opportunity

The combination of confidence and preparation is a powerful one that can bring you success of any kind. Today determine a goal you wish to achieve. Write it down to clarify it in your mind. Then believe you can accomplish it. The following tips can help.

MIND: *Set a goal, then let it happen*
When you desire something, consider using the tools of manifestation to attract it into your life. Set a goal, then let your mind (along with your angels, guides, or whatever suits your beliefs) help you reach it. No matter what your objective is, opening yourself to accept what you want is the first step to receiving it.

BODY: *Use acupressure to improve concentration*
To increase your ability to stay focused on your objective, activate the acupressure point known as Gates of Consciousness. The energy points are located at the base of your skull, on either side of your neck bone. Press your fingers to these points for about a minute, then release. Do this several times a day. You'll strengthen your memory, too.

SPIRIT: *Make a medicine bundle*
A Native American medicine bundle contains lucky objects intended to produce a certain result. Select a few objects (no more than four) that represent your intention. Add a pinch of loose natural tobacco. Place everything in a leather pouch and tie it shut. Carry it with you to help you achieve your goal.

> "LIFE HAS TAUGHT US THAT LOVE DOES NOT CONSIST
>
> IN GAZING AT EACH OTHER BUT IN LOOKING OUTWARD
>
> TOGETHER IN THE SAME DIRECTION."

—Antoine de Saint-Exupéry

Rekindle the Flame

Boredom is the kiss of death to many relationships. But the fire doesn't have to go out of a relationship over time. Keep the flames burning brightly. Here are some suggestions you can try to rekindle the spark in a partnership.

MIND: *Watch an erotic movie together*
Watching a sexy movie together can get you in the mood and perhaps give you some ideas about how to please one another. Most women don't like porn marketed to men, and prefer a bit more romance with their sex. Choose a steamy flick that has both elements and will entice both of you and whet your appetites.

BODY: *Wear risqué clothing*
Dress up for your partner in something sexy and alluring. Ask what he or she would like to see you in, or surprise your partner—whichever you think would be more enticing. If you're at home alone, you could wear slinky lingerie or silk boxers to dinner. If you go out, don't wear undergarments and make sure your partner knows.

SPIRIT: *Set the stage with candles*
Candles provide a romantic and intimate ambiance. Turn off the electric lights and illuminate your home with candles. Put them on the mantel or coffee table. Eat dinner by candlelight. Place candles in your bedroom. Light candles in the bathroom and take a bath together. Choose aromatherapy candles to add a sensual note.

"IF YOU KNOW EXACTLY WHAT YOU'RE GOING TO DO,

WHAT'S THE GOOD OF DOING IT?" —Pablo Picasso

And Now for Something Completely Different

Indulge your curiosity today and expand your horizons, by delving into something completely unknown. When you were a kid, everything was new and exciting. Recapture that youthful enthusiasm. Usually, the only way to find out if you like something is by giving it a try.

MIND: *Learn something new*

Attend a lecture or take an online webinar on a subject about which you know absolutely nothing. Without any preconceptions, you are free to explore with an open mind. Whatever you learn will be unexpected and totally new. You may find it's not something you want to pursue further, but you could be pleasantly surprised.

BODY: *Try a new type of workout*

Vary your workout program by taking a class or going with a friend to try something new and different. Most fitness and sports centers offer lots of different programs. How about yoga or tai chi? Kickboxing or karate? Pilates or belly dancing? You'll notice that you use muscles you don't ordinarily use in your familiar routine. You might really enjoy it, too.

SPIRIT: *Attend an unfamiliar ritual or ceremony*

Regardless of whether you are the religious type, you can benefit from the uplifting aspects of spiritual rituals. Attend a ritual or ceremony associated with a belief system about which you know little or nothing: Wicca, Hinduism, Islam, or something else. Open your heart and mind to the experience.

"KNOWLEDGE RESTS NOT UPON TRUTH ALONE,

BUT UPON ERROR ALSO." —Carl Jung

Know Thyself

How much do you really know about yourself? Today, consider ways to develop a deeper understanding of yourself in order to enjoy a healthier, happier, more fulfilling life. Knowledge is power, and the more knowledge you have about yourself, the better choices you can make.

MIND: *Consider doing Neurolinguistic Programming*
Neurolinguistic Programming (NLP) is a form of holistic therapy that examines your perceptions and how they affect problems in your life. So long as you continue holding on to fixed ideas, the problems will remain. By changing your brain's responses to stimuli and the signals it sends, you can resolve phobias, unhealthy thought patterns, and self-limiting behaviors.

BODY: *Use kinesiology to check out your food*
Check out the food you eat to see what's really good for you. Kinesiology is a type of muscle testing that provides instant information. Hold a food in one hand, then hold your other arm out and try to resist letting someone push it down. If the food is good for you, you'll have strength in your arm. But if the food isn't healthy for you, the strength in your arm will be greatly diminished.

SPIRIT: *Get your hands read*
The lines, mounds, and marks on your palms reveal information about every area of your life. Have a professional read your palms for you to give you insight into your past and future, strengths and weaknesses, motivations, and more. The backs of your hands, fingers, and thumbs also tell lots about you.

"WITHOUT AN OPEN-MINDED MIND,

YOU CAN NEVER BE A GREAT SUCCESS." —Martha Stewart

Open Up to Blessings

Today, open yourself mentally, physically, and spiritually to the opportunities and blessings the universe offers you. Be receptive to other people. Expect good things to happen. Say "yes" or "maybe" rather than "no."

MIND: *Keep a gratitude journal*
One of the steps to manifesting what you desire is being grateful. Every day, write down something you are thankful for. Expressing thanks for the good things you already have lifts your mind to a more positive place. With a positive mind-set, you are more likely to attract positive things, people, and situations. A negative mind-set sabotages possibilities before you even get started.

BODY: *Pay attention to your body language*
The way you sit, stand, and walk conveys a lot about your attitudes, including your willingness to receive or deflect what life brings you. Crossing your arms over your chest and crossing your legs suggests you are in protective mode—the door is closed and the lock is bolted. Practice standing up straight, holding your head high, and keeping your chest open to invite good things to come your way.

SPIRIT: *Affirm your unlimited potential*
If you think you are powerless to change your life, think again. In fact, you are capable of changing virtually anything you wish to change. You have vast, untapped potential to make whatever you choose of your life. No matter what your circumstances, affirm that you have the power to change them. Pick someone such as Oprah or J. K. Rowling to emulate.

"WE MUST EMBRACE PAIN AND BURN IT AS FUEL

FOR OUR JOURNEY." —Kenji Miyazawa

Cope with Pain

You can't avoid pain entirely; it's part of human existence. But you can choose how you wish to deal with pain, whether physical, emotional, or spiritual. Today, listen to what pain is trying to convey to you. It is usually a transitional state that may guide you to the next stage of being.

MIND: *Try hypnosis*

Hypnosis is a form of therapy that researchers at New York's Mount Sinai School of Medicine found could reduce pain from rheumatoid arthritis, cancer, burns, and other conditions. Hypnosis slows pulse and respiration, and places you in a relaxed state where you become receptive to mental suggestions that can aid various ailments. For more information, contact the American Society of Clinical Hypnotists.

BODY: *Do yoga to relieve back pain*

Yoga stretches, strengthens, and balances your body, to ease pain and to condition your body so you are less likely to experience painful injuries. To ease pain, lie on your back, bend your knees, pull them up to your chest, and wrap your arms around them. Slowly rock back and forth, gently massaging your back for several minutes.

SPIRIT: *Stop resisting*

When you see pain as an adversary or curse, you become more rigid, which can increase the pain. Instead of trying to defend against pain, attempt to see what it is saying to you. Fearing pain will give it more power. Breathe deeply, and with each breath visualize soothing blue light at the site of the pain.

"IF I HAD TO LIVE MY LIFE AGAIN I WOULD HAVE MADE A RULE TO READ SOME POETRY AND LISTEN TO SOME MUSIC AT LEAST ONCE A WEEK; FOR PERHAPS THE PARTS OF MY BRAIN NOW ATROPHIED COULD THUS HAVE BEEN KEPT ACTIVE THROUGH USE."   —Charles Darwin

Protect Your Brain

Good brains are hard to find. Take care of yours. A study conducted by the University of Virginia's Professor Timothy Salthouse suggests your brain begins to decline when you are in your late twenties. However, you can do many things to slow that decline. Here are some suggestions.

MIND: *Stimulate your brain*
In his book *Making a Good Brain Great*, Daniel G. Amen, MD, recommends stimulating your brain with new ideas and activities to protect it from age-related deterioration. Find a hobby or interest that draws on the intuitive and the analytical parts of your brain, such as painting, playing a musical instrument, woodworking, or chess. Pick something that challenges you.

BODY: *Wear a helmet*
Seventy-five percent of biking deaths result from brain injury. Protect your brain by wearing a helmet when you're motorcycling or riding a bicycle. It's wise to wear one when you are skateboarding, rock climbing, horseback riding, or playing hockey, baseball, or football as well.

SPIRIT: *Nurture your intuition*
Many sources say the right portion of your brain is linked with intuition and creativity, the left with logic and verbal ability. Protect and strengthen your intuitive brain by exercising it. Whenever your phone rings, try to guess who's calling before you look at the caller ID.

"OUR STRENGTH WILL CONTINUE IF WE ALLOW
OURSELVES THE COURAGE TO FEEL SCARED, WEAK,
AND VULNERABLE." —Melody Beattie

Understand Your Strengths and Weaknesses

We all have strengths and weaknesses, mentally, physically, and otherwise. Understanding yours can help you make the best of your abilities. Today, strive to be the best *you* that you can be.

MIND: *Accept your limitations*
Although it may be true that your only limitations are those you set for yourself, accepting these limitations allows you to stop struggling to keep up a front or to try to impress others with your abilities. Limitations are necessary—accept that you can't and don't want to do everything. Then you can devote yourself to those things you *do* want and feel are important.

BODY: *Tap chromium's health benefits*
Chromium helps your body metabolize fat, convert blood sugar into energy, and make insulin work more efficiently. It also seems to protect your heart, prevent diabetes, increase muscle mass (with exercise), and boost longevity. Make sure you get enough of this valuable mineral. You'll find it in eggs, broccoli, orange and grape juice, seafood, dairy products, and many types of meat.

SPIRIT: *Help someone whose needs are greater than yours*
One way to appreciate your blessings is to help someone who is less fortunate than you. Assist at a nursing home, homeless shelter, VA hospital, or children's cancer clinic. Witnessing the courage others display despite adversity will help you focus on what's really important. And by showing that you care, you'll strengthen their ability to cope with challenges.

"LIFE IS MEASURED BY THE NUMBER OF THINGS
YOU ARE ALIVE TO." —Maltbie D. Babcock

Rev Up Your Inner Engine

Just as your car needs to be driven fast on the highway periodically
to keep its engine clean, your mind and body need to shift into high
gear sometimes to sweep out the cobwebs. Stimulation isn't the same
as stress, although stress can be stimulating. Today, find healthy
ways to excite and enliven your mind, body, and spirit.

MIND: *Discuss a stimulating topic*
Choose a thought-provoking topic to discuss with friends or family
members. It should be something that challenges you mentally and
provokes lively debate, but not arguments. Philosophical, esoteric,
and multidimensional subjects with no right or wrong answers are
best. Art and literature offer many possibilities, too. Avoid politics
and religion, however, so as to avoid creating hard feelings.

BODY: *Eat protein to boost metabolism*
Because it takes more energy to digest protein than carbohydrates or
fats, you'll rev up your metabolism temporarily if you eat a protein-
rich meal. Complete proteins, found in meat, fish, eggs, and dairy
products, also provide all the amino acids you need to keep your
body operating optimally. Protein is necessary for building muscle
and tissue, and for good cell maintenance.

SPIRIT: *Play a drum*
Many traditions use drums in spiritual ceremonies and rituals. Drumming raises your energy, elevates your emotions, and stimulates your
awareness. It can also put you into a light trance that lets you connect
with other levels of existence. Consider drums such as the djembe,
taiko, doumbek, or bodhran (see *www.worldmusicalinstruments.com*
for information).

"AS LONG AS HABIT AND ROUTINE DICTATE THE
PATTERN OF LIVING, NEW DIMENSIONS OF THE
SOUL WILL NOT EMERGE." —Henry Van Dyke

Change Your Routine

Sometimes you just need to stir things up a bit, to keep life interesting.
A change of pace. A change of scenery. Productivity drops when you
become mentally and physically dulled because you do the same things
over and over. Today, make some healthy changes in your routine.

MIND: *Adjust your thinking*

Often we continue thinking about things in the same way for years,
without really questioning whether our ideas are in sync with our
present life situations. Reevaluate some of the attitudes you've held
for a while. Ask yourself why you still think that way and whether
doing so still serves you. Try shifting your perspective to consider
other possibilities.

BODY: *Change your scent*

Have you been using the same perfume or cologne for decades?
Maybe it's time to try something new. Over time, your body chemis-
try changes, so a fragrance that once complimented you may no longer be right. Scent quickly triggers brain responses and can increase
your energy, calm your nerves, or entice sexual feelings. See how
you react when you dab on a new fragrance.

SPIRIT: *Change your artwork*

Museums frequently rearrange the artwork they display in order to
increase interest for visitors. You can, too. Move the pictures in your
home or office around and hang them in different locations. You'll
"see them in a different light" literally. Change the photographs you
display, too. Update them with more current ones.

> "IF YOU WANT TO TURN YOUR LIFE AROUND, TRY
> THANKFULNESS. IT WILL CHANGE YOUR LIFE MIGHTILY."
>
> —Gerald Good

Show Appreciation

Look around today and take note of all the good things in your life, the little ones as well as the big ones. Recognizing and appreciating the benefits you enjoy is the first step to attracting more. Today, acknowledge your good fortune in all its forms, and express thanks, outwardly and inwardly.

MIND: *Just say "thanks"*
Tell other people when they make a difference in your life. It doesn't have to be a big deal—acknowledge small acts, too, such as when someone holds a door open for you or lets you go ahead in the supermarket checkout lane. Recognizing and appreciating other people's generosity encourages more of the same. Say "thank you" often.

BODY: *Show your body respect*
Treat your body well and it will serve you well. One of the best things you can do for yourself is to stay at a healthy weight. Check your Body Mass Index (BMI) to see where you fit into the picture: underweight, healthy weight, overweight, or obese. Go to the U.S. Department of Health & Human Services website, *www.nhlbisupport.com/bmi*, to calculate your BMI.

SPIRIT: *Respect religious freedom and diversity*
Whether or not you follow a particular religion, be thankful for the opportunity to choose your path—or none at all. Religious freedom doesn't exist everywhere, and religious differences have led to many wars. Respect other people's right to follow their beliefs and insist on being able to follow yours.

"THE BEST KIND OF FRIEND IS THE ONE YOU COULD SIT ON A PORCH WITH, NEVER SAYING A WORD, AND WALK AWAY FEELING LIKE THAT WAS THE BEST CONVERSATION YOU'VE HAD." —Anonymous

Strengthen Your Friendships

Today, work on strengthening your friendships and expanding your support network. Studies show that people with strong social networks experience less stress. They also recover more rapidly from injuries and illnesses, and are less likely to suffer from depression.

MIND: *Set up a barter system with friends*

Barter is an ancient form of currency, that lets everyone win. Set up a barter system with friends and neighbors. Maybe you can trade babysitting a friend's kids for a massage or guitar lessons. Bartering can strengthen your relationship with friends, too, because each of you values the other's skills.

BODY: *Take a daily stroll with friends*

A walk around your neighborhood will be more enjoyable if friends join you. Honor the allotted time as if it were an important appointment that you have to keep—it is! Friendships need nurturing, and your body needs exercise. A daily workout and stimulating conversation yield a twofold benefit.

SPIRIT: *Allow a friend to grow and change*

Friends who care about one another give each other space and permission to grow, change, and evolve. Honor whatever stage your friend is at now. Be supportive, even if that means letting your friend go her own way or giving him space for a time. Try not to hold on to the past or make your friends only into what you want them to be.

"SIT IN REVERIE AND WATCH THE CHANGING COLOUR

OF THE WAVES THAT BREAK UPON THE IDLE SEASHORE

OF THE MIND." —Henry Wadsworth Longfellow

Give Yourself the Gift of Time

What would you do if you didn't have anywhere to go or anything pressing to do? No deadlines, no responsibilities. Set aside a day to do whatever you want—or nothing at all. It's your choice. This is your time. Enjoy it.

MIND: *Take ten*

Ten minutes of meditation twice a day may be the best gift you can give yourself. Meditation quiets the mind to produce physical and emotional benefits. According to the National Institutes for Health, regular meditation can reduce chronic pain, anxiety, high blood pressure, cholesterol, substance abuse, and post-traumatic stress disorder. Take time today—and every day—to meditate, using whatever style you prefer.

BODY: *Take a vacation*

Prevent burnout by taking a vacation. If you can't afford to get away for an extended period of time, consider scheduling a long weekend, with or without family. *Don't* take a working vacation—leave the laptop at home. Rest, relax, recuperate, recharge, rejuvenate, and renew yourself on every level. You'll be healthier—and happier—when you return.

SPIRIT: *Spend time alone*

Set aside a block of time every day—perhaps only ten or fifteen minutes—to be alone. During this time, don't answer the phone or let loved ones disturb you. Turn inward and reflect on things that give you peace and joy. Observe nature. Enjoy a treasured possession. Stroke your pet. Consider this time precious and don't let anything else preempt it.

"What is Paradise? But a Garden, an Orchard of Trees and Herbs, full of pleasure, and nothing there but delights." —William Lawson

Pep Up with Peppermint

One of the tastiest and most versatile herbs is peppermint. Since ancient times, herbs have been used for medicinal, dietary, and spiritual purposes. According to a 2007 survey by the CDC's National Center for Health Statistics, more than half of Americans use complementary and alternative therapies, including herbal medicine. Try these self-care tips.

MIND: *Refresh your thinking with peppermint oil*
The fresh, clean scent of peppermint can stimulate your mind when your attention starts to flag. If you've been plodding along at a boring or mentally taxing task, put a few drops of peppermint essential oil on a cloth handkerchief and smell it. The scent instantly reaches your brain and boosts your alertness.

BODY: *Clear congestion with peppermint*
When inhaled, peppermint's cleansing aroma can help unblock breathing passages in your nose, sinuses, throat, and lungs. If you have a cold or flu, put a few drops of peppermint essential oil on a cloth handkerchief and breathe in its crisp, cool scent to break up congestion. Drink peppermint tea to soothe a sore throat. It's good for easing asthma and coughs, too.

SPIRIT: *Grow peppermint to attract prosperity*
Some herbalists and followers of earth-based spiritual paths believe peppermint has the power to attract prosperity. Its stimulating scent helps speed up results, too. Grow peppermint in your garden or a flowerpot. Care for your plant and, as it grows healthy, so will your finances.

"WE CAN'T SOLVE PROBLEMS BY USING THE SAME KIND OF THINKING WE USED WHEN WE CREATED THEM."

—Albert Einstein

Clarify Your Life Purpose

Today, consider your purpose in life. Your values, priorities, and goals change over time. As a child you may have had an idea about what you wanted to be when you grew up. But what was important to you at ten may not matter much at age thirty or fifty. What role do you want to play now?

MIND: *Make a difference in the world*

Devote time to a cause you feel passionate about. Helping others is a good way to help yourself, according to a study led by Peggy Thoits, sociology professor at Vanderbilt University. It showed that people who did some type of volunteer work were mentally and physically healthier than those who didn't. Having a sense of purpose also enhanced their happiness, satisfaction, and self-esteem.

BODY: *Set health goals for yourself*

Do you want to run a marathon? Lose twenty pounds? Stop smoking? Whatever your health goals are, you'll be more successful if you lay out a game plan. Determine what you are capable of realistically. Don't set the bar so high you'll give up before you reach your goal. Then put your plan into practice.

SPIRIT: *See the world through new eyes*

According to *A Course in Miracles*, a self-study program that encourages inner peace, we don't really see the world around us, we remember it. Notice how you interpret objects around you through preconceptions and past beliefs—it's the first step to seeing anew.

"ALL CREATIVE PEOPLE ARE KIDS AT HEART."

—Steve Carmichael

Give in to Whimsy

Lighten up today! Many spiritual teachers believe life wasn't meant to be so serious. In the book of Matthew, Jesus says, "The Kingdom of heaven belongs to those who are like these children." Try to approach life with an open heart and a playful mind—you may experience unexpected blessings.

MIND: *Read a Dr. Seuss book*

Dr. Seuss's wonderfully witty children's stories delight people of ages. Actors use these entertaining tales as verbal exercises—the can enhance your communication skills, too. Escape into Seuss's fanciful world. Read his books aloud—they're more fun that way. Laugh at the crazy predicaments his characters get into. Twist your tongue around his clever rhymes.

BODY: *Get a messy beauty treatment*

Delightfully messy spa treatments are becoming increasingly popular—and they're deliciously healthy. Mud baths draw off toxins from the body and exfoliate dead skin cells. They also soothe aches and pains. Seaweed wraps stimulate blood and lymph circulation to encourage detoxification of the body. For centuries, this practice has also been used to relieve arthritis and rheumatism, sprains, and skin conditions. Seaweed contains many necessary minerals that your skin absorbs.

SPIRIT: *See beyond the obvious*

Children often see things adults don't: fairies, angels, leprechauns, devas, and imaginary friends. The fact that these beings don't exist in the adult world simply means adults have lost the capacity to see them. Reawaken your perception and expand your vision. You may be amazed at what lies beyond the boundaries of the rational mind.

> "THOUSANDS OF CANDLES CAN BE LIGHTED FROM
> A SINGLE CANDLE, AND THE LIFE OF THE CANDLE
> WILL NOT BE SHORTENED." —The Buddha

Let Other People Guide and Inspire You

A Buddhist proverb says that when the student is ready, the teacher will appear. Today, let other people inspire, guide, and mentor you. You don't have to do it all yourself. Someone who has "been there, done that" can steer you in the right direction and help you avoid pitfalls.

MIND: *Join a support group*
Sharing your problems, questions, and life journey with other people can make the process easier. According to the Mayo Clinic, people who participate in support groups experience a strong emotional connection with other members and see the group as "family." One of the benefits, says WebMD, is realizing that you are not alone and that others share your problem.

BODY: *Hire a personal trainer*
Yes, personal trainers are expensive. But sometimes that investment provides the incentive you need to commit to your fitness program. Professional trainers can tailor an exercise program to your needs and abilities, so you get the most from your workouts. They'll also push you to reach higher goals than you might on your own.

SPIRIT: *Draw a tarot card every morning*
Each morning, before you start your day, ask your higher self for guidance. Then draw a single tarot from a tarot deck. The symbolism on the card will give you direction for the day. It may also signal things to pay attention to and alert you to possibilities that lie ahead.

"ALL GREAT TRUTHS BEGIN AS BLASPHEMIES."

—George Bernard Shaw

Don't Believe Everything You Read

Become more circumspect about what you believe. Every day, some new virus, threat, or scam comes along. If you accept everything you read and hear, you'll scare yourself silly. Pretty soon, you start wondering if it's safe to get out of bed. Bring your critical faculties to bear today to separate truth from fallacy.

MIND: *Check with Snopes*
Do well-meaning friends send you all sorts of "warning" e-mails about scams, charlatans, and downright dangerous people? Before you take those scary stories to heart—and pass them along—check with *www.snopes.com* to find out if they're true. Snopes' investigative team checks into these "urban legends" and debunks a lot of them.

BODY: *Stop using antibacterial soap*
Antibacterial soap helps stop the growth of bacteria and provides protection against infection. However, the prevalence of antibacterial products can lead to "superbugs" that are resistant and more dangerous. Antibacterial soap also kills the good bacteria and can prevent your body from developing its own, natural immunity. In most cases it may be best to wash your hands thoroughly with ordinary soap—fingernails, too—in water that is as hot as is comfortable.

SPIRIT: *Question religious texts*
Just because something appears in a religious text doesn't mean it's definitive. Many ancient writings have been translated numerous times, and words can mean different things in different cultures. Additionally, language evolves over centuries, which can be confusing. Use your own judgment to ascertain a book's intent.

"BY COMMON CONSENT GRAY HAIRS ARE A CROWN OF
GLORY; THE ONLY OBJECT OF RESPECT THAT CAN NEVER
EXCITE ENVY." —George Bancroft

Care for Your Hair

Is your hair in need of some TLC? Frequent washings, hair dryers and
flat irons, chemical coloring, and processing all damage your hair. In
earlier times, hair was considered your crowning glory—it's often the
first thing someone notices about you. Take care of yours today.

MIND: *Consider a new hairstyle or color*
Getting your hair done can get you out of a rut and make you feel
brighter. As you age, oil glands in the scalp dry out, causing your
hair to become brittle. Nearly half of all men can expect some bald-
ing, and most people of European descent will have noticeable gray-
ing by their fiftieth birthdays. Research natural products that restore
color and stimulate hair growth.

BODY: *Be good to your hair with botanicals*
Choose a shampoo and conditioner made from natural plants to
nourish your hair and scalp—or make your own. To treat dandruff,
add nettle extract to your conditioner. To bring out highlights in
blond hair, rinse with chamomile tea. You'll find lots of online sites
that discuss the benefits of botanicals for hair care.

SPIRIT: *What do dreams about hair mean?*
In dreams, your hair can describe how you feel about yourself. Long,
lustrous hair usually signifies a sense of power. Thinning or dull hair
may mean you feel weak or unhealthy. If someone is cutting your
hair, notice who it is. That person may be "cutting you down" and
diminishing your power.

"ALL THE ART OF LIVING LIES IN A FINE MINGLING OF LETTING GO AND HOLDING ON." —Havelock Ellis

Get with the Rhythm

Everything in the cosmos flows with its own rhythm: the tides, the planets, the plants and animals. Today, get in tune with your own rhythms. Struggling against them is like rowing against the tides. Instead, go with the flow. You'll be happier and healthier.

MIND: *Mark nature's rhythms with plants*
Stay in tune with nature's cycles by decorating with seasonal plants. Hang a wreath on your front door and change it every season (or more frequently, if you like). Plant window boxes or containers with seasonal flowers and herbs, and watch them bloom. Put fresh flowers in your home that reflect the time of year.

BODY: *Honor your body's natural rhythms*
Some of us are morning larks, others are night owls. The daily biological cycle, known as the circadian rhythm, exists not only in people but in animals, plants, and other organisms as well. Honor your circadian rhythms. Plan your most challenging activities when your energy is high, and back off when it starts to drop. You'll sleep better if you get in sync with your natural rhythms, too.

SPIRIT: *Chart your biorhythms*
Based on the date of your birth, your biorhythms are natural energy cycles that affect your body, emotions, intellect, and intuition. They continue to rise and fall throughout your life, in a wavelike motion. Each lasts for a specific amount of time. To see when your cycles peak and plummet, go to *www.biorhythm-calculator.net* and get your biorhythms calculated free.

"AN ORGASM A DAY KEEPS THE DOCTOR AWAY." —Mae West

Spark Your Sensuality

How can you add spark to your sex life? Make mutual pleasure a priority. See sex as an equal opportunity experience. A 2006 University of Chicago survey found that equality between the sexes increased sexual satisfaction for both men and women. In countries where male domination prevailed, women's satisfaction tended to be lower.

MIND: *Make a playlist of sexy songs*
Making a sensual playlist with your partner can be erotic. Find music that gets you in the mood—romantic, sensual, or down and dirty. Perhaps include some favorite make-out songs from your youth. Vary the beat so the music shifts as your arousal grows. Start with slow and romantic tunes, then pick up the pace as the excitement between you grows.

BODY: *Stimulate your erogenous zones*
Your body is replete with erogenous zones just aching to be turned on. Although your lips and tongue, nipples, vagina, and penis are the most obvious erogenous zones, consider stimulating other areas of the body: scalp, ears, neck, shoulders, hands, feet, and butt. Each of us is unique, so what turns one person on might not matter to someone else. Experiment and enjoy the process.

SPIRIT: *Make a love talisman*
Make a good-luck talisman to increase the love in your life. In a small box, place some dried red rose petals, a tiny silver heart, and anything else that symbolizes love to you. Tie a red ribbon around the box and place it under your pillow or on your nightstand to enhance love.

"A TATTOO IS A TRUE POETIC CREATION, AND IS ALWAYS MORE THAN MEETS THE EYE." —V. Vale and Andrea Juno

Love Your Tattoo

Are you thinking of getting a tattoo? According to the American Academy of Dermatology, nearly a quarter of people between the ages of eighteen and fifty have at least one. Tattooing dates back more than 5,000 years to the early Egyptians. If you're not sure, try a temporary tattoo before getting the real deal.

MIND: *Choose a meaningful personal symbol*
Since ancient times, people have tattooed themselves for spiritual, symbolic, and cultural reasons. You might wish to get a tattoo that reflects your heritage or spiritual beliefs. Or choose a symbol that has significance for you. You can even design your own. Consider it well—your tattoo will be with you for the rest of your life.

BODY: *Put sunblock on tattoos*
Over time, tattoos can lose their initially vibrancy. Red, orange, purple, and yellow are the most likely colors to fade. The most common reason for fading is exposure to ultraviolet light. To extend the life of your tattoo, wear sunblock when you go outside. Or, consider getting a tattoo in a place where it won't see the sun.

SPIRIT: *Try a henna tattoo*
Temporary *mehendi* tattoos made from the reddish-brown henna plant have a rich spiritual history. In India they are applied as part of a wedding ceremony. In ancient Egypt, they were painted on the pharaohs before mummification to aid them in the afterlife. Avoid black or dark blue "henna" tattoos made with indigo; they can cause adverse reactions.

"A WOMAN IS LIKE A TEA BAG. YOU NEVER KNOW HOW
STRONG SHE IS UNTIL SHE GETS INTO HOT WATER."

—Eleanor Roosevelt

Get Stronger

You are stronger and more capable than you think. However, the strain of daily living can take a toll on even the most powerful people. Try the following suggestions to help you become healthier in mind, body, and spirit.

MIND: *Meditate to strengthen your memory*
A study published in the *Journal of Personality and Social Psychology* found meditation helps reverse age-related memory loss in seniors. Another study, published in the journal *Intelligence*, showed that meditation helped students increase their IQs. Meditate daily to improve analytical and intuitive thinking, as well as awareness and memory.

BODY: *Eat cabbage to build strong bones*
Recent research indicates that vitamin K helps reduce age-related bone loss. One cup of cabbage boasts 85 percent of your daily value of vitamin K. This vitamin fuels the proteins that rebuild bone tissue, which deteriorates as we age. Vitamin K is also thought to positively affect calcium balance, a key mineral in bone metabolism.

SPIRIT: *Use a crystal to strengthen your perception*
Acquire a clear quartz crystal small enough to comfortably hold in your hand. Sit quietly and take several slow, deep breaths to relax. Gaze at the crystal, examining its many intricacies: wisps, inclusions, metallic-like plates, rainbows, and so on. Turn it to see it from different angles. Let your awareness explore deeper and deeper into the crystal. Spend several minutes studying and tuning in to your crystal.

"I'VE ALWAYS KEPT MY DIET SECRET BUT NOW I
MIGHT AS WELL TELL EVERYONE WHAT IT IS.
LOTS OF GRAPEFRUIT THROUGHOUT THE DAY AND
PLENTY OF VIRILE YOUNG MEN AT NIGHT."

—Angie Dickinson

Eat Grapefruit

Start your day with grapefruit. Low in calories and high in vitamins
A and C, beta carotene, and lycopene, it also contains lots of fiber. A
powerful antioxidant, lycopene (found in red and pink varieties) can
help lower blood cholesterol and protect against some types of cancer.

MIND: *Check for adverse reactions with medications*
Grapefruit interacts with many medications, including antidepressants and cholesterol and blood pressure drugs. Researchers believe
compounds in grapefruit juice may block enzymes in the intestines,
preventing them from breaking down drugs. If you are taking any
kind of medication—even over-the-counter products—check with
your doctor to make sure it is safe for you to eat grapefruit.

BODY: *Eat grapefruit for younger-looking skin*
A cup of grapefruit sections contains more than 100 percent of the
Recommended Daily Value for vitamin C. Eating foods rich in vitamin C such as grapefruit may lower your risk of age-related skin
dryness and/or getting wrinkles, according to research published in
the *American Journal of Clinical Nutrition*.

SPIRIT: *Lift your spirits with grapefruit*
The clean, refreshing scent of grapefruit essential oil can lift your
spirits and help counteract feelings of discouragement. Put a few
drops on a clean handkerchief and inhale the aroma to ease stress,
anxiety, and nervous tension. If you're feeling lethargic or apathetic,
sniff grapefruit to wake up your enthusiasm.

"IF YOU WANT TO BE OF GREATEST VALUE TO OTHERS, SEE
THEM AS YOU KNOW THEY WANT TO BE."

—Esther and Jerry Hicks, *The Law of Attraction*

Help Others Do Their Best

Today, focus on a loved one's good characteristics. When you feel
angry or discouraged with someone, remember his or her redeeming
qualities. Point these out. Praise behavior you want to see repeated.
Notice how emphasizing people's goodness strengthens their ability
to overcome their flaws.

MIND: *Emphasize a person's good qualities*

Help people become the best they can be by focusing on their assets
rather than their faults. Studies show that children live up to the
expectations of their elders; the same is true of adults. If someone
doesn't realize his goodness, reveal it to him. Encourage her by
believing in her abilities.

BODY: *Set a good example*

Help a loved one meet health goals by setting a good example—
especially if the loved one is a child. If he wants to lose weight, agree
to get in shape, too. If she wants to start eating a healthier diet, share
nourishing meals with her. Your loved one probably won't do as you
say if it's not what you do. You'll benefit, too, from taking better
care of yourself.

SPIRIT: *Encourage someone's spiritual growth*

Instead of forcing your ideas on someone else, encourage him or
her to seek out answers independently. Whether or not you are reli-
giously oriented, you can nurture someone's search for truth, perhaps by presenting various options and opinions. Trust that a loved
one will find the right path.

"No man is an island entire of itself; every man is a piece of the continent, a part of the main."

—John Donne

Support Sustainability

When it comes to saving the planet, every little bit helps. It's increasingly obvious that we are dependent on one another and our environment. Today, do your part to live more lightly on the earth and encourage health and happiness for all beings.

MIND: *Buy Fair Trade products*
When you buy Fair Trade products, you show support for a more equitable distribution of business risks and rewards between owners and workers in a global economy. The Fair Trade Federation seeks to eliminate forced child labor and to establish fair compensation for labor, workplace safety, and freedom from discrimination. Look for the Fair Trade label on products you purchase.

BODY: *Wear clothing made from natural fibers*
Clothing made from cotton, silk, linen, wool, and other natural fibers allows your body to breathe more freely than garments made from synthetic products. The fibers also wick away perspiration, so you feel more comfortable. And they don't transfer unhealthy chemicals to your skin. These renewable materials are also healthier for the earth, because they generate less chemical pollution. Choose organic materials whenever possible.

SPIRIT: *Thank Mother Earth*
Remember to thank the planet for providing the air, water, food, shelter, clothing, minerals, and everything else you need to live. Develop an attitude of gratitude for Mother Earth and her inhabitants. Become aware of your connection to everything in the world and your interrelationship with it.

"THERE IS DEEP WISDOM WITHIN OUR VERY FLESH, IF WE
CAN ONLY COME TO OUR SENSES AND FEEL IT."

—Elizabeth A. Behnke

Tune Up Your Chakras

Tune up your chakras today to optimize well-being. Eastern medicine
and philosophy recognize a system of energy centers in your body,
called chakras (pronounced *sha kras*). This Sanskrit word means
"wheel" because these centers look like spinning discs or wheels.
Each one influences the well-being of certain parts of your body, some
of which are described below.

MIND: *Balance your brow chakra*

Located between your eyebrows, where your nose joins your forehead, the brow chakra is associated with wisdom, vision, and intuition. When it is balanced, you feel connected to higher knowledge
and can figure things out without worrying. To energize this chakra,
envision indigo light glowing in this area.

BODY: *Energize your heart chakra*

Located in the region of your physical heart, the heart chakra is the
locus of love and connection with others. It is associated with both
your emotions and with physical conditions related to the heart. If
your heart chakra isn't functioning properly, you might experience
coronary problems. Energize this area by envisioning green light
glowing in the area of your heart.

SPIRIT: *Open your crown chakra*

This chakra, located at the top of your head, connects you with your
Source. When it is balanced, you feel a sense of unity and peacefulness.
You experience pure consciousness, the intelligence of the universe, the
feeling that all is one. To balance this chakra, envision violet light glowing at the crown of your head; allow cosmic consciousness to guide you.

> "UNINTENDED HURT IS AS COMMON AS BRANCHES SNAPPED IN WIND. BUT IT IS THE UNACKNOWLEDGED HURT THAT BECOMES A WOUND." —Mark Nepo, *The Book of Awakening*

Heal the Hurt

Pain and suffering are probably unavoidable so long as we are in human form. Whether an injury is emotional, physical, or spiritual, it needs to be addressed and healed, so you can move on in life. Today, focus on healing your own pain or someone else's.

MIND: *Make amends*

If you have hurt someone, accidentally or otherwise, making amends can help ease the pain and bridge the gap between you. Acknowledge your actions and apologize as quickly as possible. Say this directly to the other person if you can, or write a letter to him or her. If this isn't possible, say it mentally as a sort of prayer or blessing.

BODY: *Take arnica*

To ease the pain of bruises, sprains, and other minor aches and pains, try a homeopathic remedy known as arnica montana. Derived from a perennial plant, this natural healer comes in both pill form and salve or gel. Homeopathy is a holistic modality developed in the 1700s by German doctor Samuel Hahnemann.

SPIRIT: *Breathe blue light*

To help ease minor pain, sit or lie in a comfortable place and close your eyes. Breathe slowly and deeply, allowing yourself to relax. Imagine you are surrounded by a bubble of pale blue light. Inhale this blue light as you breathe in and imagine sending it to the painful area. Do this for several minutes, sending soothing energy to the affected site.

"IF YOU CARRY YOUR CHILDHOOD WITH YOU,

YOU NEVER BECOME OLDER." —Tom Stoppard

Reconnect with the Joy of Childhood

Have you forgotten the lighthearted days of your youth, when everything seemed bright and new and exciting? If the stresses and responsibilities of adulthood are weighing you down, take time today to recapture the joy of childhood. Let your mind, body, and spirit blossom with youthful energy.

MIND: *Bake cookies*

Do you remember baking cookies with your mother or grandmother when you were a kid? Many people say the smell of cookies baking brings back fond memories of childhood, warmth, and love. Bake cookies with your own children or a friend's. Decide together on healthy recipes. Have fun decorating the cookies and sharing them with loved ones.

BODY: *Swing*

Did you enjoy swinging as a kid? Studies have shown that the repetitive back-and-forth motion can have positive effects on people of any age. An article published in *Geriatric Nursing* in 2001 reported that ten minutes of swinging in a glider helped patients with dementia become more relaxed and less aggressive.

SPIRIT: *Watch children playing*

Sit on the sidelines of a playground, park, or beach where children are playing. Notice how spontaneous and unabashed they are, and how completely they are focused in the present. Listen to their laughter. Allow their joy to awaken childlike happiness within you.

"THE MIND, ONCE EXPANDED TO THE DIMENSIONS OF
LARGER IDEAS, NEVER RETURNS TO ITS ORIGINAL SIZE."

—Oliver Wendell Holmes

Turn on Your Brain

The jury is still out on whether there's a correlation between brain size and IQ. However, you can make the most of your brain power and hold on to what you've got longer if you nurture your mind. Today, take care of your brain in the following ways. Use it or lose it!

MIND: *Challenge your mind*
Instead of vegging out in front of the TV, read. It's okay to read books you enjoy and that let you escape from your everyday routine. But also read books that challenge your mind with their vocabulary, philosophy, or writing style. Discuss what you've read with friends to further stimulate your mind.

BODY: *Give your brain the vitamins it needs*
To function optimally, your brain needs certain vitamins. Vitamin A helps protect brain cells from harmful free radicals and improves circulation within the bloodstream, and thus to the brain. Vitamin B9 (folic acid) aids cerebral circulation by inhibiting narrowing of the arteries in the neck. Studies suggest it can reduce the likelihood of age-related dementia.

SPIRIT: *Stimulate your psychic skills*
Try this fun game to tap your psychic powers. Close your eyes while a friend puts three different pictures in three plain, identical envelopes. Then hold each envelope individually and try to "see" what's inside. You may pick up a color, shape, or feeling. Write down what you sense. When you've finished, open the envelopes and see how close you came.

"SOME PAINTERS TRANSFORM THE SUN INTO A YELLOW SPOT;

OTHERS TRANSFORM A YELLOW SPOT INTO THE SUN."

—Pablo Picasso

Mellow Yellow

Add a touch of sunshine to your day by connecting to the color yellow. A hue of harmony and balance, it falls in the middle of the visible color spectrum. It also corresponds to the solar plexus chakra in the center of your body, the locus of self-esteem and well-being.

MIND: *Paint your office yellow*
Yellow reminds us of the sun and can make you feel more positive as a result. On dark days or when you're under pressure, yellow brings a sense of lightness and cheer to your work environment. Color researchers also associate yellow with creativity. Working in a yellow room can activate your creative juices and inspire innovative approaches to problem-solving.

BODY: *Eat bananas to improve digestion*
Bananas are high in potassium and pectin, which can aid the digestive tract. They also contain a chemical that nourishes the probiotic bacteria in your colon to aid proper bowel function and improve your digestive ability. Additionally, bananas are rich in tryptophan, which when converted to serotonin, makes you feel more mellow—and when you feel relaxed you can digest your food better.

SPIRIT: *Tap citrine's cleansing power*
This yellowish gemstone is known for its ability to cleanse disruptive energy and negative emotions. Place citrines around your home to harmonize family discord. Wear or carry a citrine to induce calm and help you become less critical of yourself and others. You can also use this stone to clean your other crystals.

"HOLD A TRUE FRIEND WITH BOTH HANDS."   —African Proverb

A Show of Hands

Treat your hands kindly today. They are one of the most important and amazingly intricate parts of your body. Pay attention to the many ways you use your hands today: to feed and dress yourself, write a poem, or touch a loved one.

MIND: *Get a manicure*

Treat yourself to a little luxury today—get a manicure. Your fingertips have an abundance of nerve endings, which makes them very sensitive to touch. Having your nails done and your hands massaged can relieve stress. Manicured nails, like makeup and jewelry, add a finishing touch to your appearance. Clean, neatly trimmed and filed nails are a sign of good grooming for men, too.

BODY: *Try hand reflexology*

Usually we think of reflexology as a type of foot massage, but your hands have reflexology points on them, too. According to this holistic healing modality, each part of your hands relates to another part of your body. The fingers link to the head and neck, the middle of the palm to the torso, and the part near the wrist to the lower sections of your body. Massaging points on your hand can aid problems elsewhere in your body.

SPIRIT: *Thumbs-up*

Whenever you meet people, notice their thumbs. In the art of hand analysis, the thumbs equate to your sense of self. A large thumb indicates a strong self-image, or perhaps arrogance and egotism. A rigid thumb suggests stubbornness or a fixed nature. If the lower section is thinner than the end portion, the person is sensitive to the needs of others.

"A LAKE CARRIES YOU INTO RECESSES OF FEELING OTHERWISE IMPENETRABLE." —William Wordsworth

The Healing Power of Water

More than 70 percent of the earth is covered by water. Up to 60 percent of your body is water. Today, let yourself be nourished mentally, emotionally, physically, and spiritually by water.

MIND: *Listen to the soothing sound of water*
Listening to the soothing sounds of water can calm stress, promote mental relaxation, and help you sleep better. If you don't have the good fortune to live on the ocean, a lake, or a river, you can still enjoy the peaceful sounds of moving water. Install a fountain or water garden, inside or outside your home. Or, listen to CDs that feature the sounds of rippling brooks and waves breaking on the shore.

BODY: *Stay hydrated*
Your body is largely water, especially your brain. To make sure it operates properly, drink plenty of water. Water contributes to the proper function of your nervous, respiratory, circulatory, and elimination systems. It also aids skin and joint health. Research suggests that drinking water from plastic bottles may contribute to certain types of cancer, so choose glass or stainless steel containers instead for drinking water.

SPIRIT: *Meet the undines*
Metaphysicians speak of spirit beings known as elementals who typify the four elements: earth, air, fire, and water. The undines abide in water, and they concern themselves with the realm of the emotions. Theory says they can help you with your relationships, but you must give them a gift first. Pour a little perfume into a body of water to win their favor.

"IF IT KEEPS UP, MAN WILL ATROPHY ALL HIS LIMBS

BUT THE PUSH-BUTTON FINGER." —Frank Lloyd Wright

Educate Yourself about Electronics

Evaluate your electronics today—are electromagnetic frequencies (EMFs) harming your health? Numerous studies have linked EMFs with health risks, including leukemia, brain tumors, and chronic fatigue. The Environmental Protection Agency suggests there is "reason for concern." You can't avoid all EMFs, but you may be able to reduce your risk.

MIND: *Reduce cell phone use*

Cell phone use changes brain activity, according to a study by Dr. Nora Volkow of the National Institutes of Health and published in the *Journal of the American Medical Association*. The electromagnetic radiation increases glucose metabolism in the brain in people who use their cell phones for fifty or more minutes per day. It's too early to tell, however, if this effect is dangerous. Consider reducing the time you spend on the phone or use an earphone instead of placing the phone directly to your ear.

BODY: *Don't sleep under an electric blanket*

Electric blankets may be a factor in childhood cancers and miscarriages, according to some researchers. Dr. Nancy Wertheimer and Ed Leeper discovered a connection between magnetic fields and childhood leukemia. To be safe, switch to natural wool blankets or down comforters.

SPIRIT: *ESP: Faster than e-mail*

Try sending a friend a message using only your mind. Extrasensory perception (ESP) is immediate and knows no boundaries. If you find yourself thinking about someone you haven't been in communication with lately, that person may be trying to contact you.

"SOME PEOPLE ARE ALWAYS GRUMBLING BECAUSE ROSES HAVE THORNS. I AM THANKFUL THAT THORNS HAVE ROSES."

—Alphonse Karr

A Rose Is More Than a Rose

Today, enjoy flower power. No flower is more beloved and symbolic than the rose. Poets, artists, gardeners, and of course lovers have long drawn inspiration from the rose—you can, too.

MIND: *Say it with roses*
We associate roses with love and romance. But in the Victorian period, flowers were assigned specific meanings, and sending a bouquet was a way to send a beautiful message. Red roses signified passion; pink ones represented happiness. White roses meant innocence, but also "I am worthy of you." Yellow ones could indicate either friendship or jealousy. Send someone roses to convey your intentions.

BODY: *Drink rose hip tea*
Rose hips are the reddish-orange seedpods in roses, especially wild varieties such as sea roses. They're chock full of vitamin C—more than in oranges. Rose hips also contain vitamins A, D, E, and flavinoids. To make rose hip tea, chop five rose hips and steep them in hot water for about ten minutes. Add honey if you like. You can also find rose hip tea bags in supermarkets.

SPIRIT: *Attract love into your life*
Fill your hands with red rose petals. Take them outside your house or apartment and scatter them on the walkway leading to your home. As you do, say: "Love find your way. Love come to stay." Repeat this intention three times. Keep one rose petal and place it where you'll see it often to draw love into your home.

"ORDINARY RICHES CAN BE STOLEN; REAL RICHES CANNOT. IN YOUR SOUL ARE INFINITELY PRECIOUS THINGS THAT CANNOT BE TAKEN FROM YOU." —Oscar Wilde

Nurture Your Financial Well-Being

Especially in uncertain economic times, managing your money and finding new ways to increase your prosperity become more important than ever. Today, focus on your finances. Keep a positive attitude instead of worrying about money matters—you're more likely to attract wealth if you believe you can.

MIND: *Don't tolerate bank fees*

Does your bank add fees for various services? Many charge check cashing fees, minimum balance fees, and overdraft fees. Call your bank and ask them to waive these fees. Ask what they are willing to do to keep you as a customer. Maybe they offer a type of account that's better for you. If your bank won't work with you, find one that will.

BODY: *Meditate to reduce job-related stress*

Your health and productivity affect your earning ability. Health care and absenteeism due to workplace-related stress in the United States costs $300 billion annually. Meditation, however, reduces stress, fatigue, and health problems in workers. A study published in the journal *Anxiety, Stress, & Coping* noted meditation also improved workers' overall health and effectiveness.

SPIRIT: *Energize your home's wealth sector*

The ancient Chinese art of feng shui connects your home with your life. For example, the section at the back and left of your home, when you are standing at your front door looking in, is associated with wealth. You can energize this section to attract money by placing a healthy plant there.

"PREPARE AND PREVENT; DON'T REPAIR AND REPENT."

—Anonymous

Safety First

Remember Benjamin Franklin's words: "An ounce of prevention is worth a pound of cure." Don't leave yourself and your loved ones vulnerable to injuries and harm that could have been prevented. Think ahead and take precautionary measures to ensure your safety on every level.

MIND: *Purchase a fire extinguisher*
Does your home have a fire extinguisher? Do you know how to use it? In many cases, you can prevent a small fire from escalating into a big one that could damage your property or worse. Learn what type of fire extinguisher is best for your purposes. Position it in a readily accessible place and make sure everyone in your household knows how to use it.

BODY: *Wear a life jacket*
Even if you are a good swimmer, protect yourself when boating. Wear a life jacket whenever you are kayaking, sailing, or motorboating. An injury in a boating accident could render you unable to swim. So might cold water, cramps, exhaustion, or other physical conditions. According to the Centers for Disease Control and Prevention, nearly 4,000 people drowned unintentionally in the United States in 2007. Play it safe.

SPIRIT: *Tap the protective qualities of ash trees*
The ancient Druids respected the power and wisdom of trees. They believed the ash tree offered protection to those who sought it. Plant ash trees around your home to protect it. If that's not possible, sprinkle bits of ash bark around your property. Or, gather ash leaves and bark and add them to a protection amulet.

"HE WHO TAKES MEDICINE AND NEGLECTS TO DIET

WASTES THE SKILL OF HIS DOCTORS." —Chinese Proverb

Eat Well to Stay Well

You've heard the saying, "You are what you eat." Yet the standard American diet consists largely of unhealthy fats, sugar, animal products, and processed carbohydrates. Today, commit to eating more fruits and veggies, complex carbs, and healthy fats—and consider the tips below.

MIND: *Plan meals for a week at a time*

Instead of scurrying around trying to figure out what to make for dinner when you're hungry and tired from work, plan your meals a week in advance. Ask family members for input. Think of creative ways to use leftovers. Good planning will cut down on supermarket shopping trips. You'll save money, time, and aggravation. You'll also be less likely to stop at a fast-food place.

BODY: *Clean out your refrigerator*

Do you have food molding in the back of your refrigerator? Spoiled food poses health risks for you and your family. Go through your refrigerator and toss everything that isn't fresh. Organize what's left so you can find it easily. Clean out your refrigerator on a regular basis to prevent the possibility of food poisoning and other problems.

SPIRIT: *Use nutrients more efficiently*

Before each meal, set an intention that everything you eat will nourish your body optimally and be utilized by your system for your best advantage. Enjoy eating slowly, attentively, and in a relaxed manner. Being mentally and spiritually receptive to the nourishment your food provides will help your body assimilate and integrate nutrients more efficiently.

"DON'T SEEK, DON'T SEARCH, DON'T ASK, DON'T KNOCK,

DON'T DEMAND—RELAX. IF YOU RELAX, IT COMES."

—Osho

You Deserve a Break Today

If you're like many people, you burn the candle at both ends. There never seem to be enough hours in the day to accomplish everything. Now could be the time to reverse the trend. Instead of pushing forward, relax today.

MIND: *Break up your schedule*

You'll be more productive if you break up the pace of your day. Instead of working flat out, which can lead to burnout, design a pattern that fits your needs. For instance, work at your desk for an hour, then get up and do something else for ten minutes—go to the copy machine, take a quick walk, do the laundry, or eat a healthy snack. Balance intense mental focus with relaxation and creative time.

BODY: *Put your feet up*

Elevating your feet helps prevent varicose veins and edema, and improves blood circulation. Lie on your back on the floor. Put a pillow under your hips. Lift your feet and put them up against a wall for five minutes, twice daily. If you watch TV or read in bed, put pillows under your feet to elevate them six inches or so.

SPIRIT: *Enjoy moss agate*

This pretty green stone can refresh your mind, body, and soul by connecting you with the earth's rejuvenating powers. Carry a moss agate in your pocket to lessen past pains and help you find peace in the present. It also lets you appreciate the beauty in the world around you.

"LOVE IS A SYMBOL OF ETERNITY. IT WIPES OUT ALL SENSE OF TIME, DESTROYING ALL MEMORY OF A BEGINNING AND ALL FEAR OF AN END." —Anonymous

Show Your Love

In the crush of daily responsibilities and general busyness, we sometimes forget to show our mates how important they are to us. When we take our partners for granted, the spark between us flickers and goes out. Often it's the little things, the daily expressions of affection, that keep the fire burning.

MIND: *Send a card*

Don't wait for a birthday, anniversary, or other special occasion to send your partner a greeting card. Receiving a cheerful card that says "I love you" will brighten your mate's day—especially if he or she isn't expecting it. Send a card just to let your beloved know you are thinking of him or her.

BODY: *Hold hands*

Touching your partner often is a way to strengthen your connection and say, "I care." Nonsexual touch enhances the production of oxytocin, lowers blood pressure, and relieves stress, according to a study published in 2008 in the journal *Psychosomatic Medicine*. Holding hands is something you can do anywhere, in private or public.

SPIRIT: *Send your partner good vibes*

It doesn't matter whether you are sitting side by side or miles apart, you can send "good vibes" to your partner. Imagine a beam of light connecting the two of you at your hearts. Then imagine your love traveling along that beam of light, flowing from you to your beloved, and enhancing his or her well-being on every level.

"Even if I knew that tomorrow the world would
go to pieces, I would still plant my apple tree."

—Martin Luther

An Apple a Day

Eat an apple today, and consider not only its health merits, but also its long and diverse history. No fruit has as much mythological significance attached to it as the apple. This fruit of the goddess is linked with the many faces of femininity, from Eve's rebellion to the homey symbolism of apple pie.

MIND: *Notice an apple's symbolism*
Cut an apple open and you'll notice the seeds form a star pattern inside—the symbol of hope. It also resembles the human body, the points representing the head, arms, and legs. This symbolism suggests the positive healing properties in apples.

BODY: *Eat apples to protect against cancer*
The saying "an apple a day keeps the doctor away" may have validity. The flavonoids in apples may protect you against two types of cancer: bladder and lung. Based on studies done at the University of Hawaii's Cancer Research Center, the flavonoid quercetin found in apples may protect against certain forms of cancer.

SPIRIT: *Fruit of the goddesses*
The apple appears often in mythology, as a fruit attributed to various goddesses. In Genesis, the apple that Eve presents to Adam represents knowledge. Apples are also linked with Aphrodite, the Greek goddess of love, so sharing an apple symbolizes sharing love.

"LIGHT GIVES OF ITSELF FREELY, FILLING ALL AVAILABLE
SPACE. IT DOES NOT SEEK ANYTHING IN RETURN; IT ASKS
NOT WHETHER YOU ARE FRIEND OR FOE. IT GIVES OF ITSELF
AND IS NOT THEREBY DIMINISHED." —Michael Strassfeld

Here Comes the Sun

Become a sun worshiper today. The sun is one of our greatest
resources. Life on earth would be impossible without it. Consider
ways to utilize the sun's energy to improve your health and well-
being on every level.

MIND: *Go solar*
Research the benefits of installing a solar heating and/or hot water
system in your home. Especially if you live in a sunny area, you
could save money and reduce your dependency on nonrenewable
fuel sources. Making your home more energy-efficient may also
qualify you for tax credits.

BODY: *Expose your body to moderate amounts of sun*
We've heard lots about the dangers of too much sun, but too little can also be harmful. Studies show that sunshine strengthens
your immune system. The Center for Natural Medicine points out
that sunshine can help lower cholesterol, blood pressure, and blood
sugar. Research by Dr. Esther John of the North Carolina Cancer
Center suggests that sunlight may reduce the risk of breast cancer by
as much as 40 percent.

SPIRIT: *Install solar lights along your walkway*
Eastern philosophy says chi (the enlivening force that energizes the
earth) is attracted to light. Direct chi to your home so it can bring
positive energy to you and your family. Place easy-to-install solar
lights along your driveway or the walkway to your home—they'll
light the way at night.

"NO ONE IN THE WORLD NEEDS A MINK COAT BUT A MINK."

—Murray Banks

Be Kind to Animals

Play with your pet today. Animals give us unconditional love. They can also help you relax and improve your health. According to the Centers for Disease Control, bonding with an animal companion lowers blood pressure, decreases cholesterol, and eases depression associated with loneliness.

MIND: *Adopt a pet from a shelter*

If you are thinking about getting an animal companion, consider adopting a stray rather than buying a purebred pet. Bringing a pet home from a shelter might save the animal's life—and make your life happier. Every year millions of cats and dogs are put to sleep because they are homeless. Donate money to support the rescue efforts of homeless and injured animals.

BODY: *Eat less meat*

Even if you don't choose to become a vegetarian, you can reduce the amount of meat and animal products you consume. If you eat four or more ounces of meat a day, you have a greater risk of dying from any cause during the next ten years than people who eat less, according to the National Cancer Institute. You'll also support animal welfare and planetary health.

SPIRIT: *Connect with animal deities*

In many cultures, gods and goddesses take animal forms. The Egyptians revered Bast the cat goddess and Sekhmet the divine lioness. In Babylonion myth, a dragon called Tiamat brought light to the world. The Native Americans honor all sorts of spirit animals. Research the powers of animal deities to see how they may benefit you.

"DON'T LET YOUR MIND BULLY YOUR BODY INTO
BELIEVING IT MUST CARRY THE BURDEN OF ITS WORRIES."

—Astrid Alauda

Don't Get Bent Out of Shape

We are more alike than we are different. Today, rather than focusing
on how you are different from your neighbors, try to see how you
are similar. The world is home to all of us, and it will take all of us
to save it.

MIND: *Don't take things personally*
Often we become offended by something a person does or says,
when it might have little to do with us. Even when a criticism is lev-
eled at you, it may have more to do with that person's unresolved
issues than yours. Remember the saying, when someone points a
finger at you, three fingers are pointing back at him or her.

BODY: *Stand up straight*
Notice your posture today. Do you hunch over when you walk? Slump
at your desk? When you stand up straight, you relieve pressure on
your vertebrae and reduce the risk of back problems. Keeping your
neck straight can help prevent headaches. You'll also strengthen your
abdominal muscles by standing up straight. Good posture keeps your
body in balance and enables you to stay more flexible.

SPIRIT: *Relax your spiritual views*
Although religious groups may position themselves in opposing
camps, if you look at what the original teachers of Christianity,
Islam, and other spiritual paths have said, you may find they advo-
cate similar views. Instead of focusing on the differences between
you and someone of a different faith, try to see the similarities.

"THE FENCE THAT MAKES GOOD NEIGHBORS NEEDS A GATE TO MAKE GOOD FRIENDS." —Anonymous

Bond with Others

During humanity's early days of existence, individuals worked together, hunted together, and lived together for protection. For primitive societies, interaction was essential. It still is. Studies show people with strong social networks are healthier and happier. Reach out to others today.

MIND: *Be a good neighbor*

In our busy, technology-driven world, we are becoming increasingly isolated from one another—many of us don't even know our neighbors. Today, reach out to a neighbor. Run an errand for an elderly or shut-in person. Shovel snow from a neighbor's sidewalk. Take a neighbor flowers from your garden. Establishing a positive connection with your neighbors will benefit everyone.

BODY: *Join a yoga class*

No matter how old you are or what your physical condition is, you can do some type of yoga. One of yoga's key components is proper breathing. Even if you aren't very limber or strong, you can still benefit from yoga's gentler movements. In a class, you'll also meet people like you who are concerned about improving their health and well-being.

SPIRIT: *Participate in a spiritual circle*

If you don't belong to a particular religious faith, you can still enjoy the social and spiritual benefits of belonging to a circle of like-minded people. Some churches, such as Unity and the Unitarian Universalists are spiritual, but not necessarily religious. Or, join a meditation group, a peace group, prayer circle, twelve-step program, or other group with a spiritual focus.

"PEOPLE FROM A PLANET WITHOUT FLOWERS WOULD THINK WE MUST BE MAD WITH JOY THE WHOLE TIME TO HAVE SUCH THINGS ABOUT US." —Iris Murdoch

Flower Power

For centuries, people who understood the medicinal and magical properties of flowers concocted remedies from them to heal everything from burns to broken hearts. Flowers are one of nature's many gifts to us, for healing, food, and spiritual sustenance. Enjoy them today.

MIND: *Breathe the scent of hyacinth*

The refreshing scent of this spring flower can ease stress, lethargy, and depression. Essential oil of hyacinth increases mental alertness and sparks greater clarity. When you feel mentally burned out or overwhelmed, dab a little hyacinth oil on your wrists to help balance your emotions and quiet your thoughts. It can also inspire creative thinking and imagination.

BODY: *Cook with sunflower oil*

Sunflower oil provides essential fatty acids and is low in polyunsaturated fats, so it can be a good choice if you are trying to cut back on unhealthy fats. Sunflower oil also contains high amounts of the antioxidant vitamin E, which protects your cells. Because you can cook with it at high temperatures, substitute this beneficial oil for lard when frying food.

SPIRIT: *Make an offering of daisies*

According to mythology, Freya, the Norse goddess of love and passion, is particularly fond of daisies. If you want to solicit her help with a matter of the heart, place a vase of daisies in your bedroom as an offering to Freya. Their cheery presence will make you feel more optimistic, too.

"If I'd known I was going to live so long,
I'd have taken better care of myself." —Eubie Blake

Fit Healthy Practices into Your Daily Routine

Find opportunities to get healthy today. Your daily activities provide possibilities for well-being, in a relatively painless and practical way. Every little bit helps!

MIND: *Practice mindfulness in daily tasks*
The technique known as mindfulness meditation teaches you to pay complete attention to whatever you are doing, as a way of relieving stress. When you are raking leaves, folding the laundry, or cleaning the bathroom, focus your mind on the experience. Avoid the temptation to think about work, your relationships, or what you'll eat for dinner. In this way, every mundane chore becomes an opportunity to meditate.

BODY: *Park as far as possible from your destination*
When you go to the mall or the supermarket, park your car at the far end of the lot. That way you'll incorporate extra exercise into your shopping trip. If you weigh 160 pounds, you'll burn about 85 calories per mile walking at a moderate pace and more if you walk faster. Walking also improves circulation, respiration, and muscle tone.

SPIRIT: *Practice gratitude constantly*
Cultivate an awareness of the blessings in your life and appreciate them. Be thankful for sunshine; be thankful for rain. Be thankful for your body. Be thankful for the food you eat, your morning shower, the electricity that lets you see in the dark, and all the other little things that make your life good. Get in the habit of saying "thank you" often.

"IS EVERYTHING AS URGENT

AS YOUR STRESS WOULD IMPLY?"   —Carrie Latet

Say No to Stress

Everyone has different stressors—people or events that cause pressure—at any given moment. Remember that some stressors, like a new job offer, are good, while others, like a sick child, are bad. Indeed, even a bad stressor like a sick child can become good when you take a day off work to spend quality time with your child. Much of how you see stress is all about perspective.

MIND: *Identify your stressors*
How do you find your stressors? Imagine you are a reporter, writing a stress story from your life. Describe the situation, the people involved, and other factors that play a role in the story. Writing down a stressful situation helps you see what exactly is stressing you out so you can take steps to reduce stress.

BODY: *Cut down on sugar*
During times of stress, many people turn to sugar for a quick pick-me-up. However, after a temporarily lift, you experience a drop in blood sugar. This leaves you feeling even more anxious, tired, jittery, irritable, and tense. Your adrenals work even harder, causing more stress and more exhaustion. Reduce your intake of all sugars—including sugar substitutes—to ease stress on your body.

SPIRIT: *Awaken divine energy*
Some yogis say you can attract the conditions for peace and relaxation through various spiritual practices. Awareness can occur spontaneously, through dedicated practice, or through the transference of energy from teacher to student. Meditation, yoga, chanting, and prayer are vehicles for awakening the divine energy within you.

"A PERSON SHOULD GO OUT ON THE WATER ON A FINE DAY
TO A SMALL DISTANCE FROM A BEAUTIFUL COAST, IF HE
WOULD SEE NATURE REALLY SMILE."

—Augustus William Hare and Julius Charles Hare

Take the Waters

Our bodies are largely composed of water. Without water, we can
only live a few days. How does your inherent need for water, and
your link to it psychically as well as physically, lead you to connect
with this vital element?

MIND: *Consider a water filtration system*

Consider installing a water filtration system that removes impuri-
ties and contaminants. It's also a good idea to choose a system that
adjusts the pH value of your water to help balance your body's pH.
There are plenty of water filtration systems on the market—research
which will best serve your needs.

BODY: *Bathe in Epsom salts*

Epsom salts are high in magnesium, an essential mineral in which
many of us are deficient. The National Academy of Sciences says
magnesium deficiency can contribute to numerous ills, including
heart disease, arthritis, and digestive problems. Taking supplements
may not be effective, because magnesium isn't absorbed easily by
the stomach. However, you can obtain magnesium through your skin
by taking a bath in Epsom salts.

SPIRIT: *Infuse water with sound*

Make healing water by infusing it with sound vibrations. Sound
healing uses sound to balance body, mind, and spirit. Put spring
water in a "singing bowl" made of metal or crystal; tap the bowl to
generate healing vibrations. The resonance will imprint the water.
Drink the water to heal your entire system.

"LIFE SHRINKS OR EXPANDS IN

PROPORTION TO ONE'S COURAGE." —Anaïs Nin

Increase Your Self-Confidence

You are as powerful as you believe yourself to be. Most of us under-estimate ourselves, and resign ourselves to being less than we could be. Today, take steps to boost your self-confidence. Believe in your-self, and other people will, too.

MIND: *Join Toastmasters to present a better image*
Public speaking intimidates many people. Since 1924, Toastmas-ters International has been training people to feel confident speak-ing in front of a group. Their meetings train you not only how to get up and speak in public, but how to be a leader. Other people in the group give you feedback that can help you present yourself more effectively, whether you're interviewing for a job or giving a wed-ding toast.

BODY: *Exercise to boost self-confidence*
When you feel good about the way you look, your confidence soars. Other people feel that energy, too. If you aren't happy with your appearance, it may be time to establish a workout program to get in shape. Exercise also increases production of endorphins, serotonin, and dopamine in your brain to enhance positive feelings.

SPIRIT: *Project a powerful self-image*
Everyone is afraid at times, but even when you feel inwardly anx-ious you don't have to show it. Remember the saying "fake it 'til you make it"? See yourself glowing with radiant, golden light. Imagine every cell in your body shining as if the sun were within you. Envi-sion golden radiance flowing out to everyone you meet and impress-ing them favorably.

"AGE IS AN ISSUE OF MIND OVER MATTER. IF YOU

DON'T MIND, IT DOESN'T MATTER." —Various attributions

Turn Back the Clock

You don't have to subscribe to an arbitrary timetable. Today's sixty is yesterday's forty. In 1900, life expectancy was forty-seven years. Now you can expect to live seventy-eight years, or more. Lifestyle is the biggest factor in longevity and well-being. You *do* have a choice.

MIND: *Shift your attitude about aging*
As the average lifespan increases, our attitudes about aging are changing. Baby Boomers, in particular, refuse to accept outdated beliefs about life as senior citizens. Changing your ideas about "old age" really can help you live longer and better. Study results published in *U.S. News and World Report* in 2006 indicated that optimistic people suffer fewer heart attacks, strokes, arthritis, and other physical ailments.

BODY: *Eat nonmeat sources of protein*
Your need for protein increases as you age, but many older people eat less protein than they did when they were young. Protein isn't synonymous with meat and animal products. Increase your consumption of legumes, whole grains, nuts, soy products, and fish to reduce your fat intake, while still getting the protein you need.

SPIRIT: *Meet Hecate*
The ancient Greeks called the goddess Hecate the "guardian of the crossroads." The Holy Crone, Hecate rules the third phase of a woman's life: post-menopause. She is the divine depiction of wisdom, dignity, and the freedom that can only come for women after their children are grown. Connect with Hecate and explore the gifts of maturity.

"BREAD FEEDS THE BODY, INDEED,

BUT FLOWERS FEED ALSO THE SOUL." —The Koran

Plant Plants

Humankind is dependent on the plant kingdom, even though we sometimes appear not to realize this. Today, become more conscious of your connection to plants and the benefits they offer you. Few things nourish the mind, body, and soul like plants.

MIND: *Provide a habitat for birds*
Want to enjoy bird-watching and birdsong? Different birds require different types of habitat: tall trees, shrubs, hedges, or marsh vegetation. Research the species that are native to your area, especially those that are endangered or that could use a little extra assistance from you. Where do they like to nest? What are their main sources of food? Plant whatever will contribute to their well-being.

BODY: *Plant an herb garden*
Since ancient times, people have planted herb gardens for medicinal, culinary, and mystical purposes. Herbs are easy to grow, and nothing spikes up a recipe like fresh herbs. Choose your favorites, depending on how much room you have for planting. Even if you live in an apartment, you can grow herbs in containers. Consider raising some to eat and some to use for healing purposes.

SPIRIT: *Tap mystical qualities in plants*
Botanicals have long played an important role in talismans and amulets. If you want to attract love, for example, cultivate roses, red clover, raspberries, or myrtle. If you seek financial gain, grow mint, parsley, or money plant. Basil, fennel, and garlic offer protection. Study the mystical qualities of flowers and herbs, and plant those that serve your needs.

"The higher your energy level, the more efficient your body. The more efficient your body, the better you feel and the more you will use your talent to produce outstanding results."

—Anthony Robbins

Tune Up the Higher Chakras

Today, familiarize yourself with the higher chakras. Usually, we recognize only the seven main chakras in the body. But in actuality, there are many of these energy centers, and each has its own unique properties and influences.

MIND: *Gain inspiration through the causal chakra*
Located just behind the upper part of your skull, this chakra lets you tune out everyday noise and find peace. When your mind is relaxed, you are able to receive inspiration from higher sources. Place a piece of the stone known as kyanite near the back of your head to facilitate serenity and receptivity.

BODY: *Activate the earth star chakra to get grounded*
This energy body, located below your feet, connects you to the secure foundation of the earth. In meditation or chakra healing practices, you can strengthen your connection with the earth and draw supportive energy from her through this chakra. Placing hematite, onyx, or smoky quartz at your feet can support this chakra.

SPIRIT: *Receive Divine wisdom through the stellar gateway chakra*
The stellar gateway chakra is located above your head, and it serves as a spiritual conduit between you and your Source. Meditation can help you to open and balance this chakra, so you receive guidance from a higher level of wisdom. Positioning an amethyst here can help you move beyond illusions and self-imposed limits.

"IT'S NO STRANGER TO LIVE TWICE THAN TO LIVE ONCE."

—Voltaire

Look to the Future

How would you like to be remembered in the future? What mark do you want to leave? Often fear keeps us from facing the future. Today, instead of trying to avoid the unavoidable, embrace it and put your stamp on it.

MIND: *Write your memoirs*

Don't let invaluable stories go untold. Future generations will appreciate knowing about the experiences of loved ones who came before them. Write your memoirs for your children, grandchildren, and great-grandchildren to enjoy. Include personal details and anecdotes that will enrich their appreciation of their ancestors.

BODY: *Become an organ donor*

More than 100,000 people are waiting for new organs. You can give the gift of life after you leave this world. One organ donor can save up to eight lives. If you would like to offer someone a second chance after you pass on, register to be an organ donor. In the United States, go to the U.S. Department of Health and Human Services website, *www.organdonor.gov*, to sign up as an eye, tissue, and/or organ donor.

SPIRIT: *Consider the possibility of an afterlife*

Most religious traditions uphold the concept of an afterlife, although they don't necessarily agree on the details. A 2005 CBS News survey found that 78 percent of Americans believe in an afterlife. Belief in life after death can even enhance your time on earth, according to a study by Fordham University psychology professors who found that terminally ill patients who believed in an afterlife suffered less despair and anxiety.

"DO NOT VALUE MONEY FOR ANY MORE NOR ANY LESS THAN
ITS WORTH; IT IS A GOOD SERVANT BUT A BAD MASTER."

—Alexandre Dumas

Say Yes to Prosperity

Economic ups and downs may be outside your control. You can control your reactions to financial conditions, however. As numerous motivational leaders and writers such as Norman Vincent Peale have said repeatedly, your attitude contributes to your economic status.

MIND: *Choose to pursue wealth*

We've come to equate poverty with spirituality and selflessness, whereas the pursuit of wealth often has been perceived as a selfish desire and greed. The Law of Attraction, a concept popularized in *The Secret*, says wealth is neither good nor bad. The universe will give you whatever you think you deserve. It is up to you to choose.

BODY: *Get a massage*

Regular massages let your body relax, which reduces blood pressure and the amount of the stress-hormone cortisol in your blood. Thus, massage helps protect you against ailments ranging from the common cold to coronary disease. When you're healthy and feeling good, you can be more productive, make better decisions, and will miss less time from work—all factors that contribute to income.

SPIRIT: *Use feng shui to attract wealth*

According to the ancient Chinese philosophy of feng shui, the portion of your home that is at the back left when you enter your front door relates to wealth. Red is considered a lucky color in China, and black is the color of money. Use these colors in your home's wealth sector to help you attract prosperity.

"In Italian, a belladonna is a beautiful lady;
in English, it's a deadly poison." —Ambrose Bierce

Viva Italiano!

The Italians seem to exude a love of life unmatched by any other culture. Today, take a tip from the Italians. Enjoy the good things they value and extol: love, good food, wine, art, and opera.

MIND: *Take a more relaxed attitude toward life*
The average Italian workweek is about six hours shorter than the American one. Italians take more time off for vacation, too—the standard is four weeks compared to two in the United States. In general, the Italian attitude is more relaxed and less hurried, emphasizing the enjoyment of life rather than climbing the corporate ladder as fast as possible.

BODY: *Eat an Italian diet*
Studies show the Italian diet has many health benefits and may actually help you live longer. Consider some of the main ingredients in Italian meals. Tomatoes supply vitamins C and K. Olive oil provides antioxidant properties and monounsaturated fats. Garlic is a powerful blood cleanser. Beans add healthy fiber. Red wine can reduce the risk of blood clots. In addition, Italians don't eat much meat, preferring fish or poultry instead.

SPIRIT: *Make an amulet with Italian herbs*
Herbalists who tap the mystical properties of herbs consider basil, fennel, garlic, and oregano to provide protection. You can use these herbs to make a protection amulet. Dry the herbs, then place them in a small drawstring pouch. Hang it on your front door to safeguard your home.

"LOVE IS THE ONLY SANE AND SATISFACTORY ANSWER TO

THE PROBLEM OF HUMAN EXISTENCE." —Erich Fromm

Love Makes the World Go 'Round

Humans require love to flourish. Today, attune your thoughts to love. In his bestselling book, *Think and Grow Rich*, author Napoleon Hill explained that it is by our predominant thoughts that we thrive. You'll feel and look better when love is on your mind and in your heart.

MIND: *Do something scary with your partner*
Taking minor risks can escalate your feelings of attraction for a person. When you experience something scary, you get an adrenaline rush that boosts your excitement. Your heart beats faster—it's a little like falling in love. To heighten your thrills, enjoy an adventure together. Ride on a roller coaster, see a scary movie, or go hang gliding.

BODY: *Sample scents-uous surroundings*
Including delicious smells in your bedroom will make it seem more like a love nest than just a place to sleep. Each of us has our favorite scents, but studies indicate that many men respond to spicy smells such as cinnamon buns and pumpkin pie; women get turned on by the smell of licorice and leather. Vanilla, jasmine, musk, and orange seem to appeal to both sexes.

SPIRIT: *Get a joint astrological reading*
A type of astrology called synastry evaluates the relationship between two people. An astrologer compares the sun, moon, planets, and other factors in your birth chart to your partner's to see what your strengths and weaknesses are. You can get a computer printout version online at *www.astro.com*.

"When you are sorrowful look again in your heart,
and you shall see that in truth you are weeping
for that which has been your delight."

—Kahlil Gibran

Give in to Grief

Many people avoid grief. It's messy, uncontrollable, and even scary. No one wants to look out of control. Yet, we cannot prevent losses from occurring, and if grief is not addressed, it will soon control you. Try these ways to cope with grief.

MIND: *Honor the loss*

Honor the loss. Put flowers on a grave, write in a journal, plan a ritual, or do whatever you need to do to feel better. Seek therapy or talk with a trusted friend. When you can smile through tears, you have triumphed over grief. Your mind is healing, and the crippling stress around the loss will soon be a thing of the past.

BODY: *Cry to overcome stress*

Make time to let off steam and to honor the loss so that grief doesn't consume you. When you feel grief welling up inside you, take several deep, slow breaths. Allow the feelings to surface. Let yourself cry as loud and hard as you need to. Crying releases stress that might otherwise lead to serious illness, such as stroke or coronary problems.

SPIRIT: *Accept the cycle of creation and destruction*

Shiva, a Hindu god with arms spiraling out from his body in a circle, symbolizes creation and destruction. For Hindus, life and death are bound in a never-ending cycle. Grief, too, is a process of creation and destruction.

"SOME PEOPLE, NO MATTER HOW OLD THEY GET, NEVER LOSE THEIR BEAUTY—THEY MERELY MOVE IT FROM THEIR FACES INTO THEIR HEARTS." —Martin Buxbaum

Save Your Skin

Beauty is more than skin deep, but keeping your skin looking beautiful can help you feel better about yourself in every way. You know the basics: limit exposure to sunshine, use a good moisturizer, and drink plenty of water. Here are some other suggestions to consider.

MIND: *Research natural makeup*
Natural and organic makeup is becoming more popular and more readily available. Mineral products that rely on finely ground minerals such as mica, titanium dioxide, and zinc oxide may be healthier for your skin than conventional foundations, blushers, and powders. Choose cosmetics that lack fragrance, dyes, binders, and preservatives—they're kinder to your skin. To locate sources, visit *www.greenpeople.org/organicskincare.html*.

BODY: *Eat fruit to nourish your skin*
Beautiful skin begins inside with the nutrients you consume. Fruit is full of healthy substances, including vitamins A and C, folic acid, potassium, antioxidants, phytochemicals, and fiber. Your best bets are apples, bananas, berries, citrus fruit, and melons because of their high fiber and nutrient content.

SPIRIT: *Send positive energy to your skin*
Close your eyes and rub your palms together vigorously. Then hold your hands up about six inches in front of your face, with your palms facing you. Imagine positive energy flowing from your hands to your face, rejuvenating and refreshing your skin. See imperfections disappearing. Envision your skin glowing with good health.

"SUCCESS IS A JOURNEY, NOT A DESTINATION."
—Ben Sweetland

The Secret of Success

As many motivational teachers have pointed out, you are the only person who can bring about your success. Some people are born with silver spoons in their mouths, but others, such as Oprah and J. K. Rowling, have achieved wealth and success on their own. Underlying success is a belief in yourself.

MIND: *Be a team player*
No matter what your position within the company, you are interdependent upon the other people in the operation. A team approach will not only inspire staff members to work together for the common good, it will encourage harmony among employees. When you aim for a joint goal, where everyone prospers, your chances of accomplishing your intentions multiply exponentially.

BODY: *Energize your Center of Power*
Acupressure links the energy point known as the Center of Power with self-confidence. When you are facing a challenge or feel your self-confidence dwindling, press this point to reduce confusion, anxiety, or a sense of helplessness. Press your index and middle fingers to your solar plexus (halfway between your heart and belly button) for a minute. Repeat as necessary.

SPIRIT: *Believe your hopes are possible*
Napoleon Hill, author of the bestseller *Think and Grow Rich*, counseled that in order to receive the success you desire, you must first believe it is possible. Choose a touchstone that will serve as a reminder of your objective, perhaps something that symbolizes your goal. Whenever you start to doubt, turn to your touchstone and reaffirm your intention to succeed.

"YOU CAN LIVE FOR YEARS NEXT DOOR TO A BIG PINE TREE, HONORED TO HAVE SO VENERABLE A NEIGHBOR."
—Denise Levertov

Appreciate Pine Trees

It's no surprise that we choose to erect pine trees in the dead of winter. Their everlasting greenery reminds us that the spirit, too, is eternal. Today, regardless of the season, appreciate what pine trees offer us beyond their endearing symbolism.

MIND: *Cleanse the air with pine*
Let the clean, fresh scent of pine purify the air in your home, office, or sacred space. Whether you burn pine incense or a pine-scented candle, the area will seem fresher and more inviting as a result. In aromatherapy, the scent of pine eases nervousness and stress-related conditions, and strengthens your will.

BODY: *Sprinkle pine nuts on your salad*
Pine nuts come from various types of pine trees, and are more than just a tasty addition to salads. Chocked full of antioxidants including vitamins A and E, they counteract free-radical damage. Their oleic acid (a monounsaturated fat) contributes to healthy heart function by controlling cholesterol levels. With high levels of vitamin K, they aid blood clotting. Pine nuts even contain lutein, which benefits vision.

SPIRIT: *Pine symbolizes eternal life*
In *Tree Magick,* author Gillian Kemp connects the pine tree with celebration, partly because it remains green even during the harsh, cold winter months. Thus, the pine symbolizes life everlasting. It also represents endurance and permanence. Although we usually decorate our homes with pine boughs only during the winter, the fresh, clean smell of pine can be purifying and invigorating at any time of the year.

"WHEN WE ARE NO LONGER ABLE TO CHANGE A SITUATION,
WE ARE CHALLENGED TO CHANGE OURSELVES."

—Victor Frankl

Get Unstuck

We tend to fall into habitual patterns, thinking and doing things the
same way year after year. Today, focus on how to move beyond those
old patterns to become more creative, productive, and happy. Here
are some suggestions to try.

MIND: *Have a yard sale*
Get rid of all that stuff you no longer use or need, that is cluttering up
your home or garage. Hold a yard sale. Other people may be thrilled
to get something they need at a good price. You'll make extra cash
and free up space in your home. Coordinate with friends or neighbors and host a group sale—it's more fun that way.

BODY: *Make nutrition a priority*
Become more conscious of what you eat. Focus on what you *can* eat
rather than what you can't. Include lean proteins, complex carbohydrates, fruits and vegetables, and healthy fats in every meal. This
doesn't mean you can never enjoy your favorite junk food, only that
most of your meals and snacks will be good for you.

SPIRIT: *Cut cords that bind*
Close your eyes and imagine a situation in which you feel stuck.
Envision your hands and feet are tied. See yourself picking up a
knife and cutting the rope binding your hands, then the rope that
binds your feet. Shake your hands and feet as you experience a wonderful sense of freedom. You may receive guidance about how to
extricate yourself from the limiting situation.

"TRUE SILENCE IS . . . TO THE SPIRIT WHAT SLEEP IS TO

THE BODY, NOURISHMENT AND REFRESHMENT."

—William Penn

Quell Your Need for Noise

In a world filled with constant noise, you may have a hard time hearing the quiet voice of your inner guidance. Today, find ways to reduce the noise in your environment and within yourself. You may not be able to tune out all distractions, but you don't have to escalate them.

MIND: *Turn off media*

It may seem hard to disconnect from the continual buzz of information. If you spend most of your free time watching TV, listening to the radio, texting, or surfing the Internet, you are overdue for some quiet time. Are you using media as a way to avoid dealing with personal issues? Turn everything off for a while and look inward.

BODY: *Go for a walk*

Go for a walk by yourself, preferably in a peaceful, natural setting. Nature has a powerful rejuvenating effect on our minds and bodies. Psychotherapist Sarah Nakatsuka of Vancouver Island, Canada, even recommends walking in nature as part of her patients' treatment program. If you walk after dinner, you'll burn off calories. You may also discover the wonderful self you've been neglecting.

SPIRIT: *Be receptive to spiritual guidance*

When you are quiet, you are more able to receive guidance from higher sources. Sit peacefully with your eyes closed. Breathe slowly and relax. Envision a purple channel of light at the top of your head, stretching toward the sky. Allow insights to flow from the Divine, through this channel, and into your mind.

"I WILL LOVE THE LIGHT FOR IT SHOWS ME THE WAY; YET I WILL LOVE THE DARKNESS FOR IT SHOWS ME THE STARS."

—Og Mandino

Learn to Love the Dark

Do you feel uncomfortable in the dark? Many people associate darkness with danger or even evil—a fear on which scary movies capitalize. At night, the feminine or yin principle operates. Getting in touch with this energy can stimulate your intuition and imagination.

MIND: *Examine your ideas about the dark*
We often connect darkness with the hidden side of our personalities and the unconscious. Your attitudes about darkness can be clues to how you feel about your own "darkness" and your feminine side. Spend some time reflecting on these ideas. To achieve harmony, it's necessary to make friends with your dark side.

BODY: *Eliminate light in your bedroom*
Light affects your natural sleep patterns. When nighttime comes, your body increases its production of melatonin so you can sleep. But when you are exposed to light, the pineal gland, which is sensitive to light, stops producing melatonin. If you are experiencing a sleep disorder, eliminate all lighting from your bedroom—even a small night-light may interfere with your innate rhythms.

SPIRIT: *Become a moon worshiper*
Since ancient times, the moon and the night have been connected with the Divine Feminine. Go outside at night and gaze at the sky. You cannot see clearly, so you must use your inner sight to interpret your surroundings. Allow yourself to feel the presence of feminine mystery, magic, and power.

> "IT IS EXERCISE ALONE THAT SUPPORTS THE SPIRITS,
> AND KEEPS THE MIND IN VIGOR." —Marcus Tullius Cicero

Get Toned

Men and women weren't designed to sit around all day, doing nothing. We are creative beings who thrive on challenges. Today, apply yourself mentally, physically, and spiritually to strengthen what you've got. Your reach should always exceed your grasp.

MIND: *Tone your mental muscles*

We used to think that once nerve cells died they weren't replaced, but recent studies show that new nerve cells can arise in a few regions of the brain, even in older brains. Word games that challenge your brain can help prevent age-related deterioration. Choose a word of five or more letters. Then see how many other words you can make from those letters.

BODY: *Lift weights to build muscle*

Starting at age thirty, you begin to lose muscle mass. The good news is, you can replace lost muscle; you just have to work at it. Building muscle not only helps you look toned, it decreases your chances of getting osteoporosis. A few times a week, lift weights. Lifting 85 percent of your maximum ability is most effective for reducing body fat and boosting metabolism.

SPIRIT: *Use sapphires to improve your insight*

Crystal workers connect blue gemstones with intuition and insight. Sapphires, in particular, are believed to enhance your powers of clairvoyance. Relax and hold a sapphire in your palm. Gaze at it as your mind grows quiet. After a few moments, you may start to receive insights. Practice doing this regularly to strengthen your ESP.

"RULES ARE MOSTLY MADE TO BE BROKEN AND ARE TOO OFTEN FOR THE LAZY TO HIDE BEHIND."

—Douglas MacArthur

Break the Rules

Give yourself permission today to do some little things you don't usually think you should do. Nothing dangerous or illegal, just things you have accepted as "rules"—perhaps because other people told you this was the "right" way. Notice that the sky doesn't fall if you step outside your self-imposed limits.

MIND: *Wear your pajamas all day*
Lounging around in your pj's doesn't mean you are sloppy or indolent. It just means you want to be comfy. If you have to dress up for work during the week, give yourself a break today. The key is not to judge yourself; just see how it feels.

BODY: *Eat dessert first*
From childhood, we've been told we can't have dessert until we finish dinner. Today, change your ordinary routine and eat dessert first. So what if it ruins your appetite? You can wait a while, then eat the rest of your meal—or save it for tomorrow. Try not to hear your mother's voice scolding you; just enjoy an uncommon treat.

SPIRIT: *Find God/dess anywhere*
If you were raised to think you had to go to church or temple to connect with the Divine, try another approach. Some belief systems hold that all life is holy and that God or Goddess exists everywhere, in everything. Go to a peaceful spot in nature and observe the wonders you see. Can you sense the majesty of the Creator in the birds, trees, and rocks?

"LIFE IS RATHER LIKE A TIN OF SARDINES—
WE'RE ALL OF US LOOKING FOR THE KEY." —Alan Bennett

Flow with Life's Changing Rhythms

Life is like a beach: sometimes the waves sweep away sand; other times they bring it back. Instead of struggling against the tide, learn to go with the flow. Today, align yourself with the rhythm of the universe and let it support you.

MIND: *Recognize your mental rhythms*
Some days your mind is sharp and clear, whereas other days it seems dull or fuzzy. According to the study of biorhythms, your mental cycle lasts thirty-three days, half on the high side, and half on the low side. Try to schedule challenging projects or those that require creativity when your cycle is on the upswing. Do routine tasks on the down days.

BODY: *Try bioidentical hormones*
Hormone replacement therapy has come up against a lot of opposition for potentially increasing risks of breast cancer, heart disease, and stroke. However, bioidentical hormones differ vastly from the synthetic kind. These are natural hormones that are specifically compounded, or mixed, for the needs of each individual woman. Extracted from a chemical found in yams and soy, they can aid in the comfortable transition through menopause.

SPIRIT: *Consult with a numerologist*
Your life is a cycle, beginning on the day you were born. A numerologist can calculate your personal rhythms and cycles, to assess when you are likely to experience advantageous periods or challenging ones. Armed with this knowledge, you can make better decisions in every area of your life.

"WEALTH FALLS ON SOME MEN AS COPPER DOWN A DRAIN."

—Seneca

Learn the Value of Copper

For centuries, people have worn copper bracelets to aid arthritic pain and stiffness. However, copper's benefits are far more extensive. It's necessary for good mental and physical health as well as for high-speed Internet connections.

MIND: *Investigate copper's value*
If you're not in a position to invest in gold or silver, consider copper. Some analysts predict a burgeoning copper market. Copper is used in construction, power generation, electronics, transportation, telecommunications, the automotive industry, and heating and cooling systems. As Third World countries develop, the need for copper may skyrocket.

BODY: *Eat copper-rich foods*
Copper helps the body make red blood cells and hemoglobin (needed to carry oxygen to red blood cells) by aiding in the absorption of iron in the body. In addition, copper helps make hormones that regulate a variety of body functions, including heartbeat, blood pressure, and wound healing. Copper is found mostly in organ meats, especially liver, as well as in seafood, nuts, seeds, poultry, legumes, and dark green leafy vegetables.

SPIRIT: *Wear copper to attract love*
Some spiritual traditions connect copper with Venus, and other goddesses of love. Do you want to attract a new lover or increase the love in a current relationship? Wear a copper bracelet, necklace, or earrings to solicit aid from the love goddesses.

"THE ONLY WAY YOU MAY CORRECT THE BAD THINGS IN
YOUR PAST IS TO ADD BETTER THINGS TO YOUR FUTURE."

—Shiloh Morrison

Cleanse Yourself of Toxins

We live in an increasingly toxic world. Toxic chemicals and pollution are the most obvious forms, but attitudinal toxins in the form of
anger, violence, fear, and racism also affect us. Today, consider how
toxic substances, ideas, and behaviors may be impacting your life,
and explore ways to eliminate them.

MIND: *Express your emotions*
When you repress an undesirable emotion (such as anger, guilt, or
self-hatred) psychological damage can occur. Unexpressed emotions
can become toxic and damage you on every level. Talk to a trusted
friend, if you feel comfortable doing so. Or, consider seeking professional therapy. Acknowledging your emotions and working through
them will reduce their negative power.

BODY: *Detoxify your brain*
If you suspect that you may have been exposed to dangerous fumes
or toxic chemicals, consult a doctor for a thorough analysis and
treatment. To cleanse your brain (and your body) of common toxins, such as pollutants or household chemicals, you can try flaxseed,
licorice root, ginseng, ginkgo biloba, aloe vera, grapefruit pectin,
papayas, slippery elm bark, alfalfa, peppermint, and/or ginger. You
can take capsules or use the ingredients to make tea.

SPIRIT: *Protect yourself against psychic toxins*
Whenever someone thinks hateful thoughts or wishes another person
ill, toxic energy is generated and released into the atmosphere. To protect yourself against these bad effects, envision yourself surrounded
by a ball of white light that deflects anything that might harm you.

"ORDER IS NOT PRESSURE WHICH IS IMPOSED ON
SOCIETY FROM WITHOUT, BUT AN EQUILIBRIUM
WHICH IS SET UP FROM WITHIN." —Jose Ortega y Gasset

Establish Equilibrium

Life is a balancing act. If you are always struggling to keep too many balls in the air, it's time to focus on finding harmony. Today, attempt to establish equilibrium within and in your outer life. Balance means nothing in excess, everything in moderation.

MIND: *Make a mandala*
Mandala means "circle" in Sanskrit. These elaborate, circular paintings symbolically depict the universe, with the heavens at the top and earth at the bottom. They also represent your own inner and outer nature, thus signifying unity and harmony. Paint one to bring your mind into balance. Include symbols, images, and colors that are meaningful for you.

BODY: *Try yoga's Tree Pose*
This posture improves balance and concentration, while also strengthening your legs and ankles. Stand straight, then shift your weight to one leg. Bend the other knee, swing it out to a 90-degree angle, and bring your foot up until your sole presses against the inside of your straight leg's knee. Place your palms together in prayer pose and hold them at your chest. See if you can balance this way. After taking a few breaths, change legs.

SPIRIT: *Find equilibrium with lithium quartz*
Carry this crystal to help balance you on every level. Considered a natural antidepressant by crystal workers, its soothing properties aid you in dealing with stress and emotional issues. It also works to align your energy field and bring your system into alignment.

"EVERY THOUGHT IS A SEED. IF YOU PLANT CRAB APPLES,
DON'T COUNT ON HARVESTING GOLDEN DELICIOUS."

—Bill Meyer

Lift Your Spirits

Economic worries, crime, war, natural disasters—no wonder so many people feel discouraged or depressed these days. You know it's important to maintain a positive attitude, but that's sometimes easier said than done. If you need a lift today, consider the following suggestions.

MIND: *Ask your doctor about SAMe*
SAMe (pronounced *Sammy*) is a form of the amino acid methionine that occurs naturally in the body. It appears to increase the levels of certain neurotransmitters, and may affect moods and emotions. In nine studies, SAMe compared favorably with antidepressant drugs. Some researchers have found that SAMe supplementation has improved mood disorders, without the side effects of other antidepressants (such as weight gain, headaches, sleep disturbances, and sexual dysfunction).

BODY: *Move your body*
In his book *Integrative Medicine*, David Rakel reports that more than 10,000 trials have examined the relationship between exercise and mood, showing that exercise may be just as effective in treating depression as psychotherapy. Exercise stimulates circulation and increases blood flow to all parts of the body and brain. Walk, jog, swim, lift weights, do yoga or tai chi—it all works.

SPIRIT: *Burn calming incense*
In Buddhist tradition, burning incense is a spiritual ritual and an adjunct to meditation. Choose frankincense, lavender, lemongrass, sandalwood, or vanilla. These soothing scents will help to relax your mind and calm your spirit. All-natural incense from plant materials is better than synthetic varieties.

"Life is too short to sleep on low-thread-count sheets." —Leah Stussy

Get Your Zs

If you feel drowsy sitting at your desk, or fall asleep as soon as your head hits the pillow, you may be sleep deprived. Chronic sleep dysfunction affects forty million Americans, according to the National Institute of Neurological Disorders and Stroke. Most adults require seven to eight hours of sleep per night, but many get much less. Try these suggestions to get the rest you need.

MIND: *Visualize safety from the storm*
Instead of counting sheep, imagine you are safe in your home while a storm rages outside. The storm symbolizes your racing thoughts. In your mind, see yourself making sure all the windows and doors are shut tight. Do whatever makes you feel secure: check the furnace, unplug the computer. Then envision yourself crawling into a warm, comfy bed and snuggling peacefully under the covers.

BODY: *Try hops*
A thousand years ago English brewers began using hops as a preservative. They discovered that their pickers tired quickly when working. Science has since recognized the power of hops as a sedative. Hops calm the body, soothe muscle spasms, relieve nervous tension, and promote restful sleep. To counteract insomnia, make a tea with hops and drink it at bedtime. Capsules are also available.

SPIRIT: *Examine precognitive dreams*
Sometimes dreams give you a glimpse into future events. Precognitive dreams often seem more realistic and less symbolic than ordinary dreams. If you believe you've had a precognitive dream, take note. It might be preparing you for what lies ahead.

> "OUR MOST BASIC COMMON LINK IS THAT WE ALL INHABIT
> THIS SMALL PLANET. WE ALL BREATHE THE SAME AIR."
>
> —John F. Kennedy

A Breath of Fresh Air

With each breath you take today, become more aware of yourself, your desires and priorities, and your journey through life. Become aware of the air you breathe, without which you would soon cease to exist. As yoga postulates, through breath work you can reconnect your body and mind, and discover your spirit.

MIND: *Attend a lecture or class that intrigues you*
We don't use all of our brain power in our everyday lives. You have plenty of room in there for new ideas. Listening to new discoveries, technical advances, philosophies, and so on will excite your curiosity and stimulate your brain. Sweep the dusty old concepts away and open yourself to fresh possibilities.

BODY: *Open your windows*
Make sure your home is well-ventilated. Open the windows whenever possible and consider exhaust fans or air-to-air heat-exchanging devices that draw fresh air in through one duct and expel it through another. Make sure stoves and heaters vent outdoors. Keeping your house closed tight not only prevents harmful pollutants from dissipating, but also promotes sick building syndrome.

SPIRIT: *Connect with the air spirits*
Metaphysicians believe nonphysical entities reside in the four elements: earth, air, fire, and water. Sylphs occupy the element of air. If you look closely, you may see them as tiny sparks or Tinkerbell-like beings. Befriend these spirits and they will assist you in handling mental tasks or matters involving communication.

"I THINK WE DREAM SO WE DON'T HAVE TO BE APART SO LONG. IF WE'RE IN EACH OTHER'S DREAMS, WE CAN PLAY TOGETHER ALL NIGHT."   —Bill Watterson, *Calvin and Hobbes*

Make Love a Priority

Today, let your love shine brightly. Delight in it. Proclaim it proudly. Indulge its demands and cravings. Let it bring out your best.

MIND: *Put a love note on your partner's pillow*
Write a love note and pin it to your partner's pillow. It can be something as simple and heartfelt as "I love you." Or, copy a favorite love poem that expresses your sentiments. If you prefer, write something racy—tell your lover what you'd like to do with him or her tonight. Add a piece of dark chocolate.

BODY: *Make love in different places*
Your home offers plenty of great places to have sex. Changing locations can add spice to your love life. Some tried-and-true spots include the kitchen table, the counter, the laundry room (with one of you on the washer during the spin cycle), over the back of the couch, and the shower. Use your imagination.

SPIRIT: *Design a special love symbol together*
Create a special symbol that only the two of you will understand. It could combine letters from both of your names, images that you both enjoy, or anything else that represents love and togetherness to you. Display the symbol in your office, print it on a T-shirt, or utilize it in any way that will make you think of your lover whenever you look at it.

"THE WORST ENEMY TO CREATIVITY IS SELF-DOUBT."
—Sylvia Plath

Believe in Yourself

Motivational speakers and spiritual teachers agree that if you believe in yourself, you can accomplish great things. Self-doubt, however, is like water thrown on a fire. Today, consider the following suggestions to help you overcome self-doubt.

MIND: *Use your imagination*
According to Dr. Frank Lawlis in *The IQ Answer*, "The mechanism in the brain follows the imagery process . . . we only know our world through our senses and our interpretations of those sensations." When you engage in imagination, the imagery stimulates the same neurological network as the actual experience. Your prefrontal cortex seeks to create what you think you want. Thus, envisioning exactly what you want helps you create the desired outcome.

BODY: *Let aromatherapy increase your self-confidence*
Scents trigger the brain's limbic system, causing nearly instantaneous responses. Some aromas have been shown to strengthen feelings of self-confidence, including bergamot, frankincense, orange blossom, and sandalwood. Put a few drops of these essential oils on a cloth handkerchief and sniff them periodically throughout the day. Or, blend them with a carrier oil (such as grape seed oil) and apply them to your skin.

SPIRIT: *Wear tiger's eye*
This golden stone has long been associated with personal power and wealth. Linked with the radiant energy of the sun, it gives you the confidence to take action and make decisions. Carry one with you when you have an important meeting—it will help you make a good impression.

"THE HUMAN FOOT IS A MASTERPIECE OF ENGINEERING

AND A WORK OF ART."   —Leonardo da Vinci

Treat Your Feet with Respect

Most of us will experience foot problems at some time in our lives. It stands to reason that the more you abuse your feet, the more likely you are to suffer pain later on. Your feet do yeoman's service—treat them with the kindness and respect they deserve today. You'll feel better all over.

MIND: *Purchase comfortable shoes*
Those stiletto platform shoes may be ruining your feet. Pitch those dominatrix heels into the back of your closet and buy some comfortable shoes that let you walk with ease. Consider having a podiatrist make custom orthotics to provide proper support and balance for your feet.

BODY: *Soak your feet*
Treat your feet—soak them in a hot spa bath, scented with aromatherapy bath salts. Make your own using Dead Sea or Epsom salts. Add fifteen to twenty drops of your favorite essential oil to three cups of salt and mix well. To promote relaxation, use essential oil of lavender, lemongrass, or vetiver. Put an ounce of aromatic salts in a spa footbath and enjoy.

SPIRIT: *Walk barefoot in nature*
Let your spirit connect with Mother Earth by walking barefoot. Take off your shoes and feel the soft grass caress your feet. Let your feet sink into warm sand as you stroll along the beach. Your feet have dozens of sensitive, reflexology points that send healing signals to every part of your body. Feel the earth nurturing you with every step.

"TIME YOU ENJOY WASTING, WAS NOT WASTED."

—John Lennon

Take It Easy

Give yourself permission to take it easy today. Make relaxation and fun a priority. You may not be able to avoid all chores, but fit a healthy amount of downtime into your schedule.

MIND: *Balance work and play*

What's your work-to-play ratio? Keep a journal for at least a week to assess how much time you devote to work and how much to play/relaxation. (Don't count sleeping.) You may be surprised to discover how lopsided your scale is. If you log in sixty hours a week working, commuting, and getting ready for work, but only ten hours relaxing, it could be time to make some adjustments.

BODY: *Try valerian instead of Valium*

Called "the Valium of the nineteenth century" (though it has no chemical similarity to Valium), the herb valerian (*Valeriana officinalis*) is a common sedative used worldwide. In Europe, it is prescribed for anxiety. Herbalists treated nervous tension and panic attacks with valerian. This safe non-narcotic herbal sedative is often combined with other herbs to make pain-relieving remedies, as it can relax muscle spasms. Although valerian has been widely studied, how it works remains a mystery.

SPIRIT: *Practice awareness*

Buddhist monk Thich Nhat Hanh teaches that mindfulness—awareness of what's around you at the present moment—is key to inner peace. Stop and notice a tree outside the window, a picture on your desk, or that beautiful apple on your lunch tray. Take several minutes to just explore the object with one or more of your senses.

"FROM THE BITTERNESS OF DISEASE MAN LEARNS
THE SWEETNESS OF HEALTH." —Catalan Proverb

Make Wellness a Priority

What does wellness mean to you? Back in 1948, the World Health Organization pointed out that wellness is "not merely the absence of disease or infirmity." Wellness "is a state of complete physical, mental, and social well-being." Spiritual wellness also contributes to health on every other level.

MIND: *List your wellness needs*

Take some time to explore what you need to do to meet all of your physical, relational, and emotional needs every day, in order to maintain wellness. Make a list and prioritize them. Attending Pilates class might be sixth on your list; reading a bedtime story to your children might be number two. Are you meeting these needs daily and weekly?

BODY: *Try Zumba*

Want to have fun while you work out? Try Zumba, an energetic dance-fitness program that lets you burn off calories and tone your body by dancing to lively Latin music. Introduced in 2001, Zumba now claims more than ten million weekly participants. Many dance studios, fitness centers, and even YMCAs now teach Zumba. Or, visit *www.zumba.com* to find a class in your area.

SPIRIT: *Practice detachment*

Recognize that you are not attached to conditions that surround you. Learning to detach can help you find greater peace. When you possess objectivity, difficult emotions no longer dictate your actions. Detachment doesn't mean not caring. In fact, detachment can be a form of showing love and respect for others, trusting them to make their own choices.

"THE MORE TRANQUIL A MAN BECOMES, THE GREATER IS HIS SUCCESS, HIS INFLUENCE, HIS POWER FOR GOOD. CALMNESS OF MIND IS ONE OF THE BEAUTIFUL JEWELS OF WISDOM."

—James Allen

Be More at Ease

Today, find ways to be more at ease and to slow the hectic pace of life. Speeding up and multitasking don't enable you to accomplish more; they may actually make you less effective. You'll be happier and healthier, too, if you lighten up and approach your day in a more relaxed manner.

MIND: *Wear pastels to lighten up*

Psychological researchers have found that colors have the ability to influence emotional and physical reactions temporarily. To lighten your mood, wear pastels. Yellow can help you feel more optimistic; light blue gives a sense of peace and calm; pink makes you feel more friendly and affectionate.

BODY: *Don't eat on the run*

If you eat standing up, while you're working at your computer, or in your car, you aren't getting the most from your meals. Sit down and enjoy what you eat. Relax; chew slowly and completely. This enables digestion to start in your mouth, so your body assimilates nutrients better. You'll probably eat less this way, too.

SPIRIT: *Use a mala*

A mala is a string of smooth beads used by Buddhists, Hindus, and others as an aid to meditation and prayer, in a manner similar to a rosary. The practice of using malas dates back to about the eighth century. A typical mala contains 108 beads, made of wood, gemstones, or other materials.

"WE ARE LIVING IN A WORLD TODAY WHERE LEMONADE IS
MADE FROM ARTIFICIAL FLAVORS AND FURNITURE POLISH
IS MADE FROM REAL LEMONS." —Alfred E. Neuman

Eat Healthier

Do you really know what you're eating? If many of your meals come
from fast-food take-out establishments, you can be pretty sure you
are ingesting things that may not be good for you. Learn more about
the food you consume and become more discriminating.

MIND: *Read labels*

The U.S. Food and Drug Administration requires all packaged foods
to display a Nutrition Facts Label. This label provides consumer information about calories, fats, cholesterol, sodium, sugar, fiber, proteins,
vitamins, and minerals that are contained in the food. Compare products before you buy them. Two items that seem nearly identical may
contain different amounts of healthy or unhealthy ingredients.

BODY: *Stop drinking sodas*

Soft drinks are highly acidic, and colas are the most acidic of all.
Studies show that cancer cells grow in an acid environment. When
your body's pH level is acidic (less than 7, which is considered neutral), you are at higher risk for developing cancer. One of the easiest
ways to raise your body's pH is to stop drinking sodas.

SPIRIT: *Dowse for food allergies*

You may not realize you have food allergies because your reaction
isn't strong enough to cause a trauma. But food allergies can still
impair your well-being. Here's an easy way to check. Hold a pendulum over a particular food and ask "Is this good for me?" If the pendulum swings side-to-side, the answer is "no."

"A DREAM IS THE MIND'S WAY OF ANSWERING A QUESTION
IT HASN'T YET FIGURED OUT HOW TO ASK." —*The X-Files*

What Are Your Dreams Trying to Tell You?

The symbolic nature of dreams can make them challenging to understand. Consider the main themes and images in your dreams. Notice how a dream feels to you. Pay attention to puns, too. If you dream you only have one leg, it could mean you don't have a leg to stand on with regard to a certain situation.

MIND: *Know when your dreams are speaking to you*
A dream that repeats is trying desperately to get your attention. Usually, dreams speak in symbols. For instance, if you've been ignoring a dream's message, you might dream of a teacher shouting to a classroom of unruly students, "You're not listening to me."

BODY: *Dreams can pinpoint health issues*
Sometimes dreams alert you to health issues or problems, using the language of symbolism to communicate. If you dream about a stopped-up toilet, your elimination system may need cleansing. Dreams may also suggest possible treatments. Notice if you are eating a particular food in a dream and what your reaction to it is—this could signal dietary needs.

SPIRIT: *Look for spirit animals in your dreams*
Native Americans speak of spirit animals in the nonphysical realms who offer guidance to humans. Often they appear to us in dreams. When you dream of an animal, consider the characteristics of its earthy counterpart to determine its message. Dreaming of a fox may advise being clever; a squirrel may suggest stockpiling resources.

"HAPPINESS OFTEN SNEAKS IN THROUGH A DOOR

YOU DIDN'T KNOW YOU LEFT OPEN." —John Barrymore

Find Excuses to Enrich Your Daily Life

You've heard the saying, "Life is what you make of it." Today, make the most of those ordinary moments that you usually waste. The key is to stay attentive and seek to enrich your appreciation of the possibilities available in your daily life.

MIND: *Find excuses to talk to your children*

According to A. C. Nielsen statistics, parents average 3.5 minutes per week in meaningful conversation with their children. By comparison, the average child watches 1,680 minutes of television per week. Find opportunities to share ideas with your kids. Schedule activities and outings that will provoke discussion. Invite them to share their opinions, instead of discouraging them.

BODY: *Find excuses to exercise*

Your daily routine and activities offer plenty of opportunities for sneaking in exercise. For instance, take the stairs instead of the elevator. Do semi-squats while you are waiting "on hold." Position your phone a distance from your desk so you have to get up to answer it. Rake leaves rather than blowing them away.

SPIRIT: *Find excuses to be amazed*

Pay attention to things you ordinarily overlook or take for granted. Notice the iridescent colors on a beetle. Watch how acrobatically a squirrel leaps from branch to branch. Observe a delicate blade of grass pushing up through a concrete sidewalk. Once you start looking for them, you'll find lots of things to be amazed about.

"BE INFINITELY FLEXIBLE AND CONSTANTLY AMAZED."
—Jason Kravitz

Stay Limber

Staying active is essential in order to stay limber, not only physically but mentally and spiritually as well. If you don't exercise your mind and body, they will stagnate like a body of water blocked with debris. Today, find ways to keep flexible.

MIND: *Learn a foreign language*
Keep your brain limber by learning a foreign language. According to a University College of London study, published in 2004, learning a new language not only lets you converse with and connect to more people, it also builds gray matter and keeps your mind flexible. You assimilate new information, strengthen memorization skills, and relearn rules about grammar.

BODY: *Do the twist*
Loosen up periodically while sitting at your desk. Turn as far as you can to your left, holding on to the back and arm of your chair for leverage. Hold this position for a count of fifteen, then slowly unwind. Then do the same thing, turning to your right. Repeat this three times, every hour to keep your back, neck, and shoulders limber and relieve muscular strain.

SPIRIT: *Have a spiritual adventure*
Have you wanted to visit a sacred place, such as Machu Picchu in Peru or the caves of the ancient Anasazi in New Mexico? Don't let self-limiting thoughts such as being too old or out of shape keep you from having the adventure you seek. For twenty-eight years, beginning at age forty-four, Mildred Lisette Norman Ryder, known as "Peace Pilgrim," walked 25,000 miles, crossing the United States seven times.

"FEAR IS ONLY AS DEEP AS THE MIND ALLOWS."

—Japanese Proverb

Reduce Your Fear Factor

In our society, fear is endemic. Studies indicate that people who regularly watch the news and violent TV shows believe the world is more dangerous than it actually is. Instead of focusing on fearful matters, today find ways to keep fear at bay.

MIND: *Don't watch violent shows*

Check movie ratings and reviews before going to the theater. Even a PG-13 film may have plenty of graphic violence, so be sure to read why the movie has been given its rating. Don't watch violent TV programs, either. According to A. C. Nielsen statistics, the average child sees 8,000 murders on TV by the time he or she finishes elementary school.

BODY: *Stop worrying about your health*

Focusing on illness may actually contribute to physical ailments. Anxiety, stress, and your mental attitude adversely impact physical health. Ohio State University researchers Ronald Glaser and Janice Kiecolt-Glaser found that stress can impair your immune system, keeps wounds from healing, and interferes with the effectiveness of vaccines. Caregivers whose lives center around suffering are particularly susceptible to stress-related immune system weakness.

SPIRIT: *Learn about near-death experiences*

Many of us are afraid of dying, although according to the work of bestselling author, Dr. Raymond Moody, most near-death survivors say they no longer fear death. A 1997 *U.S. News and World Report* survey found that fifteen million adults in the United States had had near-death experiences. Read about or talk to someone who has undergone a NDE—it could lessen your fear.

"MAN'S HEART AWAY FROM NATURE BECOMES HARD."

—Standing Bear

Go Green

Many of the keys to health and happiness can be found in nature. Today, focus on reducing stress, on yourself and on the earth. Eating natural food, using natural products, and developing a green awareness promotes wellness at every level.

MIND: *Buy green cleaning products*
Instead of using laundry detergent, dishwashing liquid, and floor and bathroom cleansers laden with chemicals or petroleum derivatives, buy green cleaners. Natural cleaning products are safer for your family, pets, and the environment. Visit *www.seventhgeneration.com* for information about natural household products.

BODY: *Wash fruits and vegetables before eating*
Most fruits and vegetables are grown with pesticides and herbicides, unless they are certified organic. Wash them well, rubbing them under running water. You can make a vegetable wash with equal parts of white vinegar and water. Soak fruits and veggies for a minute or so to remove bacteria and chemicals, then rinse. You can use a soft brush to clean apples, potatoes, and other firm fruits and vegetables.

SPIRIT: *Send messages of peace to heal the planet*
Write a letter to Mother Earth, telling her how much you love and appreciate her. Thank her for supporting and nourishing you all these years. If you wish, express thanks for specific things. Promise to do your best to show her the respect she deserves. Make the letter as personal and heartfelt as possible. When you've finished, burn the letter to release your intentions into the universe. Sprinkle the ashes on the ground.

"SOMETIMES YOUR JOY IS THE SOURCE OF YOUR SMILE,
BUT SOMETIMES YOUR SMILE CAN BE THE SOURCE OF
YOUR JOY." —Thich Nhat Hanh

Do Things That Make You Happy

If you rarely feel happy, you may be suffering from depression. Depression is the most serious example of burnout. According to Mental Health America, more than nineteen million Americans suffer from depression or depression-related illnesses. Consult your doctor to address serious depression. Simultaneously, do things that make you happy.

MIND: *Make an album of happy pictures*
Collect your favorite photos of good times. They may feature family, friends, pets, vacations to pleasant places, or anything that evokes happy memories. Compile an old-fashioned photo album and look through it whenever you feel sad or discouraged. Or, put together an online album and share your happy moments with others.

BODY: *Laugh more often*
Lighten up, enjoy life, and laugh at life's stressors rather than fretting about them. A 2000 study at the University of Maryland Medical Center found that patients with heart disease were 40 percent less likely to laugh than those without heart disease. Cardiologists found that hearty laughter actually improved the lining of blood vessels as well as lowered blood pressure and heart rate.

SPIRIT: *Make someone else happy*
Sometimes the best way to be happy yourself is to bring joy into someone else's life. Visit people in a hospital or nursing home. Do a favor for a neighbor. Give your subway seat to someone who needs it more. Pay someone a compliment. Possibilities abound.

"A MAN IS NOT OLD UNTIL REGRETS TAKE

THE PLACE OF DREAMS." —John Barrymore

Age Gracefully

A hundred years ago, most people died before the age of fifty. In 2009, according to the Administration on Aging, the United States had nearly forty million persons aged sixty-five or older. Whether you want to live to be 100 or want to enjoy good health for as long as possible, numerous studies show that your attitude, lifestyle, and diet play a big role in your overall well-being.

MIND: *Memorize your grocery list*

Enhance your memorization skills at every opportunity to help prevent age-related mental decline. Turn a trip to the supermarket into a game. After you've written your shopping list, memorize it. Then leave the list at home and try to recall the items on it. How well did you do?

BODY: *Protect against heart disease with psyllium*

Approximately fifty-two million Americans have elevated cholesterol levels. If you're one of them, psyllium may protect you against heart disease and diabetes. This water-soluable fiber reduces blood cholesterol and can also curb appetite. Take it as a powder, whole husks (in soups), or capsule form. Drink at least one glass of water or juice after taking a capsule.

SPIRIT: *Accept yourself*

No matter how old you are, accepting yourself where you are at now in life's journey is the key to peace and contentment. It may sound clichéd, but if you aren't satisfied with yourself, do something to change what you don't like—you are the only one who can.

> "PERFECTIONISM IS NOT A QUEST FOR THE BEST.
> IT IS A PURSUIT OF THE WORST IN OURSELVES,
> THE PART THAT TELLS US THAT NOTHING WE DO
> WILL EVER BE GOOD ENOUGH." —Julia Cameron

Just Do Your Best

In his book *The Four Agreements,* Don Miguel Ruiz recommends always doing your best. However, he also reminds you that your best will vary from day to day. Doing your best will let you get more out of life and gain greater respect for yourself.

MIND: *Stop trying to be perfect*
Consider Voltaire's warning: "The perfect is the enemy of the good." Trying to be perfect can make it impossible for you to act. Instead, do the best you can. Give yourself permission to make mistakes. No baseball player ever hit a home run without having struck out many times.

BODY: *Don't become a slave to your diet*
Once you've chosen a dietary program, do your best to stick to it. But that doesn't mean you can never enjoy a favorite treat or eat something that isn't healthy. Try a 90/10 rule. Ninety percent of your daily food intake should be part of your diet and food that you know is good for you. Allow yourself 10 percent that's not part of your plan.

SPIRIT: *Be patient with yourself*
Life is not meant to be a struggle. When you know you have done your best, that's enough. Pushing yourself harder will only create strife. You may even suffer setbacks. Guilt, self-recrimination, and regrets won't contribute to your well-being or enable you to achieve your goals any faster.

"ONE CAN ENJOY A WOOD FIRE WORTHILY ONLY
WHEN HE WARMS HIS THOUGHTS BY IT AS WELL
AS HIS HANDS AND FEET." —Odell Shepherd

Get Fired Up

We associate fire with vitality, enthusiasm, and passion. Metaphysically, fire is one of the four elements that comprise our universe (along with earth, air, and water). Practice connecting with the energy of fire today. Express its qualities as you go about your day.

MIND: *Sit before a fire*
Build a fire in a fireplace, or a safe spot outdoors. Watch the fire burn and feel its warmth. Notice deeper sensations and awarenesses. Do you feel more alive and inspired? Does the fire relax your mind, producing a trancelike state, while stimulating your vitality? Sit before the fire as long as you like. Write your impressions in a journal.

BODY: *Use the Breath of Fire to get energized*
A breathing technique from the kundalini school of yoga called the Breath of Fire quickly revs up your energy. Sit, stand, or assume another yoga posture. Inhale and exhale through you nose, using short, fast snort-like breaths. As you inhale, relax your stomach muscles. As you exhale, pull your stomach in quickly. Continue for thirty seconds or more for a surefire energy boost.

SPIRIT: *Call upon the salamanders*
In some earth-centered traditions, salamanders are nature spirits that embody the qualities of fire. You can invite them to help you when you need vitality, creativity, or courage. Light a candle to attract them. As you gaze at the candle, you may see them dancing in the flame.

"IT'S AN ILL WIND THAT BLOWS NO GOOD."

—John Heywood

Turn Negatives into Positives

Positive and negative can be viewed as two sides of the same coin. Do you see a problem or an opportunity in a situation? If challenges arise today, try to find ways to make the best of them.

MIND: *Find opportunities in travel delays*

When your flight is delayed, or your train doesn't arrive on time, turn a negative into a positive. Read a book. Send a few e-mails or text messages. Call a friend. Take some quiet time for yourself. If you're traveling to a new place, take this opportunity to review your guidebook of must-see places. Instead of seeing this as time wasted, relish it as extra moments to do what you please.

BODY: *See illness as a message from your body*

It may be hard to see anything good about an illness. But when you take a holistic perspective, an illness may tell you something you need to know. For instance, if you have been working too hard and come down with a cold or flu, your body may be saying it's time for a rest.

SPIRIT: *Transform your awareness*

The Law of Attraction and other spiritual teachings say that you attract what you put your attention on. If your thoughts and feelings are centered in fear, anger, or other negative things, that's what you will draw to you. The good news is, you can transform negative situations into positive ones by changing your perceptions.

"IF YOU HOLD YOURSELF DEAR,

PROTECT YOURSELF WELL."

—The Buddha

Be Content with Who You Are

Contentment depends upon self-acceptance. Regardless of how you look, what you do for a living, where you live, or how others see you, set an intention to appreciate yourself today. Life isn't easy—give yourself credit for making it this far.

MIND: *Look at what you've accomplished*
At the end of the day, look at what you've done, not what you didn't do. Most of us have long to-do lists, and we don't always finish everything. But that doesn't mean you didn't accomplish much. If you made a list, you might realize you did dozens of things—give yourself credit for your accomplishments, large and small.

BODY: *Consider food as a lifestyle choice*
You've heard the saying "you are what you eat." Choose to eat a diet that will enable you to be the person you want to be. Protect your body and keep it in good shape by eating a diet that is low in fat and cholesterol, and high in antioxidant-rich fruits and vegetables. Include whole grains and plenty of fiber. A healthy diet will let you be happier with who you are.

SPIRIT: *Choose a companion crystal*
A companion crystal is a special one that becomes a dear and personal friend. Choose a clear quartz crystal that is small enough to carry in your pocket or purse. Spend time bonding with it, sharing your thoughts and feelings. Treat it with respect and it will aid you in every area of your life.

"In true love the smallest distance is too great,

and the greatest distance can be bridged."

—Hans Nouwens

Make Your Partnership a Priority

Relationships are challenging, no doubt about it. One of the biggest challenges can be making time to really nurture your relationship, rather than expecting it to just take care of itself. A satisfying relationship, however, is one of the most important requirements for happiness in life. Make the effort—it's worth it.

MIND: *Spend quality time with your partner*
In many relationships, work, family responsibilities, and outside activities interfere with personal time together. Take a day off and spend it with your partner. Don't take the kids. Leave the laptop at home. Turn off your cell phone. Do something you both enjoy but never seem to do anymore, such as having a picnic lunch or sharing a bottle of wine while you watch the sunset.

BODY: *Enjoy eating erotically*
Have fun eating foods that remind you of sex organs, such as bananas, mangoes, cucumbers, oysters, or clams—and eat them provocatively. Or, try a centuries-old Japanese practice called Nyotaimori, which involves eating sushi directly off a person's naked body, as if she were a living serving tray.

SPIRIT: *Honor your partner*
The word *namaste* means "I honor the divine within you." See your partner as a spiritual being having an earthly experience. Look beneath the things that annoy you to realize the divine nature at his or her core. When you find yourself criticizing or getting frustrated with your partner, say aloud "namaste" to remind yourself.

"IF YOU REALLY WANT TO DO SOMETHING, YOU'LL FIND A WAY. IF YOU DON'T, YOU'LL FIND AN EXCUSE."

—Jim Rohn

Take Charge of Your Life

If you want to hit a home run, you have to step up to the plate. You are the only person who can guide your life. The Law of Attraction says you can do, be, and have whatever you want. But first you must see yourself that way and be willing to pursue your dreams.

MIND: *Don't see yourself as a victim*

Don't assume a victim mentally. No matter what your situation, there's always something you can do to improve it. That may be changing your perception of a problem or your reaction to it. If you perceive yourself as a victim, you give others power over you instead of assuming your own power, which can be an excuse for doing nothing.

BODY: *Choose to be healthy*

Approximately 1.6 million out of a total 2.1 million deaths a year in the United States are related to poor nutrition, according to former Surgeon General C. Everett Koop. You can improve your health by choosing to eat a healthy diet. Extensive information is available about nutrition, in magazines, books, on TV and the Internet. It's up to you to put that information to use.

SPIRIT: *Nurture your inner self*

What makes you feel joyful? Listening to music? Reading poetry? Taking a nice, long bath? Make time for things that nurture your spirit. Don't put them at the bottom of your to-do list—make them priorities. If you don't, nobody else will.

> "ONE PERSON WHO IS TRULY UNDERSTANDING,
> WHO TAKES THE TROUBLE TO LISTEN TO US AS WE
> CONSIDER A PROBLEM, CAN CHANGE OUR WHOLE
> OUTLOOK ON THE WORLD." —Dr. Elton Mayo

Become More Attentive

It's been said that we have two ears and two eyes, but only one mouth because we gain more knowledge from paying attention than from talking. Today, practice observing and listening in order to expand your understanding.

MIND: *Listen up*

One surefire way to improve your communication skills and memory is to pay attention to what's being said. Most of us only half-listen to the people we're conversing with—while someone else is talking, we're formulating what we're going to say in response. Give whoever is speaking the benefit of your full attention and really listen. You may be surprised at what you can learn.

BODY: *Eat dark chocolate to stay alert*

Chocolate contains phenylethylamine, a strong stimulant related to the amphetamine family, known to increase the activity of neurotransmitters in parts of the brain that control your ability to pay attention and stay alert. One or two bites of dark chocolate will also give you a quick, feel-good lift.

SPIRIT: *Use your fingers to stimulate awareness*

Meditators sitting in the so-called lotus position often hold their thumbs and fingers together to increase mental relaxation. This gesture activates sensitive points in your fingertips that connect to the intuitive, creative part of your brain. To stimulate awareness at this level, press the tips of your thumbs to your index and middle fingers for about a minute.

"DISEASES OF THE SOUL ARE MORE DANGEROUS AND
MORE NUMEROUS THAN THOSE OF THE BODY."

—Marcus Tullius Cicero

Reduce Your Risk of Stroke

The incidence of stroke is about four out of 1,000 people. It is the third leading cause of death in the United States. You can reduce your chance of stroke by making lifestyle changes. Holistic physicians recommend addressing health on every level: mind, body, and spirit.

MIND: *Know your risk for stroke*
Stroke is usually caused by a blood clot or buildup of cholesterol plaque that blocks an artery in the brain. High blood pressure, heart disease, smoking, high cholesterol, and diabetes increase your risk of stroke. If you have a high risk for stroke, take concrete steps to safeguard your brain from this devastating blow.

BODY: *Favor curry*
Turmeric, an ingredient in curry powder, aids digestion by stimulating the flow of bile and the breakdown of dietary fats. According to *Earl Mindell's Herb Bible*, "The herbs that are combined to make curry help prevent heart disease and stroke by reducing cholesterol and preventing clots." German research indicates that turmeric can also protect against gall-bladder disorders and is an effective treatment for gall-bladder disease.

SPIRIT: *Embrace peace and stillness*
Being more peaceful and calm can benefit your mind, body, and spirit. Lie on your back on the floor. Light an aromatherapy candle or a stick of incense, preferably one scented with lavender, clary sage, frankincense, or vanilla. Turn out all the lights. Close your eyes and relax for at least ten minutes at the end of the day.

"THE HEART IS LIKE A GARDEN. IT CAN GROW
COMPASSION OR FEAR, RESENTMENT OR LOVE.
WHAT SEEDS WILL YOU PLANT THERE?" —The Buddha

Sow Seeds for Your Future

An acorn contains everything necessary to produce an oak tree. Your
thoughts, emotions, and actions are like seeds, each containing the
potential for something more to grow from them. Today, consider
what many spiritual traditions teach: "As you sow, so shall you reap."

MIND: *Pay attention to the seeds you sow*
According to the Law of Attraction, with your thoughts you sow
the seeds of your future reality. Whatever thoughts you plant in the
universe will eventually grow into the conditions in your life. Therefore, it is wise to pay attention to your thoughts and weed out the
ones that you don't want to materialize.

BODY: *Munch on pumpkin seeds*
Pumpkin seeds nestle in the core of the pumpkin, encased in a white-
yellow husk. This super seed contains a number of minerals—zinc,
magnesium, manganese, iron, copper, phosphorus—along with
proteins, monounsaturated fat, and the omega fatty acids 3 and 6.
Pumpkin seeds help prevent prostate cancer in men, protect against
heart disease, and also have anti-inflammatory benefits.

SPIRIT: *"Seed" crystals for protection*
To protect your property and yourself, you can plant crystals around
the perimeter of your yard, home, or elsewhere. Choose tiny quartz
crystals and tell them that you want them to safeguard you and your
home. Then bury the crystals in the earth, a few inches deep. They
will continue to provide a psychic barrier.

"BE MODERATE IN ORDER TO TASTE

THE JOYS OF LIFE IN ABUNDANCE." —Epicurus

Balance Your Body Functions

Holistic healing is all about achieving balance in mind, body, and spirit. The key to well-being is bringing your system into balance. Today, seek to bring all aspects of your life into a state of equilibrium.

MIND: *Benefit from biofeedback*

Biofeedback is a complementary therapy that trains your mind to control such functions as heart rate, blood pressure, breathing, and pain. Sensors are attached to your body to measure your responses to stress and other stimuli. Biofeedback uses imagery, sound, and verbal cues to improve your ability to regulate your body's processes. For more information, check with the Biofeedback Certification Institute of America, *www.bcia.org*.

BODY: *Boost your metabolism*

All activity in the body occurs through a process called metabolism in which cells break down chemicals and nutrients to generate energy and form new molecules. Efficient metabolism requires blood loaded with oxygen, glucose, and nutrients. Enzymes are the molecules that make metabolism happen, and nutrients are vitamins and minerals that act as essential coenzymes. Eat a healthy diet, add exercise, and keep your body in top running form.

SPIRIT: *Tune in to the sound of Creation*

The sound current of AUM, the Mother of all Sounds (the cosmic vibration of atoms in creation), can take you to a place of *Samadhi*, or at-one-ness with the Divine. Whether you chant the sound or listen to it on a CD, concentrate not only on the sound, but on its vibration to achieve balance.

"STRESSED SPELLED BACKWARDS IS DESSERTS.

COINCIDENCE? I THINK NOT!"   —Anonymous

Sweet Poison

It's estimated that the average American eats 130 pounds of sugar annually. As sugar consumption has increased, so has diabetes. Monitor the amount of sugar you ingest. It might not be obvious—many products you might not expect may contain sugar and other sweeteners.

MIND: *Know the facts about sugar*
The typical American diet is packed with sugar, and most of it is hidden. No RDA for sugar exists, but experts recommend that 55 to 60 percent of total calories in your diet should come from carbohydrates, with less than 10 percent coming from simple sugars. The USDA advises people who eat a 2,000-calorie healthful diet to limit themselves to about 10 teaspoons (40 grams) of added sugars per day.

BODY: *Be cautious about sugar substitutes*
Some sugar substitutes are more dangerous than the substance they are replacing. Aspartame, for example, has come under attack for producing symptoms including headaches, memory loss, nausea, dizziness, and more. Recent evidence suggests that some sugar substitutes may actually increase your hunger for sweets and starches. Stevia and erythritol (Truvia) are safer choices.

SPIRIT: *Increase the sweetness in your life*
Our cravings for sweets can be a symptom that we seek more sweetness in our lives emotionally and spiritually. Do you feel a lack of love and joy? Does your life seem more bitter than sweet? Giving what you wish to receive is the first step. Find ways to share the sweetness that is in you, and you'll find more coming back.

"LIFE IS A GREAT BIG CANVAS, AND YOU SHOULD THROW ALL THE PAINT ON IT YOU CAN." —Danny Kaye

Seek a Long and Healthy Life

Science has managed to extend our lives quite impressively. Yet attitude and lifestyle, as much as technology, are responsible not only for the length of your life but its quality as well. Today, take steps to ensure you have the life you desire.

MIND: *Join a social club*

The more people participate in social relationships, the better their overall physical and mental health. The MacArthur Foundation Study on Aging revealed that the two strongest predictors of well-being among the elderly are frequency of visits with friends and frequency of attendance at organization meetings. The more diverse your circle of social support, the better off you are likely to be.

BODY: *Lose that belly fat*

In a study of Kaiser Permanente patients in California, middle-aged people with belly fat were nearly three times more likely to experience dementia in their later years than people with little to no belly fat. Doctors recommend a combination of weight training and aerobic exercise that targets the whole body (not just the abdominals), a low-fat diet, and minimal sugar to lose that belly fat.

SPIRIT: *Seek quality of life*

Although achieving a ripe old age is certainly something to aspire to, in the final analysis, quality of life is more important than quantity. We don't know when we're going to die. Therefore, it makes sense to live as if this were your last moment on earth.

"THE PRODUCE MANAGER IS MORE IMPORTANT TO MY
CHILDREN'S HEALTH THAN THE PEDIATRICIAN."

—Meryl Streep

Know Your Fruits and Veggies

We all know we're supposed to get plenty of fruits and vegetables in
our diets. But which ones are the best? Do your homework and learn
which provide which nutrients. Visit Dr. Decuypere's website, *www
.healthalternatives2000.com*, for an easy-to-read chart of different
fruits and vegetables.

MIND: *Know the benefits of different fruits*
Most fruits contain vitamins A, B1, B2, B6, C, E, and K as well as folate,
niacin, and pantothenic acid. They also provide necessary minerals.
However, the amounts vary. For instance, cantaloupe is high in vitamin
A. Guava has lots of vitamin C—more than three times that of oranges
or grapefruit. Blueberries are a good source of vitamin K. Research the
percentages of each and compare them to the USDA guidelines.

BODY: *Drink 100 percent fruit juice*
When choosing fruit juices, check the labels. Fruit juice contains fructose, the naturally occurring sugar in fruit. Fruit drinks, fruit cock-
tails, and fruitades contain fructose plus added sugar. When the label
states "100 Percent Fruit Juice," the juice only has the naturally occurring fructose and no added sugar. Juice with added sugar contains
more calories.

SPIRIT: *Substitute fruit juice for wine*
Some spiritual and secular rituals use wine as part of the ceremony.
If you prefer not to consume alcohol, substitute fruit juice. Grape and
cranberry juice provide antioxidant benefits, just like red wine does.
Sparkling apple cider offers the same delightful fizziness as champagne.

> "HE CAUSETH THE GRASS TO GROW FOR THE CATTLE,
>
> AND HERBS FOR THE SERVICE OF MAN."
>
> —Psalm 104:14 KJV

Herbal Health

Recent studies show that more than 75 percent of Americans now use some form of alternative healing for their health care. Herbs are among the oldest forms of medicine, used around the world for thousands of years. You may wish to consider herbal teas, capsules, and other remedies to promote well-being on every level. *Earl Mindell's Herb Bible* is a good source of information.

MIND: *See herbs from a doctor's viewpoint*

If you are interested in having a doctor's opinion on any herbal remedies you would like to investigate or to take, you may want to gift him or her with this book: *Rational Phytotherapy: A Physicians' Guide to Herbal Medicine.* Volker Schultz, Rudolf Hänsel, and Varro E. Tyler, PhD, ScD, wrote it especially for physicians. It may help you communicate with your doctor about herbal options.

BODY: *Take echinacea for the common cold*

Used for centuries by the indigenous people of North America, this plant supports the immune system and can make you less susceptible to common colds and flu. It contains the enzyme hyaluronidase, which protects against viruses. If you already have a cold, echinacea can ease your discomfort and help you get better faster.

SPIRIT: *Tap the spirits of herbs*

Metaphysicians and holistic healers believe all plants have spirits. Harvesting fresh herbs enables you to get the benefit of this spiritual component. Dried and packaged herbs from the supermarket may be fine for flavoring food, but they lack the vital essence of the plants.

"I WILL NOT LET ANYONE WALK THROUGH MY MIND WITH THEIR DIRTY FEET." —Mahatma Gandhi

Clean Up Your Act

Cleanliness has long been linked with spirituality as well as practicality. The word *hygiene* derives from *Hygiea*, who was the Greek goddess of health. To improve your health on every level, practice cleanliness in body, mind, and spirit.

MIND: *Vacuum up mental stress*
Sit in a quiet place and close your eyes. Take several slow, deep breaths to relax. When you feel ready, imagine the stress and problems in your life as dirt on a carpet. Then envision yourself using a vacuum cleaner to suck up all the dirt that has been distressing you. Continue vacuuming up annoyances until your mental environment is clean and you feel relaxed.

BODY: *Clean up your environment*
Free radicals are the natural by-products of many processes within and among cells. Keeping free radicals under control protects your heart and your brain. A wide variety of environmental agents including photochemical air pollutants—pesticides, solvents, anesthetics, exhaust fumes, and the general class of aromatic hydrocarbons—cause free-radical damage to cells. Because free radicals are also created by exposure to tobacco smoke and radiation, cleaning up your environment can benefit your health.

SPIRIT: *Clean your kitchen*
The ancient Chinese philosophy known as feng shui links dirt and clutter with blocked energy. These blockages can damage your health, finances, and relationships. The kitchen, according to feng shui, relates to health and vitality. Clear clutter from your kitchen. Repair nonfunctioning appliances.

"WHEN YOU ARE LOOKING IN THE MIRROR, YOU ARE LOOKING AT THE PROBLEM. BUT, REMEMBER, YOU ARE ALSO LOOKING AT THE SOLUTION." —Anonymous

Challenge Yourself to Be More Conscious

One way to be more at peace with yourself and with the world you live in is to become more conscious of yourself. Do you go through your days operating on autopilot? If so, set an intention to be more aware of your thoughts, words, and deeds today.

MIND: *Replace profanity with a sharpened vocabulary*
Obscenity has infiltrated our lives and language. Rather than flinging profane words in the heat of an argument, make it your goal to broaden your vocabulary and to use words that really express how you feel. Tax your brain by challenging it to learn and remember a lexicon that will express your frustration gracefully.

BODY: *Be aware of your body*
Do you stand tall when you walk? Do you sit up straight in your chair? Is your body tense? Make a point of noticing your body today. If you catch yourself slumping, straighten your spine so rejuvenating energy can flow freely. If you realize you aren't breathing deeply, shift to deep belly-breathing to bring more healthy oxygen into your system.

SPIRIT: *Become aware of your energy field*
Your subtle energy field, also called your aura, surrounds your physical body. Hold your hands about a foot apart, palms facing. Slowly move your palms closer together. Do you notice a tingling, a slight pressure, warmth, or other sensation when your palms are only a few inches apart? That's your aura.

"THE BRAIN IS A MONSTROUS, BEAUTIFUL MESS. ITS
BILLIONS OF NERVE CELLS . . . LIE IN A TANGLED WEB
THAT DISPLAYS COGNITIVE POWERS FAR EXCEEDING ANY
OF THE SILICON MACHINES WE HAVE BUILT TO MIMIC IT."

—William F. Allman

Build a Better Brain

No one knows how much our brains are capable of. But we do know
that certain practices can help you strengthen your gray matter and
protect it from age-related decline. Here are some ways to care for
your brain.

MIND: *Play the name game*
Practice enhancing your memorization skills. At social events when
you are introduced to someone new, repeat the person's name to
yourself three times and then use it in conversation. Meet as many
people as possible. Test yourself the next morning to see how many
you can remember.

BODY: *Check for lead exposure*
In high doses, lead, which once was commonly used in household
plumbing, can cause severe brain damage and even death; in low
doses, it can cause nerve system damage in fetuses, infants, and children. Individuals living in homes constructed between 1910 and 1940,
when lead service pipes were commonly used, are most at risk. If you
suspect your home may have lead contamination, get it tested.

SPIRIT: *Call upon Megatron*
The archangel Megatron is known as the Angel of Thought. He is
believed to help us communicate with the Divine and receive wisdom from the higher realms. Create an affirmation, such as, "My
mind is filled with joyful, loving thoughts." Reflect on this affirmation to invite Megatron's assistance.

"IF IT WEREN'T FOR THE FACT THAT THE TV SET
AND THE REFRIGERATOR ARE SO FAR APART, SOME
OF US WOULDN'T GET ANY EXERCISE AT ALL."

—Joey Adams

Exercise to Keep Your Edge

Whether you are performing a concerto or playing tennis, practice
makes perfect. To maintain your edge, you must make the most of
your abilities. Today, find ways to exercise your mind, body, and
spirit to keep them in optimal working order.

MIND: *Do mental workouts*

Exercising your mind is as important as exercising your body. Experiments with rats showed that the animals who had a stimulating environment (running mazes) had wider and longer dendrites (which conduct nerve impulses) and more synapses than those with no stimulation. If you must watch TV, choose shows that stimulate your mind such as programs on the Learning Channel or history documentaries.

BODY: *Walk more*

Walk to places you ordinary drive to: a friend's house, the post
office, the coffee shop. Can you meet the kids at school and spend
time walking home together as a family? By decreasing the amount
you drive and increasing the amount you walk, you're doing your
health and the environment a favor.

SPIRIT: *Strengthen your intuition*

Start paying more attention to the voice inside that offers guidance.
Your feelings signal whether you are on the right path or the wrong
one. Often we dismiss our moods and emotions, following the intellect instead. But logic has its limits. If something doesn't *feel* right,
trust the feeling. Go with it. The more you exercise your intuition,
the sharper it will become.

"OPTIMISM IS THE FAITH THAT LEADS TO ACHIEVEMENT.
NOTHING CAN BE DONE WITHOUT HOPE AND CONFIDENCE."
—Helen Keller

Increase Your Optimism

It's easy to get pulled down by the negativity of those around you. But remember the ancient axiom: "like attracts like." Maintaining a hopeful and optimistic attitude invites people and situations that are aligned with that vibration.

MIND: *Don't think in absolutes*

When we're in a rut, we tend to think things will continue to get worse. We may start to think they will never improve. But the truth is, life is like hilly terrain with many ups and downs. When you start thinking, *I always get taken advantage of*, or, *My partner never gives me what I need*, stop yourself immediately. Not only is that type of thinking inaccurate, it's self-defeating.

BODY: *Try St. John's wort*

According to Michael T. Murray, ND, author of *Natural Alternatives to Prozac*, patients reported that St. John's wort improved psychological problems, depression, anxiety, and sleep disorders without side effects. In his book *Herbs for Your Health*, herbalist Steven Foster warns that St. John's wort should primarily be used as a safer, nonaddictive antidepressant aid until the true causes of the depression are uncovered and treated properly.

SPIRIT: *Meditate with chrysoprase*

A beautiful green stone called chrysoprase can help you realize that you are part of the whole of the universe. Meditate with it to release childhood traumas and connect with the Divine. Chrysoprase enables you to move beyond discouragement and emotional blocks to align with your ideals.

"LOVE ONE ANOTHER AND YOU WILL BE HAPPY.

IT'S AS SIMPLE AND AS DIFFICULT AS THAT."
—Michael Leunig

Keep Your Love Alive

If you or your partner travel a lot, you may experience more relationship stress than other couples. Shakespeare wrote that absence makes the heart grow fonder, but frequent periods of separation can strain even a good partnership. Make sure your beloved is thinking of you when he or she is in a motel someplace far away.

MIND: *Tuck a love note in your partner's suitcase*
Write a love note to your partner when he or she is going away on a trip. Make it as romantic or racy as you choose. Seal it with your favorite scent. Then tuck it in your lover's suitcase, in a place where he or she is sure to find it.

BODY: *Have Skype sex*
When your lover is away, tune in to Skype and enjoy virtual sex. One way to turn on you partner is to masturbate while he or she watches. Ask what he or she would like to see you do. Discuss it in advance, so you can fantasize before the big date. Use sexy clothing, toys, lube, and music to enhance the experience. Be both exhibitionist and voyeur.

SPIRIT: *Give your partner a heart stone*
Some stones naturally form in the shape of a heart. Others can be intentionally shaped that way by stonecutters or lapidaries. Give your partner a heart-shaped stone as a keepsake when he or she is away. The stone serves as a symbol of your love.

"LET THE WORLD KNOW YOU AS YOU ARE,

NOT AS YOU THINK YOU SHOULD BE." —Fannie Brice

Improve Your Circulation

Like fish who must swim to stay alive, we must grow, move, seek, and interact with others in order to thrive. Stagnation, whether in the mind, body, or spirit, is the kiss of death. With the rapidly expanding technology available today, your opportunities are virtually unlimited.

MIND: *Get out and circulate*

Don't isolate; circulate. The benefits of creating a social network are multifaceted. Studies show that a strong support network and circle of friends can boost your immune system and make you more resistant to illness. Networking with businesspeople puts you on the inside track for jobs and moneymaking opportunities. Online groups can also provide information about subjects that interest you and expand your horizons.

BODY: *Get a massage*

When your muscles are tight, it is more difficult for fluid to pass through them. Poor circulation increases the amount of strain on your heart. Massage therapy loosens contracted muscles to increase circulation, which enables the blood to transport oxygen, energy, and nutrients to your cells. Improved circulation also enables your body to rid itself of waste products more effectively. Plus, a massage feels terrific!

SPIRIT: *Attend spiritual gatherings*

You can maintain your spiritual fitness by attending conferences, workshops, and other gatherings of like-minded people. Particularly if your beliefs aren't mainstream, you may start to question yourself if you isolate. Sharing ideas and comradery with others who understand can give you a sense of connection and confidence.

"MAN IS HARDER THAN IRON, STRONGER THAN STONE AND MORE FRAGILE THAN A ROSE." —Turkish Proverb

Tap the Strength of Iron

Iron provides a good example of how a substance's energy manifests on various levels. Iron has long been linked with the blood and all that conveys, including strength, courage, and vitality. This metal also enabled our ancestors to produce more efficient tools and weapons. If you feel weak mentally, physically, or spiritually, perhaps iron can benefit you.

MIND: *Know when you may need more iron*
Some people are at risk for iron-deficiency. These include infants, children, and women of childbearing age who lose iron-rich blood each month during their periods. The elderly may have decreased iron absorption. Strict vegetarians who eat only plant foods may not absorb iron well. If you fall into one of these categories, get screened periodically.

BODY: *Eat foods rich in iron*
Iron is also needed for a strong immune system and for energy production. In the United States, iron deficiency is common and can lead to anemia, fatigue, and infections. Foods rich in iron include beef liver, fortified cereals, lean red meats, nuts, seeds, poultry, bran, spinach, salmon, legumes, lentils, whole-wheat bread, and wheat germ.

SPIRIT: *Wear iron for strength*
Since ancient times, iron has been associated with the war god Mars and hence with strength in combat and competition. You can tap this energy to provide protection, increase vitality, or give you courage and stamina in the face of challenges. Wear or carry an object made of iron to augment your own energy.

"WE ARE NOT HUMAN BEINGS ON A SPIRITUAL JOURNEY.

WE ARE SPIRITUAL BEINGS ON A HUMAN JOURNEY."

—Stephen Covey

Life Is a Trip

Ours is a mobile society and many of us spend a great deal of time in cars, trains, or airplanes. In mythology, however, journeys are symbolically portrayed as forms of self-discovery and growth. Today, intend to have a safe and pleasant journey, wherever you go.

MIND: *Learn more about your car*

Most of us know little about how our cars operate; we simply trust that they will get us where we want to go. Understanding how your car functions can give you a sense of power. Read your owner's manual. Learn how to change your oil. Learn to change a tire. Learn to use battery cables. You might even want to take an adult education class in automotives.

BODY: *Choose alternative means of transportation*

Instead of driving everyplace you go, find alternate ways to get there. If you live in a city, take a bus or subway. Consider riding a bicycle or walking if you are only going a short distance. It's a good way to fit exercise into your daily routine. Reducing the miles you drive will save you money in gasoline and help the environment.

SPIRIT: *Understand your personal journey*

Where are you going in life and what route are you taking to get there? Spiritual teachers often extol the virtues of the journey, not only the destination. As you travel toward your objective, don't miss out on the lessons, opportunities, and adventures along the way.

"IF YOU PUT A SMALL VALUE UPON YOURSELF, REST
ASSURED THAT THE WORLD WILL NOT RAISE YOUR PRICE."

—Anonymous

Enhance Your Sense of Self

Strengthen your sense of self today. Self-confidence is being secure
in yourself, rather than looking to others for validation. The Hindu
system of chakras (the body's energy centers) links the solar plexus
chakra, located halfway between your heart and your navel, with
confidence.

MIND: *What really matters to you?*
Make a list of ten things that matter to you. You might consider fam-
ily togetherness or good health or self-expression to be important.
Each person's list will be different. Refine the ten things on your list
until you are clear about your priorities. Be as specific as possible.
Devoting yourself to these things will enhance your sense of self.

BODY: *Energize your solar plexus chakra*
To energize your solar plexus chakra, step your right foot forward
approximately two feet. Stretch your right arm out in front of you
and make a fist. Bend your left arm, placing your left hand on the
back of your head. Gaze at your right hand as you twist to the right,
until you reach your stopping point. Gently release by unwinding
your torso and lowering your arms. Reverse arms and repeat.

SPIRIT: *Fix it or forget it*
In the ancient Chinese philosophy of feng shui, items in your home
that are broken, worn, faded, or not functioning properly suggest that
certain areas in your life are also in need of repair. Fix or replace
damaged furnishings, broken appliances, and burned-out lights so
they don't impair your happiness.

"FREEDOM IS THE OXYGEN OF THE SOUL."

—Moshe Dayan

Free Yourself from Limitations

Many of the limits in our lives are self-imposed. Today, attempt to relax those limitations and experience the freedom that comes as a result. Loosen your fetters and express your true self.

MIND: *Free your mind*

When you hit a mental roadblock, instead of worrying endlessly, take a walk, enjoy a shower, or do something repetitive, such as knitting. Occupying part of your brain with a repetitive action frees up the creative side of your brain to solve problems. This is why we often have great ideas when we are relaxed and not thinking about anything in particular.

BODY: *Dance freely*

You don't have to follow carefully prescribed dance steps to get the health benefits of dancing. *Trance dance*, *ecstatic dance*, and *spiritual dance* are terms used for free-form dancing, which enables people to dance their own way, with or without a partner. These expressive movements are centered in ancient cultural traditions. You'll find free-form dance groups in most major cities, and perhaps in your own community.

SPIRIT: *Dream freely*

In a dream state known as "lucid dreaming," you are aware that you are dreaming. This allows you to guide the action of the dream and the outcome. Some researchers believe lucid dreaming helps you learn to handle situations in waking life, too. When you are dreaming, try to recognize that you are in a dream. Then attempt to redirect the action, according to your wishes.

> "NOBODY CAN GO BACK AND START A NEW BEGINNING, BUT ANYONE CAN START TODAY AND MAKE A NEW ENDING."
> —Maria Robinson

You're Never Too Young or Too Old to Improve Your Lifestyle

The sooner you embrace a healthy lifestyle, the better your chances of enjoying a long and fulfilling life. Even if you are past midlife, studies suggest you can still improve your quality of life and perhaps increase your longevity. Don't delay. Your future begins now.

MIND: *Believe in anti-aging possibilities*

Recent studies have shed light on how age affects the brain and how we can keep our mental faculties sharp regardless of the number of years under our belts. Senility is not a forgone conclusion for anyone; many common types of mental degeneration are the result of lifestyle and can be reversed with a change in diet or medication. Believe in the possibility and take proactive steps to keep your brain young.

BODY: *Eat probiotic-rich yogurt*

Probiotic means "pro life." Foods rich in probiotics encourage the growth of friendly bacteria in your gut. Many people develop difficulties with digestion and assimilation as they age. In a study published in the *Journal of Digestive Diseases,* individuals with gastrointestinal disturbances benefited from eating probiotic yogurt. If you suffer from irregularity or gastrointestinal discomfort, give probiotics a try.

SPIRIT: *Walk a spiritual path*

For centuries, pilgrims have trod paths for spiritual renewal. Jerusalem's Via Dolorosa, the path leading to Mecca, or to the Bodhi tree in Bodhgaya, India, are some famous ones. Perhaps there's a spiritual trail in your part of the world. If not, consider walking one of the ancient mystical routes to renew your spirit.

> "Vision is the art of seeing the invisible."
>
> —Jonathan Swift

Beyond the Obvious

What seems obvious in most cases is merely a matter of training. We perceive the world as we have been taught to see it. However, you can choose how you wish to view your life.

MIND: *See yourself as ageless*

Stop beating yourself up over another gray hair or a new wrinkle. Ask yourself how you would feel if you had no idea how old you were. Forget for a moment that you even have a body. Imagine yourself as ageless, timeless, and perfect. Make time every day to perceive yourself in this expanded way. Allow yourself to appreciate a grander, more spectacular you.

BODY: *Get your trace minerals*

Minerals that are needed in smaller amounts than the major minerals are referred to as trace minerals or trace elements. Even though our bodies only require a small amount of these minerals, they are still important to health. Eating a healthy, varied, and balanced diet is the best way to ensure you consume safe and adequate amounts of these other trace minerals; however, you can also purchase trace mineral supplements in health food stores.

SPIRIT: *Action without action*

There is a concept in Taoism called "not doing," or *wu-wei*. It emphasizes living from the spirit, expressing harmony and love in all you do. The power behind wu-wei is synchronicity. When you send forth a loving idea or intent, you align with the energy of the Tao. Your own power works with the laws of the universe.

"Enjoy life—there are no re-runs."
—Shirl Lowery

Build Self-Care into Your Day

Part of your daily schedule should include taking care of yourself, mentally, physically, and spiritually. Set thirty-minute blocks of time to devote to each. If you think you don't have time, cut back on TV viewing.

MIND: *Meditate thirty minutes a day*
Meditation is one of the best ways to beat stress. Hundreds of studies show that daily meditation will reduce both mental and physical stress. Ideally, you'll want to spend thirty minutes each day meditating. If you wish, you can break that into two segments: fifteen minutes in the morning and fifteen minutes at night. But even a few minutes per day will have positive effects.

BODY: *Exercise thirty minutes a day*
The U.S. federal guidelines for exercise say that getting at least thirty minutes a day most days a week will help prevent heart disease, osteoporosis, diabetes, obesity, and perhaps Alzheimer's. Regular exercise can also help preserve your mental acuity. Exercise has a lot of connotations, but exercise can mean walking around the neighborhood, dancing, or doing tai chi. What's important is that you do something that requires some physicality, limbers up your muscles, and improves your circulation.

SPIRIT: *Nourish your spirit thirty minutes a day*
Spend thirty minutes a day doing something that nourishes your spirit. What inspires feelings of love, peace, and joy for you? It might be reading to your children, working in your garden, or listening to music. Tend to your inner being, as well as your outer one.

> "ONE OF THE SYMPTOMS OF AN APPROACHING
> NERVOUS BREAKDOWN IS THE BELIEF THAT ONE'S
> WORK IS TERRIBLY IMPORTANT." —Bertrand Russell

Rx: Relax

Do you often find yourself nervous, anxious, irritable, or tense? If so, you're not alone. According to a *Prevention* magazine survey, three-quarters of those polled said they experienced "great stress" one day a week. How does stress affect your life, and how can you deal with it?

MIND: *Consider how emotions affect your decisions*

When you are stressed out, you may not make sound decisions. If you are upset, anxious, or in a bad mood you may subconsciously revisit a situation from your past that hooks into your emotional state, and make a decision based on that earlier situation. Realizing this can let you put off making decisions (if possible) until you are in a better frame of mind.

BODY: *Tense and release your muscles*

A highly effective relaxation technique popularized by Herbert Benson, MD, called the "Relaxation Response" involves tensing, then releasing each of your muscles, one at a time. Start with your toes and work up slowly to the crown of your head. Tense each muscle group for about ten seconds, then relax. This practice allows you to increase the degree of relaxation you achieve.

SPIRIT: *Relax with flower essences*

Flower essences contain no actual plant substance. They are made by capturing only the spirit, or "essence," of the plant in water. To counteract stress, put a few drops of one of these essences under your tongue: Star of Bethlehem, impatiens, or vervain.

"LOVE IS, ABOVE ALL, THE GIFT OF ONESELF."

—Jean Anouilh

Give the Gift of Love

A relationship is like a garden. It needs tending to stay healthy. Give yours plenty of care and feeding. Pull the weeds. Shine plenty of light on it, and your love will blossom.

MIND: *Avoid fault-finding*
Focusing on your partner's faults, rather than his or her good qualities, is likely to exacerbate them. Examine your own faults and fix what you don't like about yourself first. Allow your inner strength and joy to be at the heart of who you are. As you become more content with yourself, you will likely notice that you also come to appreciate your partner more. His or her little flaws may not bother you as much as they once did.

BODY: *Get dirty on the dance floor*
George Bernard Shaw called dancing "a perpendicular expression of a horizontal desire." The tango is often referred to as the dance of love. Certainly dancing in your partner's embrace can be a sensual and erotic experience. Enjoy one another's bodies. If the venue allows, consider "dirty dancing" as a warm-up for later on.

SPIRIT: *Imprint water with loving energy*
Set a tarot card that symbolizes love, such as The Lovers or The Two of Cups, face up on your nightstand. Place a glass of water on the card. (Use a glass without words or pictures on it.) Allow at least five minutes for the water to absorb the energy of the image on the card. Drink the water with your partner to enhance loving feelings.

"WHEN WE ENGAGE IN WHAT WE ARE NATURALLY SUITED
TO DO, OUR WORK TAKES ON THE QUALITY OF PLAY AND IT
IS PLAY THAT STIMULATES CREATIVITY." —Linda Naiman

The Joy and Power of Creativity

Creativity isn't simply painting a beautiful picture or writing the
Great American Novel. Anything that inspires imagination—
cooking, gardening, building model airplanes—is a creative
endeavor. Today, connect with the joy of creativity.

MIND: *Do what you love, love what you do*
Do something to express your creativity—and enjoy the experience. When your creative juices are stimulated, you tend to do your
best work and feel good while doing it. In 2004, Harvard Business
School researcher Teresa Amabile examined 12,000 journal entries
from 238 diverse individuals to learn more about the link between
creativity and happiness. She and her team of associates "found that
creativity is positively associated with joy and love."

BODY: *Stimulate the locus of creativity*
Creativity, according to Eastern medicine, is centered in the sacral
chakra in the lower belly. The womb, where life itself is created, is
located here. However, you can spark other forms of creativity by
activating this energy center. Try belly dancing. Swirl a hula hoop.
Or, simply rock your pelvis back and forth rhythmically as you
breathe deeply into your belly.

SPIRIT: *Connect with the Creative*
Engage in a creative activity—you may feel guided or inspired by a
joyful force outside yourself. Some spiritual traditions refer to the
divine force of the universe as the Creator or the Creative, and most
include creation myths, which often link love with creation.

"IF WE PAUSE AND BREATHE IN AND OUT, THEN WE CAN
HAVE THE EXPERIENCE OF TIMELESS PRESENCE, OF THE
INEXPRESSIBLE WISDOM AND GOODNESS OF OUR OWN MINDS."
—Pema Chödrön

The Breath of Life

Breathe more deeply today. Deep, slow breathing produces increased oxygenation, which means that a lower blood flow can carry the same amount of oxygen. Your heart doesn't have to work as hard to supply the body with oxygen, which leads to lowered blood pressure and heart rate.

MIND: *Breathing and meditation*

Meditation and deep, slow breathing (*pranayama*) balance the body, brain, and environment, returning your experience of the world to a more neutral, peaceful state. Close your eyes and relax your mind. Breathe slowly and deeply, keeping your attention on your breathing. Meditation and breathing are a formidable force that can create sunshine within while thunderstorms rage outside.

BODY: *Breathing and yoga*

When you do pranayama, you use your body to control the flow of air in and out, and the flow of prana (life energy). When you practice hatha yoga, with conscious breath awareness, movements such as twists, elongations, and bends allow energy to travel through the body in a way that is revitalizing, rejuvenating, and restorative.

SPIRIT: *Breathing and spirit*

As Deepak Chopra explains, "If you are aware of the breath and its power for mind and body, you'll recognize that the breath is the force of the spirit as well. The word 'inspiration' means to inspire and when we're inspired with the touch of spirit we also make the best use of our breath."

"IT IS THE MIND THAT BUILDS UP THE BODY STRONG AND SHINY [THAT ALSO] WASTES IT TO SKIN AND BONE."

—Sri Sathya Sai Baba

Stay Healthier Longer

Everyone wants to enjoy a healthy life. Even if you are fortunate to be born with good genes for health, you still have to do the maintenance. You wouldn't expect your car to keep performing well if you didn't take care of it. The same is true of your body.

MIND: *Find a new hobby*

According to Daniel G. Amen, MD, in *Making a Good Brain Great*, it's better to learn something new than to repeat the same activities. "When the brain does something over and over, even a complicated task, it learns how to do it using less and less energy." Find a hobby that requires coordination between multiple brain regions, such as knitting, gardening, or writing poetry.

BODY: *Maintain a sense of humor*

Keeping your sense of humor can help you stay healthier longer, according to Sven Svebak of the medical school at Norwegian University of Science and Technology. Many elders count humor among their secrets of longevity. Taking life less seriously can help you enjoy yourself more at any age.

SPIRIT: *Tap the earth's healing energy*

On the ground or floor, place four bayberry candles and four clear quartz crystals at the four compass points, forming a square about four by four feet. Step into the middle of this square. Imagine the earth's nurturing energy flowing up through your feet and into your body, revitalizing you.

"I NOT ONLY USE ALL THE BRAINS THAT I HAVE,
BUT ALL THAT I CAN BORROW." —Woodrow Wilson

Stay Sharp

Stop numbing your brain with stupefying substances, or by watching mindless programs on TV. Seek stimulation on many levels instead. Engage in a variety of activities, including socializing with friends, reading, writing, exercising, and eating a healthy diet in order to keep your cognitive skills well honed.

MIND: *Write your family's story*
Recalling previous events requires a strong memory (which may be aided by going through photo albums, letters, etc.). Additionally, the act of writing improves visual-spatial ability and challenges your communication skills. Consider writing your family's story, either for posterity or simply to give your mind exercise. Who knows, if you've got a truly extraordinary family, you might even pen the next bestseller.

BODY: *Drink tea to sharpen your mind*
Instead of turning to coffee when your mind starts to dull, drink tea instead. Many herbal teas may provide benefits that coffee can't. For instance, ginseng helps you cope with stress. Gotu kola strengthens brain function. Yerba mata boosts metabolism, reduces fatigue, and sharpens the mind. Many herbal teas are caffeine-free, yet aid mental processes.

SPIRIT: *Reflect on a Medicine Wheel*
The Native American Medicine Wheel is a symbolic representation of spiritual energy, depicted graphically as a circle divided into four sections aligned to the four directions: north, south, east, and west. The north quadrant signifies spirituality and is a place of peace, quiet, and contemplation. Meditate on this direction as you seek within for wisdom.

"EVERY MAN TAKES THE LIMITS OF HIS OWN FIELD OF VISION FOR THE LIMITS OF THE WORLD."

—Arthur Schopenhauer

Vitalize Your Vision

Today, open your eyes to the wonders of your world. Most of us see only a portion of what exists around us. The tendency to restrict our visual awareness has increased with the proliferation of personal electronic devices. Challenge yourself to increase your perceptual abilities.

MIND: *Envision having perfect vision*

Rub your palms together until they feel warm. Close your physical eyes and cup your palms over your eyes for a minute or two. In your mind's eye, imagine your lenses, retinas, optic nerve, and every part of your eyes functioning optimally. If you like, envision washing your eyes to improve your vision. Repeat an affirmation such as: "I see clearly now and my eyes are perfectly healthy."

BODY: *Take vitamin A*

Vitamin A promotes healthy vision, especially night vision. One form called carotenoids includes beta carotene, which is readily converted by the body to vitamin A. A deficiency of vitamin A can cause night blindness and other eye problems. Too much vitamin A can lead to problems, too. Check with your doctor to determine how much vitamin A you need.

SPIRIT: *Protect your home with an eye amulet*

The ancient Turks and Greeks believed in the curse of the "evil eye" and used eye amulets to guard against it. Often these amulets consisted of concentric circles rendered in dark blue, light blue, and white that resemble eyes. Hang one near the entrance to your home to repel unwanted energies.

> "WE MUST RECOGNIZE THAT DIFFERENCE IS A
> REASON FOR CELEBRATION AND GROWTH, RATHER
> THAN A REASON FOR DESTRUCTION." —Audre Lorde

Never Stop Growing

The opposite of growth and change is stagnation. Once you stop expanding your horizons you face the prospect of deterioration mentally, physically, and spiritually. Indulge your curiosity. Set goals for yourself. Challenge yourself; don't take the easy way out.

MIND: *Turn everything into a learning event*

Everything you do offers opportunities for learning. A trip to an art museum lets you learn about the artists and the eras. Attending a concert can encourage you to learn more about musical styles and the cultures that spawned them. Athletic events also provide venues for expanding your knowledge. See how much you can learn and share your insights with friends.

BODY: *Challenge yourself*

If you repeat the same workout routine day after day, your body will find a way to accomplish the same tasks with less effort. Therefore, it's important to change your exercise pattern. If you are doing strength training, increase the amount of weight you lift. Or, add more repetitions. Do resistance training. Try a new form of exercise that works muscles you may not have been using.

SPIRIT: *Tap the power of three*

In numerology, feng shui, tarot, and other metaphysical schools of thought, the number three represents growth and actualization. You can invite growth into your home or place of business by grouping objects in combinations of three. Position furnishings, artwork, plants, and candles in this arrangement.

"A FOOL SHOWS HIS ANNOYANCE AT ONCE, BUT A PRUDENT MAN OVERLOOKS AN INSULT." —Proverbs 12:16 NIV

Decrease Irritations

You can never escape from all of life's irritations. You can change the way you deal with them, however. Be creative about finding ways to cope with annoyances. Listen to music with earphones to drown out ambient noise, for instance. Stress can only affect you if you react to a stressor.

MIND: *Detach from annoyances*
Instead of getting angry at the annoyances in your environment, mentally detach from them. If you can deal with an irritation directly, do so. But if you can't, try not to take the annoyance personally or react to it. A bad economy, commuter traffic, and miserably hot and muggy weather are beyond your control. Don't let them ruin your day.

BODY: *Protect yourself against mosquitoes*
Mosquitoes are not only pesky, they are carriers of illnesses such as malaria, West Nile virus, and dengue fever. Experts say one in ten people are particularly attractive to mosquitoes, but they don't know why. High concentrations of cholesterol or steroids may attract them. It's the females that bite, and they use blood to strengthen their young. Burning citronella candles or incense can dissuade mosquitoes. Use mosquito nets when camping.

SPIRIT: *Your spirit is indestructible*
The slings and arrows of outrageous fortune, as Shakespeare termed them, cannot affect your spirit. Your spirit is indestructible. When someone or something annoys you, imagine yourself as the light being you are and let those "arrows" go right through you harmlessly.

"WRINKLES SHOULD MERELY INDICATE
WHERE SMILES HAVE BEEN." —Mark Twain

Don't Just Get Older, Get Better

Aging is a fact of life, but it is also what you make of it. No matter what your age, value it and make the most of it. Each time of life offers unique possibilities. Cherish them.

MIND: *Reconsider retirement*

You've heard about the woes of retiring and not having a plan. Work provides interaction with others, daily challenges that stimulate you, and a sense of purpose. It may be to your advantage economically to delay retirement, too. Waiting longer to retire will increase your Social Security benefits and enable you to put more into your nest egg. If you are healthy and enjoy your work, consider working a few more years.

BODY: *You're only as old as you feel*

You've heard this saying, and there's certainly some truth to it. Your diet and lifestyle affect not only how long you live, but your quality of life. Augment your well-being by eating foods high in omega-3 fatty acids. These fatty acids possess a natural anti-inflammatory. Certain fish, such as bluefish, herring, mackerel, salmon, sardines, and tuna, are high in omega-3s. Eat these three times a week.

SPIRIT: *Respect your elders*

In Native American and some Eastern cultures, elders are respected for the wisdom they've acquired over time. In Western society, older people are often looked at as "has-beens" or burdens. Spend time listening to an elder. You may be delighted to hear about his or her experiences and insights.

"IF YOU WERE GOING TO DIE SOON AND HAD ONLY ONE
PHONE CALL YOU COULD MAKE, WHO WOULD YOU CALL AND
WHAT WOULD YOU SAY? AND WHY ARE YOU WAITING?"

—Stephen Levine

Keep Your Love Alive

Despite the high divorce rate in Western society, true love is still an ideal most people strive to attain. Medical science now recognizes that love has health benefits, too. Today, consider what love means to you and how you can enrich the love in your own life.

MIND: *Make a commitment*

When you commit to a mutually rewarding intimate relationship, your brain produces the hormone oxytocin, known as "the bonding hormone." A Harvard University study found that married women are 20 percent less likely and married men 100 to 200 percent less likely to die of stress-related causes such as heart disease, suicide, or cirrhosis of the liver than single people.

BODY: *Boost your libido with ginkgo biloba*

Ginko biloba may be good for your libido. Ginkgo has reportedly aided men who suffer from impotence induced by antidepressant medications. Plan to take ginkgo for at least eight weeks before improvement shows. Caution: Ginkgo may interfere with certain drugs. If you want to take ginkgo, consult your doctor first.

SPIRIT: *Celebrate your relationship*

Honor your love with a ritual. Many people renew their wedding vows as a way to proclaim their undying love for one another. Whether or not you are married, you can honor your commitment with a celebration that commemorates your first meeting, first love-making, moving in together, or another meaningful date.

"THE WORDS 'I AM' ARE POTENT WORDS;

BE CAREFUL WHAT YOU HITCH THEM TO." —A. L. Kitselman

Connect with Who You Really Are

We are taught to think of ourselves as physical beings. However, holistic healing and many spiritual traditions teach that you are a multidimensional being. Science points out that you are comprised of energy. Today, get in touch with your true self.

MIND: *Chant to connect with chakra energy*
A particular sound is associated with each of the body's energy centers, or chakras. Chanting these lets you access the essence of the chakras. Focus on the root chakra and chant "lam." Focus on the sacral chakra and say "vam." Move your attention to the solar plexus chakra and intone "ram." The heart chakra's mantra is "yam," and the throat chakra's is "ham." At the third eye chakra, chant "om." Observe silence in connection with the crown chakra.

BODY: *Do yoga*
The ancient practice of yoga combines mind, body, and spirit to produce harmony. *Time* magazine says that fifteen million Americans do yoga as part of their fitness regimen. Yoga strengthens your body, quiets your mind, relieves tension, increases your self-knowledge and awareness, improves your quality of life, and changes how you see the world. Many schools of yoga exist; find one that is right for you.

SPIRIT: *You are more than your mind and body*
Your thoughts shift from moment to moment. Likewise, your body changes continually throughout your life. So, you cannot be your mind, nor your body. Only your spirit remains eternal. This is the *real* you.

"The marigold abroad her leaves doth spread

Because the sun's and her power is the same."

—Henry Constable, "Diana"

Make Friends with Marigolds

Enjoy sunny yellow and orange marigolds today. These hardy and cheerful annual plants can survive in many climates, and are a sure sign of summer. They also have long-standing medicinal, environmental, and mystical properties. Some are even edible, and add a spicy or tangy touch to salads and vegetable dishes (make sure they are safe before you ingest them).

MIND: *Plant marigolds in your garden*
The distinctive smell of marigolds is offensive to many insects. Plant a border of marigolds around a vegetable garden to deter pests who might eat or damage your crops. They can also dissuade rabbits from munching on your veggies. Marigolds look pretty, too. When you use plants for pest control, you protect yourself and the earth from the dangers of insecticides.

BODY: *Heal minor wounds with calendula cream*
Calendula is a type of marigold, with numerous healing properties. This gentle remedy soothes cuts, scrapes, burns, cracked and chapped skin, eczema, and other minor skin problems. You can find calendula in cream or salve form in health food stores or online. Apply it directly to your skin, according to directions, to bring healing relief.

SPIRIT: *Spark your "second sight"*
Ancient lore connects marigolds with clairvoyance, or "second sight." Early herbalists used them to divine the future, especially in matters of love. Put dried marigold flowers in a cloth bag and sleep with them under your pillow to help induce visionary dreams and insights.

"Worry is interest paid on trouble

before it comes due." —William Ralph Inge

Easy Does It

Do you tend to push yourself too hard, trying to do too much, too fast? This syndrome is endemic in Western society. Today, move out of the fast track. Embrace ease instead.

MIND: *Ease mental strain*
When your mind feels like it's ready to melt down, try this simple visualization exercise to ease the overload. Close your eyes and imagine your mind is an overstuffed closet. Envision yourself taking some large suitcases and packing them with all the stuff you no longer need. When you've emptied the closet of junk, take the suitcases to the train station and put them on a railroad car. Feel the relief of being rid of all that "baggage."

BODY: *Ease muscle stiffness*
Ease the muscle stiffness that comes from sitting at a desk all day long. Every hour or so, stretch. While sitting, lean first to the right side, bending as far as you comfortably can. Then lean to the left side, again bending as far as you comfortably can. Then stand and stretch, first to the right side and then to the left. Bend over and touch your toes (or whatever you can reach). Lean back and stretch, gently arching your back like a bow. Ahhhh.

SPIRIT: *Ease burdens with jasper*
A wonderful stress-buster, jasper supports you during difficult times. Wear it to give you courage to deal with challenges. By aligning you with the earth's nurturing energies, jasper lets you take hold of problems and resolve them.

"As the sun is not sullied by the defects of external objects, so the inner soul of all beings is not sullied by the misery of the world." —*Katha Upanishad*

Use Eastern Wisdom to Eliminate Toxicity

Westerners have come to appreciate the ancient healing traditions and spirituality of the East. Acupuncture, yoga, ayurvedic medicine, meditation, and feng shui are only a few of the jewels we've gleaned from Asian cultures. Consider how the following practices may benefit you.

MIND: *Detox with mudras*

Curl the ring and middle fingers of each hand to touch the tip of the thumb of the same hand. Hold this posture for fifteen minutes, three times per day. Use this *mudra*, or gesture, to help you eliminate toxicity and make space for new beginnings, new ideas, and new projects. As you inhale, imagine purifying life energy entering your system. With each exhale, expel what you no longer need.

BODY: *Get an ayurvedic body treatment*

Ayurveda is an ancient system of medicine native to India. One ayurvedic treatment known as *Abyangha* involves applying warm oil to your entire body. The oil is infused with herbs. An ayurvedic bodyworker applies the oil to your body in a way that supports circulation, loosens toxins, and relaxes the mind.

SPIRIT: *Clean your chi*

The ancient Chinese art of feng shui says your home is a reflection of you. A vital energy known as chi flows through you and through your home. To keep it healthy, keep your home neat, clean, and orderly. Dirt and clutter have a negative effect on chi.

"When the heart is at ease, the body is healthy."

—Chinese Proverb

Listen to Your Heart

Heart disease is the leading killer of Americans today, accounting for more than a third of all deaths. Once considered a man's disease, coronary heart disease is now a major cause of death among women, too. Take steps to prevent heart disease—many of the risk factors are controllable.

MIND: *Know your risk for coronary disease*
Several risk factors are known to directly contribute to a higher risk of heart disease for both men and women; the more factors a person exhibits, the greater the risk. Risk factors include elevated cholesterol, elevated triglycerides, smoking, high blood pressure, diabetes, sedentary lifestyle, obesity (especially when the fat is concentrated above the waist area), and stress.

BODY: *Eat a heart-healthy diet*
Coronary heart disease is easier to prevent than it is to treat, especially if you have a family history of heart problems. A key to keeping coronary heart disease at bay is maintaining a healthful diet that is low in fat and cholesterol and high in antioxidant-rich fruits and vegetables. Basically, a low-fat diet would have less animal protein, very little fried food, and increased amounts of whole grains and vegetables. Be good to your heart, and it will be good to you.

SPIRIT: *Heal your heart with rhodochrosite*
This beautiful pink variegated stone is associated with unconditional love and compassion. Worn against your heart, it helps to heal emotional and relationship issues. It can also enable you to express your feelings more comfortably, and to release old hurts.

"Pleasure is Nature's test, her sign of approval.
When man is happy, he is in harmony with himself
and his environment." —Oscar Wilde

Healthy Pleasures

We've been taught to value hard work and sacrifice, while looking
skeptically at pleasure. However, the Law of Attraction suggests we
should do otherwise. It tells us that when we feel good, our energy
level increases, and so does our ability to create the lives we desire.
Indulge in healthy pleasures today.

MIND: *Elevate mind and mood with bergamot*
This fragrant herb has uplifting properties that may rival antidepressants. Blend essential oil of bergamot with grape seed or jojoba
oil and rub some on your wrists. When you're feeling anxious,
depressed, or mentally disoriented, sniff the soothing aroma. It may
even trigger romantic thoughts. (Caution: bergamot can make your
skin more sensitive to sunlight.)

BODY: *Take a milk and honey bath*
Supposedly, Cleopatra used to enjoy milk and honey baths. Taking one
will not only make you feel like royalty, you'll be rewarded with softer
skin. Combine a half cup of honey with two cups of powdered milk.
Add these to hot water (after you've turned the water off). When the
milk and honey have dissolved, sprinkle in rose petals or lavender buds.

SPIRIT: *Dance for joy*
Spinning as you dance can evoke elevated states of consciousness.
Perhaps you've heard of "whirling dervishes," Sufi dancers whose
graceful, twirling movements encourage trancelike states of consciousness. Some pagans engage in a spirited and joyous winding
dance known as the "spiral dance." Try dancing in circles and see
what you experience.

"SO MANY OF OUR DREAMS AT FIRST SEEM IMPOSSIBLE,
THEN THEY SEEM IMPROBABLE, AND THEN WHEN WE
SUMMON THE WILL, THEY SOON BECOME INEVITABLE."

—Christopher Reeve

Manifest Your Dreams

Everything in our world began with someone's dream or vision. But you must bring your dreams down to earth if you want them to materialize. Today, focus on making your dreams realities.

MIND: *Organize goals into steps*

Poet Robert Browning wrote that a man's reach should exceed his grasp. That's a lofty and inspiring intention; however, you must also believe that you can attain your dreams. Break your goals down into steps. Like a mountain climber, you will come to plateaus during your journey. Part of growth is realizing this is not your final destination and seeing where to go from here.

BODY: *Activate your intentions with acupressure*

Bring your dreams into focus by activating the acupressure point known as "Middle of the Person" in the indention between your upper lip and the bottom of your nose. Press it for a minute or so to relieve confusion or uncertainty, and improve concentration. Do this periodically throughout the day to strengthen your willpower and clarity.

SPIRIT: *Create an altar*

An altar is a flat surface decorated with objects that support your dreams, intentions, and path in life. Choose items that will remind you of what you want to create. The objects you display on your altar will help you transition to a different place of awareness from your daily activities, and remind you of your purpose.

"TO ERR IS HUMAN, BUT TO REALLY FOUL THINGS UP
REQUIRES A COMPUTER." —*Farmer's Almanac*

Computer Consciousness

Computers have transformed our lives forever. According to the Nielsen Company's study "An Overview of Home Internet Access in the U.S.," more than 80 percent of Americans have computers in their homes. Consider the following suggestions for dealing with this mixed blessing in a healthy way.

MIND: *Ease computer-related stress*
Computers make our lives easier in some ways, but more frustrating in others. Because we're so dependent on technology, when the computer goes down, the stress begins. You can't prepare for all eventualities, but you can take protective measures. Back up your work regularly to a travel drive. Keep hard copies of anything that's really important. Update virus protection software regularly.

BODY: *Ease keyboarding strain*
Repetitive keyboarding can lead to carpal tunnel syndrome and other painful conditions. Exercise your hands and wrists every hour to ease strain. Hold your hands up, fingers straight and together, then bend them 90 degrees. Twist your hands from side to side. Curl your hands, then open them and spread your fingers. Ball your hands into fists and make circular motions. Repeat several times.

SPIRIT: *Spiritual information at your fingertips*
No matter where you live, you can now enjoy online many spiritual and inspirational classes and lectures that used to be only available in major cities. You can also read electronic versions of esoteric books, as well as blogs and websites dedicated to various spiritual paths.

"GREAT MINDS DISCUSS IDEAS; AVERAGE MINDS DISCUSS
EVENTS; SMALL MINDS DISCUSS PEOPLE."

—Eleanor Roosevelt

Increase Your Attention Span

Increasing your ability to focus on a task can help you become more successful. It's estimated that the maximum attention span for adults is about twenty minutes, and three to five minutes for children. Here are some ways to help increase your attention span and your family's.

MIND: *Increase your reading time*
Spend time each day reading a book or magazine. *Publishers Weekly*, the principal trade magazine for the book business, says the average person spends 2.1 hours a month reading. Reading improves your creative ability by stimulating the formation of mental images as you read words. It also improves your vocabulary and can help you retain cognitive abilities later in life.

BODY: *Don't go to school or work on an empty stomach*
Eat a healthy breakfast. Instead of grabbing a donut and a cup of coffee, get protein, fruit, and fiber in your meal. Glucose levels are low in the morning, which makes it hard to concentrate. Eggs, whole wheat toast, meat, cheese, whole grain cereal, yogurt, and fruit are some good options that will give you the energy you need to start the day.

SPIRIT: *Study tarot cards*
Use the rich symbolism and colors on tarot cards to strengthen your attention and awareness. Choose a card and study the images depicted on it. Although each card has a particular meaning, artists depict this according to their own preferences. What symbols do you observe? How do you interpret the images?

"ADOPT THE PACE OF NATURE: HER SECRET IS PATIENCE."

—Ralph Waldo Emerson

Go Natural

Strengthening the bond between humans and nature may be our only hope for survival. Today, consider ways you can take a more natural approach to living. Care for the earth, and she will care for you.

MIND: *Consult a naturopath*

Medical professionals specially trained in natural medicine, called naturopaths, are fully licensed MDs who generally recommend natural approaches for the treatment of health problems. If you prefer a more natural approach to healing, consult a naturopath. To find a naturopath in your area, contact the American Association of Naturopathic Physicians at *www.naturopathic.org.*

BODY: *Eat garlic for natural healing*

The sulfur compounds in garlic are the key elements in preventing cardiovascular disease and for use as an antibiotic. In one study, garlic was tested on mice against an antibiotic-resistant strain of staphylococci. The results showed that garlic protected the mice against the pathogen and significantly reduced inflammation. Another study at the University of North Carolina found that eating one clove of garlic daily may reduce your risk of stomach and colon cancer.

SPIRIT: *Commune with nature spirits*

According to some spiritual traditions, our world is populated by nature spirits. To most people, these beings are invisible. However, you can connect with them if you are patient and perceptive. Sit quietly in a natural setting. Ask these spirits to advise you about how to care for the earth. Be sincere. Bring offerings of food or drink. Even if you don't see them, you may sense their presence.

"ALL THAT IS NECESSARY FOR EVIL TO TRIUMPH IS FOR
GOOD MEN TO DO NOTHING." —Edmund Burke

Save the Rainforests

The rainforests are essential for life on our planet—get involved
in protecting them. Rainforests purify our air by absorbing carbon
dioxide emissions and help relieve global warming. They also provide a habitat for nearly half the species on earth.

MIND: *Support the rainforests*
It is estimated that nearly half of the world's ten million species of
plants, animals, and microorganisms will be destroyed or severely
threatened over the next quarter of a century due to rainforest defor-
estation. Harvard's Pulitzer Prize–winning biologist Edward O.
Wilson estimates that we are losing 50,000 species a year! Rainforests currently provide sources for one-quarter of today's medicines.
Visit *www.rainforest-alliance.org* for more information.

BODY: *Support body function with rainforest plants*
Rainforest plants contain many biodynamic compounds with unre-
alized potential for use in modern medicine. Leslie Taylor's book
Herbal Secrets of the Rainforest lists many of these healing plants.
For instance, cat's claw aids the intestinal immune system and
arthritis. Damiana regulates hormone function. Guarana promotes
energy. If we preserve and cultivate these plants, we can continue to
benefit from them.

SPIRIT: *Learn about shamanism*
A shaman is someone who understands both the spirit world and
the natural one, and uses that knowledge to provide healing, guidance, and protection to his people. Among the indigenous people of
North, Central, and South America, shamans have long served as
medicine wo/men and visionaries. In the 1970s, the books of Carlos
Castaneda introduced millions to the concepts of shamanism.

"FOR WHATEVER WE LOSE (LIKE A YOU OR A ME)

IT'S ALWAYS OUR SELF WE FIND IN THE SEA."

—e. e. cummings

Go Down to the Sea

Perhaps we feel drawn to the sea because it is our mother, the source from which humankind emerged countless millennia ago. Or, maybe it is because our bodies are largely composed of slightly salty water. Whatever the reason, you can draw solace from the sea today.

MIND: *Let the sea soothe you*

One reason people flock to the sea is that this is one of the few places we find all four elements—earth, air, fire (sun), and water—in one spot. The repetitive rhythm of the waves breaking on the shore forms a type of meditation that can induce a trance. Sit by the sea and let its soothing sounds ease your mind. If that's not possible, listen to a CD of ocean waves.

BODY: *Eat sea vegetables*

Sea vegetables contain vitamins A, B complex, C, and E, as well as the fifty-six minerals and trace minerals your body requires to function properly. They also have omega-3 fatty acids, but very little fat—factors that can help you lose weight. Try arame, kelp, dulse, kombu, nori, and/or wakame in soups, stir-fry, and sushi.

SPIRIT: *Collect shells*

Collecting seashells is a relaxing pastime that connects you with nature. Shells have long served as tokens. Sailors, for instance, gave heart cockles to their sweethearts as talismans. In *Ocean Oracle,* Michelle Hanson proposes that each shell also has a deeper meaning and that shells can be used to gain insights.

"A MAN CAN'T RIDE YOUR BACK UNLESS IT'S BENT."

—Martin Luther King, Jr.

Be Good to Your Back

Three-quarters of all Americans will suffer from lower back pain at some time in their lives. Protect your back. Regular chiropractic adjustments and massage therapy can help prevent injury and pain. Here are some other suggestions.

MIND: *Meditate to soothe your back*
Sit with your spine straight. Take slow, moderately deep breaths. Imagine soothing green light moving up from the earth to the base of your spine. Visualize this light continuing slowly up your backbone, illuminating each of your chakras along the way. Feel muscle stiffness easing. Envision the light rising until it reaches the top of your head. Spend at least five minutes in this meditation.

BODY: *Use yoga to ease back stiffness*
Back pain is the second leading cause of absenteeism from work in the United States (after the common cold). Although we may link back problems to strain, such as lifting something heavy, sitting at a desk all day can also contribute to back pain. Try a yoga posture to keep your back limber. Lie on your back and pull your knees up to your chest. Wrap your arms around your legs. Roll gently from side to side, giving your back a pleasant massage.

SPIRIT: *What is your back trying to tell you?*
In her bestselling book *You Can Heal Your Life,* Louise Hay links back problems with problems in the psyche. Money woes are associated with lower back pain. Guilt can cause problems in the midback. Feeling unloved may manifest in the upper back. Design positive affirmations to help correct these issues.

"How can a nation be great if its

bread tastes like Kleenex?"   —Julia Child

Eat Whole Grains

Dietary guidelines set by the U.S. Department of Health and Human Services and the U.S. Department of Agriculture recommend eating three ounces of whole grain per day. However, most Americans eat highly refined grains that provide little nourishment and plenty of empty calories. Switch to hearty, whole grains—you may find you actually like them better.

MIND: *Know your grains*
In Western cultures, wheat has long been a principal staple and still plays a major role in most diets. However, many people can't properly digest the gluten in wheat, and may suffer adverse reactions when they eat it. Gluten is also present in rye and barley. Determine whether you are gluten intolerant. If so, consider switching to quinoa (pronounced *keen wah*). Include rice in your diet, too.

BODY: *Are you getting enough fiber in your diet?*
Despite efforts by government health agencies to boost fiber intake, the typical American still consumes an average of only 11 grams a day. The National Cancer Institute recommends doubling that amount. Studies have shown that consuming between 20 and 30 grams of fiber a day can dramatically reduce your risk of many cancers. Introduce fiber into your diet gradually.

SPIRIT: *Meet the grain goddesses*
Early cultures linked certain deities with grains and honored these deities to ensure a bountiful harvest. In ancient Rome, the goddess Ceres was revered as the giver of grain. We get our word *cereal* from her name. The ancient Greeks called her Demeter.

"THE BEST WAY TO DETOXIFY IS TO STOP PUTTING TOXIC THINGS INTO THE BODY AND DEPEND UPON ITS OWN MECHANISMS." —Dr. Andrew Weil

Understand Cancer

According to the American Cancer Society, "Cancer is the leading cause of death in economically developed countries." Smoking, lack of exercise, and an "American-style diet" are leading risk factors for cancer. Be proactive. Reduce your chances of cancer today.

MIND: *Know your risk for cancer*
The National Cancer Institute designates four groups of risk factors for cancer: behavioral, environmental, biological, and genetic. Although you may not be able to do much about genetic risks, you can address the others. Tobacco use, excessive consumption of alcohol, overexposure to sun, environmental chemicals and toxins, poor diet, and physical inactivity are among the main risk factors. For more information, visit *www.cancer.gov*.

BODY: *Eat red vegetables to reduce your risk of cancer*
Lycopene is a natural pigment that gives tomatoes and watermelon their deep red color. This powerful antioxidant and phytochemical may reduce the incidence and severity of some cancers. In one study, men with prostate cancer who took thirty milligrams of lycopene per day for three weeks had a reduction in tumor size and malignancy.

SPIRIT: *The curative power of hope*
Herbert Benson, a cardiologist and associate professor of medicine at Harvard Medical School, explains that "hope in something beyond the illness . . . gives purpose to life." He points out that when you remain hopeful, rather than anguishing about an illness, it enables the body to use its innate healing powers and increases the chance of recovery.

"The disparity between a restaurant's price and food quality rises in direct proportion to the size of the pepper mill." —Bryan Miller

Perk Up with Pepper

Pepper has been used in India for more than 4,000 years, making it one of the oldest spices known to humankind. A welcome digestive aid, it helps break down proteins and relieves myriad gastrointestinal woes. No wonder fresh-ground pepper is so popular in chichi restaurants.

MIND: *Wake up your mind with black pepper*
The stimulating properties of black pepper extend beyond its familiar gastronomical benefits to entice the mind as well as the stomach. Its aromatherapy properties include activating energy and willpower; therefore, it can aid you in making decisions or taking action when you feel timid or uncertain. When you're feeling mentally dull, black pepper's spicy scent sharpens your attention and helps you concentrate.

BODY: *Sprinkle pepper on your food to stimulate digestion*
Black pepper not only brings out the taste of many foods, it improves appetite and digestion by stimulating the secretion of hydrochloric acid in the stomach. It helps to prevent gas in the intestines. Like many hot and spicy herbs, black pepper perks up your metabolism and makes you sweat, so you burn more calories.

SPIRIT: *Use pepper to spark your spirit*
Early herbalists connected pepper with the planet Mars and the Roman god of war. Thus pepper, when used in talismans, confers confidence, bravery, and assertiveness. Lore also suggests black pepper can spark an ambivalent mind to action and heat up a lover's ardor.

"SEX IS ONE OF THE NINE REASONS FOR REINCARNATION.

THE FIRST EIGHT ARE UNIMPORTANT." —Henry Miller

Expand Your Sexual Repertoire

Sex in TV, movies, books, and magazines has become more graphic and widespread. However, this proliferation hasn't deepened or heightened most people's sexual pleasure. Many couples now express ennui about sex. Try these tips to turn up the heat in your love life.

MIND: *Read the Kama Sutra*
The most popular sex book of all time, the *Kama Sutra* offers lots of positions you can try. However, this ancient book is more than just a guide to sexual positions. It also addresses love and many of the aspects of lovemaking, from courtship to foreplay and beyond.

BODY: *Do everything but . . .*
If your sex life has gotten in a rut, try not having intercourse for a while. Pretend you're a teenager again, experimenting with sex. Engage in mutual masturbation or oral sex if you like. But don't go all the way. Make a point of licking, kissing, and caressing areas you haven't paid attention to lately. Studies show that long-time companions often rush foreplay. Give yourself a week or two before resuming intercourse.

SPIRIT: *Explore the spiritual nature of sex*
Sex occupies a place of honor in many spiritual traditions. An experience called high sex or ecstatic sex takes orgasm to a higher level that involves not only the genitals, but the entire body, mind, and spirit. It is considered a connection with the forces of Creation. Margot Anand's book *The Art of Sexual Ecstasy* is a good resource for learning more.

"As I see it, every day you do one of two things:

build health or produce disease in yourself."

—Adelle Davis

Commit to Being Healthy

Staying healthy is a way of life, which is why fad diets and exercise programs rarely work long term. Health is also a state of being you embrace with your mind, body, and spirit. Make that commitment today.

MIND: *Believe that optimal health is possible*
Experts in the field of mind-body health acknowledge the link between mind and body. People who believe they can obtain optimal health are more likely to see those results than people who don't feel that way. Use your mind to envision the healthy lifestyle you desire. Affirmations and visualizations can support your intention and help bring about your objective.

BODY: *Eat real food*
A major part of Michael Pollan's philosophy in *Food Rules* is to eat real food. He advocates using fresh fruits, vegetables, and whole grains, along with small amounts of fresh meat, poultry, and fish to build meals from scratch. Avoid packaged and prepared foods. If a product contains ingredients you wouldn't add in yourself, such as monoglycerides, put it back on the shelf.

SPIRIT: *Support recovery with faith*
When you experience illness, faith can be an important factor in your recovery. A study published in the *Southern Medical Journal* in 2004 found that cancer patients who expressed a higher degree of spirituality experienced greater quality of life than those who didn't have a spiritual focus. Many people recover from illnesses through their unshakeable belief that they will be well again.

> "I KNOW GOD WILL NOT GIVE ME ANYTHING
> I CAN'T HANDLE. I JUST WISH THAT HE DIDN'T
> TRUST ME SO MUCH." —Mother Teresa

Avoid Overload

Many of our lives are overloaded at every level, with work, stress, home and family responsibilities, food, material goods, noise—the list goes on. We have too much, and yet we feel lacking. One way to start dealing with this pattern is to break things down into smaller, more manageable portions.

MIND: *Take breaks from the computer*
If you spend much of your day in front of a computer, consider breaking away at regular intervals. Eyestrain, headaches, back and neck problems, and carpal tunnel syndrome are linked to extended computer use. Look away from your monitor every ten minutes and gaze at something far away. Stand up every hour and take a brief walk, even if it's just to the water cooler.

BODY: *Eat small meals throughout the day*
Rather than eating three big meals a day, try grazing and eating smaller meals throughout the day. Experts theorize that if you eat healthily throughout the day, your body burns more calories and your metabolism increases. When you keep your body busy digesting calories, you're also less likely to spike your blood sugar.

SPIRIT: *Allow time for spiritual renewal*
Give yourself spiritual renewal breaks. Shifting your focus from the daily grind to a more peaceful place can ease stress and bring things into perspective. Every hour or so, stop what you are doing. Say a prayer, meditate, or just concentrate on your breathing.

"FEW MEN DURING THEIR LIFETIME COME ANYWHERE
NEAR EXHAUSTING THE RESOURCES DWELLING WITHIN
THEM. THERE ARE DEEP WELLS OF STRENGTH THAT
ARE NEVER USED." —Richard E. Byrd

Take Care of Your Bones

Osteoporosis is a disease that thins bone tissue as you age. It weakens your bones, making fractures more likely. Ten million people in the United States have osteoporosis. Reduce your chances of becoming one of them.

MIND: *Know your risk for osteoporosis*
Some people are more susceptible to osteoporosis than others. Women become more vulnerable after menopause. Caucasians, people with small bones, smokers, people who drink alcohol, sedentary people, and women who have never borne children are at greater risk for osteoporosis. You can slow bone deterioration with diet, nutritional supplements, and exercise.

BODY: *Thwart the onset of osteoporosis*
As you age, your bones break down faster than new bone can be formed. To help offset this, supplement with calcium and vitamin D. An easy way to get it into your diet is to drink juice fortified with calcium and vitamin D. Also do weight-bearing exercise: walking, climbing stairs, or lifting weights helps to strengthen your bones.

SPIRIT: *Make friends with an oak tree*
The mighty oak has long been linked with strength. The Druids attributed mystical properties to the oak tree, and held rituals in oak groves. Sit or stand near an oak tree and try to connect with it intuitively. Relax your mind. Let the tree speak to you. What wisdom does it convey?

"YOU CANNOT SHAKE HANDS WITH A CLENCHED FIST."

—Attributed to both Golda Meir and Indira Gandhi

Become the Peace You Seek

Peace begins within each of us, and can then spread out into the world. Each of us is a microcosm of the macrocosm that is our world. Today, devote yourself to expressing peace in your own thoughts, words, and deeds.

MIND: *Contemplate peaceful words*
Notice how certain words and thoughts cause you to tense your muscles. Meditation teachers say that while you are meditating, your heart should be soft and your belly should be soft. Overall, you should be relaxed, released, and open. During meditation, choose one or more peaceful words to focus on. Notice how doing so makes you feel calm and centered.

BODY: *Calm down with theanine*
The amino acid theanine is found in green tea. You can also purchase it in capsule form in health food stores and online. Theanine's properties help you unwind at night so you sleep better, but also aid mental functioning and clarity during the day. Like meditation, theanine can calm brainwave frequencies and encourage them to ease into a slower alpha wave state. That means you'll be more relaxed and more creative as well.

SPIRIT: *Find peace in patience*
Accepting yourself and others is a way to avoid stress and fear. Be kind and exercise patience, most of all to and with yourself. Spend some time observing the sensations and thoughts that enter your consciousness. Remain a detached observer. Allow them to pass without analyzing, resisting, or reacting in any way.

"THE EGYPTIANS WERE BURIED WITH THEIR SPICES. I KNOW WHICH ONE I'M TAKING WITH ME WHEN I GO."

—Erma Bombeck

Enjoy the Gifts of Ginger

The spicy Asian herb, ginger, has been used for thousands of years, both for culinary and medicinal purposes. One of the most versatile healers, it aids respiratory, digestive, muscular, and circulatory complaints. Add zing to your meals and to your health with ginger.

MIND: *Promote mental clarity with ginger*
When you feel mentally sluggish, turn to ginger. The crisp, stimulating scent of ginger can revive your flagging spirits, increase awareness, and spark imagination. Put a little ginger essential oil on a cloth handkerchief and sniff it. Your mind will feel instantly sharper and clearer. Ginger's aroma can also aid dizziness or vertigo.

BODY: *Improve digestion with ginger*
A popular seasoning in Asian cooking, ginger can aid many digestive problems. Its cleansing properties help ease indigestion and stomach upsets, as well as diarrhea. Spicy ginger is also stimulating, so it can be useful for people who have lost their appetite. Grind it fresh for salads and stir-fry dishes, or drink refreshing ginger tea.

SPIRIT: *Stimulate action with ginger*
Some metaphysicians and herbalists link ginger with Mars, the planet of action. If you want to speed up a situation that is taking too long, make a good-luck charm and add a little dried ginger powder to it. You can use ginger to hasten love, money, success, or any other intention.

"FRANCINE SAYS YOU LOVE HER GINSENG TEA.

IT'S GREAT FOR THE SEX DRIVE." —From *Point of No Return*

Go for Ginseng

Here's another valuable root that's been used for millennia in Eastern medicine to heal a wide range of ailments. Its diverse and extensive healing benefits make it worth including in your personal pharmacopeia. Note: Siberian ginseng isn't actually ginseng, though it has many of the same health benefits.

MIND: *Balance your mind-set with ginseng*
Herbalists and practitioners of Eastern medicine categorize herbs as "heating" or "cooling" and use them to heal conditions accordingly. Asian ginseng is considered heating; American ginseng is considered cooling. When you need a mental pick-me-up, try the Asian variety. If you want to calm mental stress, use the American version.

BODY: *Pump up your sexual prowess*
Ginseng has long been reputed to increase sexual energy and performance. Studies published in 2011 indicate there's truth to this tale. Researchers from the University of Guelph (Ontario) say the Asian variety of ginseng does, indeed, offer aphrodisiac properties. The studies showed ginseng helped men deal with erectile dysfunction. It also improved menopausal women's sex drive. An added benefit: ginseng doesn't produce the unwanted side effects of medications like Viagra and Cialis.

SPIRIT: *Spice up your love life*
Make a spicy good-luck charm for love with ginseng. Metaphysicians and herbalists suggest that part of its power derives from the fact that the root looks like a tiny human being. Make a small sachet that includes powdered ginseng and place it under your lover's pillow.

"Don't dig your grave with your own knife and fork."
—English Proverb

A Is for Antioxidants

Just because you are getting older doesn't mean you have to suffer from diseases that have been associated with aging. Lifestyle changes can make all the difference in how good you look and feel. Begin with A for antioxidants.

MIND: *Understand free radicals*
Free radicals are unbalanced oxygen molecules containing an extra electron. Problems occur when free radicals attack cell membranes, inhibiting the cells' ability to reproduce or protect themselves. The effects of too many free radicals include signs of aging, including wrinkles, age spots, and poor skin quality; an abundance can also lead to more serious problems, including cataracts, heart disease, and certain kinds of cancer. Anti-aging researchers say that the answer can be found in chemicals known as antioxidants, which eat up excess free radicals.

BODY: *Be pro-antioxidants*
Antioxidants can slow the aging process and prevent many common diseases, including heart disease, high blood pressure, and cancer. Antioxidant-rich foods include apples, berries, red grapes, broccoli, spinach, tomatoes, garlic, green tea, whole grains, and soy. Make sure to get plenty of these foods into your diet to stave off the damage done by free radicals.

SPIRIT: *Cleanse your energy field with peridot*
Since ancient times, peridot has been considered to have cleansing and protective properties. Our ancestors believed the stone repelled evil spirits. Wear or carry this stone to help you release negative emotions such as jealousy, resentment, anger, and stress that can lead to illness.

"YIELD TO TEMPTATION.

IT MAY NOT PASS YOUR WAY AGAIN."

—Robert Heinlein

Seek Sensations

Sex keeps you happy. It helps you manage stress. It keeps you connected to the person you love. Make your sex life a fulfilling one.

MIND: *Contemplate the qualities you most desire*
Imagine your ideal partner. List the qualities you find most attractive. Kindness? Self-confidence? Fidelity? Your A list should include the most crucial qualities; your B list can include other important characteristics that aren't deal-breakers. The clearer you are, the better your chances of attracting that person.

BODY: *Get lubed*
Lubricants can make sex a lot easier and more pleasurable. Water-based lubes are the most popular. They don't stain or irritate, and they're safe to use with condoms. Oil-based lubes, such as olive oil, avocado oil, or safflower oil, can be used during sex play, but they can break down latex. They feel more natural and silky than water-based lubes. Silicone lubricants are very slippery and great for use in the water, but should not be used with condoms or sex toys.

SPIRIT: *Energize your relationship with feng shui*
According to the ancient Chinese art of feng shui, the back right-hand section of your home (when you enter your front door) is the relationship area. To energize this sector, put a vase of bright red roses there. Roses are potent symbols of love, and red is the color of passion.

"WE MUST ALWAYS CHANGE, RENEW, REJUVENATE
OURSELVES; OTHERWISE WE HARDEN."

—Johann Wolfgang von Goethe

Rejuvenate Your System

The body has a remarkable ability to heal itself. Your cells are constantly dying and new ones are continually being made. It's never too late to begin a program of self-health—today is the perfect time to start.

MIND: *Join the club*

Numerous studies have shown that interacting with other people is revitalizing. For instance, breast cancer patients who lacked a strong social network were four times more likely to die than those who had lots of good friends, according to Harvard researchers. If you like to travel, take a trip with a tour group. If cooking is your thing, join a cooking club. Play bridge or mahjong regularly. Friendships can be formed quickly through shared interests.

BODY: *Try schizandra*

This five-flavor fruit known as "magnolia vine" has long been a staple in Chinese medicine. High in antioxidants, the plant has been effective in helping the liver rejuvenate tissue damaged by viral hepatitis. Herbalists also believe it improves endurance, aids metabolism, regulates sugar levels, and alleviates stress response. Some even say it can enhance concentration, vision, and hearing. Take it as a supplement or drink it as a tea.

SPIRIT: *A spiritual path may heal*

Commitment to a spiritual path may provide the key to better health, according to a report in the *Journal of the American Medical Association*'s Archives of Family Medicine. It suggested that a spiritual perspective may aid people who are recovering from illness, perhaps by offering them hope and solace.

"Peace is not something you wish for; it's something you make, something you do, something you are, and something you give away."

—Robert Fulghum

Promote Peace

If we want to have peace in our communities and in our world, we must first find peace within ourselves. Today, seek inner peace. Then share it with others.

MIND: *Make peace with yourself*

Self-acceptance is an essential part of contentment. When you observe the thoughts that pass through your mind, observe your reactions to them as well. What you may not expect is the criticism that you often level at yourself—for example, thinking "wrong" versus "right" thoughts about yourself, your actions, or lack of action in recalled situations. Such thinking comes from conditioning and past experience, and has no use in growing and understanding.

BODY: *Use acupressure to relieve anger*

When you feel angry, impatient, anxious, or frustrated, activate the acupressure points known as "Union Valley." You'll find them in the webbing between your thumbs and forefingers. Use the thumb and index finger on one hand to press this area on the other hand. Then reverse hands. You'll soon feel your irritations diminishing and your mood growing more peaceful.

SPIRIT: *Hang a prayer flag*

Buddhists hang prayer flags near their homes and temples to help bring peace to the world. They decorate these pieces of colored cloth with peaceful messages and symbols. Make your own prayer flag. Write a blessing on it, then hang it outside. When the wind blows, it will carry your intention far and wide.

"AND WE HAVE MADE OF OURSELVES LIVING CESSPOOLS, AND
DRIVEN DOCTORS TO INVENT NAMES FOR OUR DISEASES."

—Plato

Plant Power

Is herbal medicine right for you? Investigate it today and see. In
The New Holistic Herbal, David Hoffmann writes, "Herbalism is
based on relationship—relationship between plant and human, plant
and planet, human and planet." This holistic approach makes herbal
healing appealing to many people who recoil from the impersonal
nature of drug-based medical practice.

MIND: *Consider healing with herbs*
Herbal remedies have become immensely popular as natural health
promoters, and as complements to over-the-counter drugstore medicines as well as prescription drugs. Major U.S. research centers are
now investigating the healing potential of herbs and other alternative medical approaches. Always consult with your physician before
ingesting herbs, particularly if you are pregnant.

BODY: *Try herbs to ease soreness*
If your muscles are sore from working out, or your joints ache with
arthritis, healing herbs can help ease pain and stiffness. Angelica is a
warming and stimulating herb that's good for rheumatism. Devil's claw
is a potent anti-inflammatory that has been compared to cortisone. Bog-
bean is cleansing and cooling; use it to relieve muscle pain. Some herbs
are available in salves or lotions. Others can be put into poultices.

SPIRIT: *Connect with the spirit of the herb*
Plants, like humans, have a life force that flows through them. This
life force gives them their potency. Choose fresh herbs for medicinal
and spiritual purposes, rather than dried ones from the supermarket
or mall vitamin store.

"IF WE COULD GIVE EVERY INDIVIDUAL THE RIGHT
AMOUNT OF NOURISHMENT AND EXERCISE, NOT TOO
LITTLE AND NOT TOO MUCH, WE WOULD HAVE FOUND
THE SAFEST WAY TO HEALTH." —Hippocrates

Nourish Yourself Wisely

Being conscious of how your diet, behavior, ideas, and activities
contribute to your health is essential to self-care. Inform yourself.
Pay attention to your patterns. Listen to your inner guidance. The
more aware you are, the more likely it is that you will use good
judgment.

MIND: *Learn the facts about supplements*
To learn about the current state of scientific research on supplements, visit *http://ods.od.nih.gov/health_information/ibids.aspx*,
created by the Office of Dietary Supplements at the National Institutes of Health. It lists scientific studies on everything classified as
dietary supplements. The site permits you to search at no charge on
hundreds of topics.

BODY: *Eat before you grocery shop*
Don't shop hungry. If you do, you're more likely to make impulse
purchases and buy items that aren't healthy for you. A 2009 study
revealed that when you're hungry, food looks more attractive (even
foods you might not eat otherwise). To outwit temptation, eat a
small, healthy snack before you go to the supermarket.

SPIRIT: *Understand your need for spiritual growth*
Some esoteric teachers say it is the destiny of each person to evolve
spiritually. If you feel you need a teacher to guide you, you can
attract this person into your life. Just open your mind and heart, and
ask to meet the right individual. A Buddhist proverb says "When the
student is ready, the teacher will appear."

"Two roads diverged in a wood, and I,

I took the one less traveled by,

And that has made all the difference."

—Robert Frost

Follow the Fundamentals

Robert Frost's poem reminds us we can choose which road to take: the road to health or the road to illness. We all know what we should do, but many of us don't do it. Follow these fundamental guidelines and you will be on your way to wellness.

MIND: *Evaluate your diet*
Eat six to eleven servings of grains, three servings of vegetables, two servings of fruit, two or more servings of low-fat dairy products, two to three servings of lean meat, poultry, fish, dried beans, eggs, or nuts per day. Your goal should be to include all of these options as often as possible. If you don't, choose one food group at a time and gradually improve your daily eating pattern.

BODY: *Exercise often*
Yoga, tai chi, and other mind-body exercises relax the mind and body by linking movement to the breath. These activities burn off physical tension, relax your muscles, and ease your mind. Regular exercise, even if it's begun at an advanced age, can help stave off heart disease, type 2 diabetes, and other illnesses, as well as maintaining brain health and bone density.

SPIRIT: *Become aware of your connection to everything*
When you walk around your neighborhood, try to sense your connection with everything around you: people, animals, birds, plants. Observe the sky and the earth. When you realize you are part of everything, you can be at peace anywhere.

"When people go to work, they shouldn't have to leave their hearts at home."

—Betty Bender

Be More Content at Work

A Conference Board study, reported by CBS News in 2010, found that only 45 percent of Americans are happy in their jobs. That's the lowest level of satisfaction reported in twenty-two years. If you aren't content with your job, try these suggestions.

MIND: *Visualize your ideal job*
Think about your dream job and how passionate you would feel doing it. Whether you are seeking a new job or want to improve the one you already have, see it clearly in your mind *the way you want it to be*. Visualize all the aspects of the job that you consider important. Get your mind and your emotions engaged. Believe in your ability to succeed.

BODY: *Relieve a headache with acupressure*
On-the-job stress and long hours at the computer can bring on a tension headache. To ease the pain, close your eyes and press your index and middle fingers to the spot between your eyebrows, where your nose meets your forehead. This is known as the "third eye" point. Hold for at least a minute. Release, and press again. Repeat as necessary.

SPIRIT: *Value your intuition*
Don't just rely on your rational mind; let your intuition help you make the right decisions in your job. When you run up against a problem you can't solve, take a break. Sit quietly and close your eyes. Take a walk. Lie down if possible. When your mind relaxes, your intuition can kick into gear.

"BY OURSELVES WE CAN ENJOY LIFE, BUT TO REALLY
APPRECIATE LIFE WE MUST FIND COMPANIONSHIP."
—Anonymous

Share Your Life with Others

Share your life with other people today. Human contact contributes
to health and happiness on every level. A study published in the
International Journal of Stress Management found that when people exercised together they felt more energized and also calmer. And
many studies have shown that sociable people tend to enjoy a higher
level of wellness than loners.

MIND: *Teach a class*

Teach a continuing education class. In addition to the joy that comes
with sharing your life wisdom, teaching helps strengthen mental
function through reading, self-learning, and lecturing. Everyone is
adept at something. Choose your specialty and approach a local continuing education program. You don't need a teaching degree, just
experience and enthusiasm.

BODY: *Work out at a fitness club*

Instead of exercising alone, work out with a group of other people at a
fitness club or your local YMCA. You'll pick up on the energy of the
group and be inspired to push just a little harder. You can also learn
new techniques, either from other members or from a professional
staff person. It's more fun, too, and you may make some new friends.

SPIRIT: *Meditate with a group*

Meditating with a group can be a powerful spiritual experience. The
combined energies of the people involved produce a highly charged
atmosphere that is more than the sum of its parts. In other words,
you may feel more relaxed, uplifted, and peaceful than if you medi-
tated alone.

"IF YOU HAVEN'T ANY CHARITY IN YOUR HEART, YOU HAVE THE WORST KIND OF HEART TROUBLE." —Bob Hope

Do unto Others

The world's spiritual teachings say that when we help others we help ourselves as well. If you believe that we are all connected, then this idea makes sense. Today, consider the Golden Rule: Do unto others as you would have them do unto you.

MIND: *Donate possessions you don't need*

A nonprofit organization called One Sight distributes eyeglasses to people in underprivileged nations. Your old glasses could help one of the 300 million people worldwide who cannot see clearly. Donate clothing, housewares, and furnishings to the Salvation Army, which helps millions of people worldwide. Donations of goods and cash are welcomed by scores of charitable organizations; your donations are tax deductible.

BODY: *Share the gift of touch*

Touch is one of the oldest healing modalities. You don't have to be a professional massage therapist to give a loved one a back rub. Or, massage the person's hands and/or feet. Use aromatherapy lotion or oil: peppermint to stimulate, lavender to relax. If you prefer, give someone a head massage or brush his or her hair. When you've finished, perhaps your friend will reciprocate.

SPIRIT: *Empower others*

You can be a catalyst for others and help them live the lives they dream of. Remind them that they have the power to change. Help them see how their negative thoughts are undermining their happiness. Be supportive of their efforts. Honor their inner goodness, even if they can't see it themselves.

"Only a hard heart can break!"
—Thorwald Dethlefsen and Rudiger Dahlke, MD,
The Healing Power of Illness

Live from the Heart

Heart disease is the leading cause of death for both men and women, causing more than a quarter of the deaths in the United States each year, according to the Centers for Disease Control. Is there a link between coronary disease and feelings of lovelessness? Holistic healers might say "yes."

MIND: *Speak from the heart*
If you knew this was your last day on earth, what would you say to the people you love? Don't wait until your dying day to reveal your feelings to loved ones—do it every day. Speak from the heart. Tell friends, family members, and others how much they mean to you. Express gratitude for their presence in your life.

BODY: *Use yoga's Fish Pose to open your heart*
Lie on your back with your legs out straight. Slide your hands under your buttocks. Tighten your abdominal muscles and raise your chest, supporting yourself on your forearms and buttocks. Arch your spine and chest; press the back of your head to the floor. Feel your heart chakra and chest opening as you take several breaths. Lower your torso again to the floor and relax.

SPIRIT: *Use flower essences to support loving feelings*
Flower essences contain the spirits of plants. Developed by English physician Dr. Edward Bach in the 1930s, they work on the etheric body to ease emotional and physical complaints. Bleeding heart, baby blue eyes, California wild rose, and forget-me-not are some to consider.

"ANY COLOUR—SO LONG AS IT'S BLACK."   —Henry Ford

Basic Black

No color carries as much symbolism as black. For centuries, we've connected black with things we feared: death and evil. However, the modern fashion world embraces black because it is not only stylish, it's practical as well. It can eliminate wardrobe dilemmas, leaving you more time for other things.

MIND: *Simplify packing for trips*
When traveling, choose black as your "staple" for clothing. You'll reduce the amount of luggage you need and simplify the process of packing. Black is appropriate for daytime or evening wear; it's visually slimming and doesn't show dirt easily. It combines with any color, so you can mix-and-match it with other garments or create different looks by changing a few accessories.

BODY: *Eat black garlic*
If you've avoided the health benefits of garlic because eating it causes bad breath, try "black" garlic. This "superfood" is garlic that has been fermented using a heat process. Black garlic is softer and sweeter than raw garlic, and has more antioxidants as well. Unlike raw garlic, it won't give you garlic breath, so you can enjoy it anytime. Because of its smooth texture, it makes a delicious and healthy spread for crackers.

SPIRIT: *The power of black*
Black holds spiritual significance. In China, black is associated with prosperity, and feng shui practitioners use it to attract wealth. In the West, ministers' and nuns' robes were traditionally black. Wiccans link black with power and protection, because black pigment contains all the colors of the spectrum. Use black to convey the meaning you choose.

"WE CAN NEVER OBTAIN PEACE IN THE OUTER WORLD
UNTIL WE MAKE PEACE WITH OURSELVES."
—His Holiness the 14th Dalai Lama

Gain Wisdom from Tibet

Until the latter half of the last century, most Westerners were unaware of Tibet's rich spiritual, cultural, and healing traditions. The 3,000-year-old mind-body-spirit practice of Tibetan medicine is now available throughout the United States. It emphasizes balance, natural remedies, and energetic harmony—qualities you may wish to investigate further.

MIND: *Implement peace*
The Dalai Lama, Tibet's leader, received the Nobel Peace Prize in 1989. One of his goals is to facilitate peace between Tibet and China. Regardless of how you view the Tibetan situation, you can implement peaceful practices in your own life, as recommended by the Dalai Lama: honor the rights of all beings, practice nonviolence, respect the natural environment, and seek peaceful resolutions to conflicts.

BODY: *Drink Tibetan pu-reh tea*
Long prized in Asian medicine for its many healing properties, this fermented tea is often drunk to aid weight loss. Researchers at St. Antoine Hospital in Paris found that consuming pu-reh helped patients reduce lipids by 25 percent. The tea can also relieve various digestive complaints, improve circulation, and ease hangovers.

SPIRIT: *Contemplate the lotus symbol*
In Tibetan Buddhism, the lotus symbolizes enlightenment. Because this beautiful flower grows from the mud at the bottom of a swamp, the lotus represents the ability to transcend the muck of everyday life to attain a heightened state of clarity. Tibetan art often depicts the Buddha seated on a lotus flower. Contemplate the symbol to help you rise above destructive thoughts and emotions.

INDEX

Contains material adapted and abridged from: